The Philippine Islands Vol.-48

by

Ed. Emma Helen Blair and James Alexander Robertson

The Philippine Islands Vol.-48
by Ed. Emma Helen Blair and James Alexander Robertson

ISBN: 978-93-59399-03-4

Published by

DOUBLE 9 BOOKS

2/13-B, Ansari Road, Daryaganj
New Delhi – 110002
info@double9books.com
www.double9books.com
Tel. 011-40042856

ABOUT THE EDITOR

Emma Helen Blair (1869-1951) was an American historian and author known for her significant contributions to Philippine history and also scholarship. Born on July 19, 1869, in Ohio, she pursued her education at Ohio Wesleyan University and later at Columbia University. Blair's passion for history and research led her to collaborate with James Alexander Robertson, an esteemed scholar, in editing and compiling "The Philippine Islands, 1493-1898" series. This monumental project spanned fifty-five volumes and covered the colonial history of the Philippines from the 16th to the 19th century. The comprehensive series showcased her expertise in meticulously examining and also presenting historical documents and narratives. Her work significantly contributed to a deeper understanding of the Philippines' complex past and its interactions with various colonial powers. Her commitment to historical accuracy and attention to detail earned her a reputation as a meticulous and reliable historian. Beyond her contributions to Philippine history, and main thing that Emma Helen Blair also authored "The Philippine Policy of Secretary Taft" and co-wrote "A History of the Philippine Islands" with Robertson. Both of these works further demonstrated her dedication to scholarship and the exploration of the Philippines' political and social developments.

James Alexander Robertson was born in Corry, Pennsylvania, in 1873. He was the sixth of eight children born to Canadian parents who became naturalized citizens of the United States after moving to Corry in 1866. His father, John McGregor Robertson, was a builder from Verulam, Ontario, close to Peterborough. His mother, Elizabeth Borrowman Robertson, immigrated to Canada as a child from her native Scotland. When Robertson was seven years old, his mother died. After three years, he and his family relocated to Cleveland, Ohio, where James finished his secondary education. In 1892, he enrolled in Adelbert College at Western Reserve University for graduate study. He studied in Romance languages, majoring in Old French, and received his Bachelor of Philosophy degree from Western Reserve University in 1896.

CONTENTS

PREFACE

The contents of the present volume (dated 1751–65) include accounts of the missionary efforts of the Augustinian and Dominican orders, and events in Filipinas from 1739 to the beginning of the English invasion; and the survey of the condition and needs of the islands which is presented in the memorial by the royal fiscal Viana. A valuable feature in the missionary reports is the ethnological information furnished therein regarding the savage tribes of Central Luzón; and the self-sacrifice and devotion of the missionaries themselves appear in striking contrast with the unscrupulous greed displayed, as one of the short documents shows, in the management of the friar estates near Manila. The times are troublous for the colony: several insurrections occur among the natives, the Acapulco galleon of 1743 is captured by the English, the Moro pirates ravage the archipelago with enormous destruction of life and property, and the Spaniards are defeated by them. Governor Arandia attempts to establish reforms, and thus incurs much odium; he is engaged in numerous controversies, and finally dies. Viana's memorial presents a vivid picture of the distressed condition of the Philippine colony after the English invasion, its urgent need of relief, and the ways in which this may be accomplished.

A letter by Fernando VI to the Manila Audiencia (November 7, 1751) expresses his approval of the proceedings of Auditor Enriquez in pacifying the insurgent Indians of certain villages near Manila and in Bulacan—a revolt caused by the usurpation of Indian lands by the managers of the friar estates, and the fraudulent proceedings of government officials who aided such usurpation. Enriquez had pacified the natives, deprived the friars of such lands as they held illegally, and distributed these among those natives who were aggrieved; he also investigated the titles by which the orders held their estates, and regulated the proper boundaries of their lands. The king also commands the Manila government to exercise vigilant care for the welfare of the Indians, and to notify them that in their difficulties they must have recourse to the royal fiscal for redress or aid.

In a rare pamphlet published at Manila in 1755, apparently written by one of the Jesuit missionaries in Leyte, are enumerated various instances when the raids of Moro pirates against the Visayan villages in 1754 are repulsed by the natives, under the direction of their spiritual guides; and one of these, the defense of Palompong, is related at length. An official report (in MS.) made by the Augustinian provincial (1760) shows the parishes and missions then in charge of his order in the Philippines, with the population (classified as to sex, age, etc.) of each one.

In the eighteenth century several important missions were conducted by the Augustinians and Dominicans among the savage and untamed head-hunting tribes of Central Luzón. Those of the former order are recorded by Fray Antonio Mozo in his Noticia histórico natural (Madrid, 1763); he presents much valuable information regarding those people, whose first contact with European civilization was mainly found in their intercourse with those missionaries. This begins, for the Italons (now called Ibilao) and Abacas in 1702, when the Augustinians attempt to christianize them—with fair success, considering the wildness and ferocity of those people. They also carry the gospel among the Isinay, a work which the Dominicans had been compelled to abandon as hopeless; and within a quarter of a century the entire tribe have been baptized and civilized by Fray Alejandro Cacho. In 1740 these Isinay missions are ceded to the Dominican order. Among all these wild peoples, the missionaries have introduced not only the gospel, but instruction in farming and irrigation, and supplies of cattle and plows; and, wherever possible, they have formed "reductions" or settlements of their converts, usually in localities best adapted to the cultivation of the soil.

The Augustinians carry on their missions among the Ilocans, the Tinguians, the Igorots, the Zambals, and the Negritos—this last having stations throughout the islands; also in Cebú and Panay, and in China. Mozo narrates the progress of these missions, but devotes much of his space to accounts of the wild tribes and their peculiar customs and beliefs; this is especially fortunate for our purpose in regard to the Negritos, about whom less has been known than about the other Philippine peoples, Mozo's residence of three years among them rendering his observations extremely valuable. He also gave particular attention to the practices and medicines used by the natives in sickness, and to the plants which are useful therein. Among these missions the most arduous, according to our writer, was that to the "apostates" and infidels who had taken refuge in a certain mountainous and densely-wooded district; these renegades and heathen dwelt together, each making the other worse. Among these people were preserved many of the ancient pagan customs which the missionaries had in most places been able to extirpate; and these are described by Mozo. Even in this hard field, "multitudes of infidels were baptized and hundreds of apostates reclaimed." The Augustinians also conduct missions in the interior of Cebú and Panay, where not only are the mountains rugged and the forests dense, but there are wizards among the natives who "by conversing with the demon do things which cause terror;" some account of their practices is given, as also of the converts gained by missionaries among those people. He then describes some of the medicines that are used by the natives. Among these are the gall and fat of the python; a stone which, when applied to a woman's thigh, would facilitate childbirth; and a plant which intoxicates and infuriates those who go into battle. Another plant temporarily paralyzes the muscular system. Mozo concludes with an account of the Augustinian missions in China, which does not concern our work.

Some account of the Dominican missions in Central Luzón is given by Bernardo Ustáriz (Manila, 1745) and Manuel del Río (Mexico? ca. 1740). In Paniqui the missionaries have formed within six years seven native churches, with nearly a thousand converts; they are erecting substantial wooden buildings for religious purposes, and have opened new roads and repaired old ones in order to facilitate intercourse between the provinces. A neighboring tribe of head-hunters have harassed the Christian districts, but a government expedition is sent against them and checks their insolence; this success greatly increases that of the missions, to which hundreds of natives flock for instruction and baptism. Río gives a more detailed account of the Paniqui mission, and of its early beginnings. Some of the first missionaries were poisoned by heathen savages. The most interesting feature of the Dominicans' labor in this region is their opening a high-road from Asingan, Pangasinan, to Buhay in Ituy.

A brief résumé of events during the period 1739–62 is compiled from the histories of the time; we have used for most of it Zúñiga's narrative, copiously annotated from Concepción's and others. The royal fiscal Arroyo is imprisoned by Governor Torre, in accordance with an order issued by his predecessor; finally, the king orders restitution of the fiscal's office, salary, and confiscated goods, but this finds the unfortunate prisoner dead (1743). In the same year the English commander Anson captures the Acapulco galleon "Covadonga," which causes heavy loss to Manila. Two years later, Governor Torre dies, after a troublous administration in which he incurs general odium. A revolt of the natives in Balayan and Taal is promptly quelled. Torre is succeeded by the bishop of Nueva Caceres, Juan de Arrechedera, a Dominican; his administration is vigorous, and he does much for the defense of Manila against possible enemies. In 1747 the new archbishop of Manila arrives in the islands, but Arrechedera retains the office of governor. An insurrection of the natives in Bohol is easily quelled. The king of Spain writes conciliatory letters to the sultans of Mindanao and Joló, who profess friendship, but prove to be scheming and unreliable; they permit Jesuit missionaries to enter their countries, but these are soon obliged to take refuge in Zamboanga. A rebellion in Joló obliges its ruler to flee to Manila. In 1750 a new governor arrives there, Francisco de Ovando; he finds much to do in making the little navy of the islands effective and in equipping a squadron against the Moros. He sends Alimudin back to his kingdom; but at Zamboanga the sultan's actions are so indicative of treachery that he and all his household are arrested and sent to Manila. War is then declared against the Joloans, and another expedition is sent to attack them, but the Spaniards are obliged to fall back on Zamboanga. This is followed by piratical ravages throughout Filipinas, causing enormous losses of property, and of persons taken captive by the Moros. Ovando sends the captive Alimudin with a fleet to restore him to the throne of Joló; but at Zamboanga he is suspected of disloyalty and treachery, and is sent back to Manila as a prisoner. The Spaniards attack the town of Joló, but are repulsed; this encourages the pirates to renew their raids, and the Visayan Islands (and even Luzón) are cruelly harried. Ovando is succeeded (1754) by Arandia as governor; he institutes reforms in all directions, thus drawing upon himself much animosity, in both secular and ecclesiastical quarters; and he makes treaties with the Joloans. The Dominican missions are reestablished in the Batanes Islands; and that order takes charge of the Isinay missions in Luzón, which are conferred on it by the Augustinians. Zúñiga records his opinions regarding the character of the Filipino natives and the proper methods of conducting missions among them. In 1757 certain ecclesiastical controversies in Tungquin are ended by decrees issued at Rome. Arandia expels the heathen Chinese from the islands, and builds for their trade the market of San Fernando. He becomes involved in numerous controversies with the religious orders, and draws upon himself much popular hatred — largely due to the acts of his favorite Orendain. He makes the utmost exertions for the service of his king and the islands, and finally, worn out by these fatigues, dies (May 31, 1759), an event probably hastened by poison. The government is assumed by Bishop Espeleta, who even usurps it from Archbishop Rojo for a time; but the latter becomes governor (1761) by royal decree. He releases Orendain, who had been imprisoned for his official acts, and provides comfortable quarters for the captive sultan of Joló. In the following year occurs the siege and capture of Manila, which will be related in VOL. XLIX.

Nearly half of this volume is occupied by the valuable memorial written in 1765 by Francisco Leandro de Viana, then royal fiscal at Manila, "Demonstration of the deplorably wretched state of the Philipinas Islands." We are told that the Council of Indias refused to print this document, a fact which indicates both the apathy and the corruption existing in the Spanish court. Viana was a man of keen and logical mind, clear and far vision, and great enthusiasm and energy; and he evidently felt a deep sense of official responsibility and ardent zeal as a Spanish patriot. In this memorial he describes the weakness, danger, and almost destitution of the Philippine colony, and shows the necessity of either abandoning it entirely or providing for it suitable means of support; demonstrates that the latter course should be adopted, and that it can be pursued if the natural resources of the islands are developed. Viana sets forth the advantageous location of the islands from both the commercial and strategic points of view, and asserts that the English covet the islands as a vantage-point for themselves, especially as a basis for their explorations on the western coast of North America—of which, and of certain Spanish explorations made in 1640, he gives some account—and for attacks on the Spanish possessions in America. If Spain keeps the Philippines, they must be put into a condition of defense, for which Viana makes various suggestions, some as less costly alternatives for others. The military forces of the islands should be enlarged, and the pay of both officers and men increased, so that they may have the means to support themselves decently. After this is accomplished, "the reduction of all the Indian villages ought to be resolutely undertaken, as a matter that is absolutely essential." This would result in a great increase of the tribute-money, and in many benefits to both the government and the Indian natives. Viana proposes an increase in the rate of the tribute exacted from the natives, and various economies in the administration of the islands; and urges that the Moros be thoroughly punished. He devotes a long chapter to "arguments which justify the increase of tributes." The expenses of administration in the islands have steadily increased since their conquest, as also have the needs of the Spanish crown; yet the Indians have not been further taxed to meet these demands, as have the people of Spain; they should now pay their share of the burden, and, moreover, they are taxed very moderately. They are idle, improvident, and extravagant; they might be rich, if they would labor even moderately; and an increase in their tributes would require but little additional work from them, which would also help to correct their slothfulness. This vice, however, is also the bane of their Spanish masters, whom Viana bitterly rebukes; but he urges that the Indians be compelled to do a certain amount of work, especially in agricultural production. The various rebellions of the natives of Filipinas constitute another valid reason for increasing their tributes. Viana declares that, in proposing this measure, he must at the same time protest against the misuse or theft of its proceeds; and he rebukes, in scathing terms, the recklessness, extravagance, and dishonesty of the Spanish officials, and the unpunished corruption and misgovernment that prevail in Spain's colonial administration. The increase of tributes can be secured only by maintaining in the islands a military force sufficient to punish and prevent the Moro raids, and to keep the Indians in wholesome awe; and the alcaldes-mayor of the provinces should be more carefully chosen and better paid. All military supplies should be kept at Cavite instead of (as now) Manila. As an alternative for increasing the tributes, Viana suggests the establishment of church tithes, by which the royal treasury would be relieved of the heavy burden of supporting the ecclesiastical estate; or the imposition on the Indians and mestizos of a tax for the support of the military posts in the provinces.

Part ii of Viana's memorial is devoted to "navigation and commerce; the method for establishing them in these islands, and their great benefits." He begins by showing the necessity of navigation and commerce for the maintenance of every nation, which he illustrates from the history of the several European nations, deploring the neglect of these industries by the Spaniards. The latter, notwithstanding the contrary claim made by the Dutch, are free to navigate by way of Cape of Good Hope; and all powers have an equal right to sail the high seas. Viana enumerates the advantages of the Cape Good Hope route for commerce—convenience, promptness, saving of expense, a wider market for the commodities of both Spain and the Philippines, better administration of the colony and stricter enforcement of the laws. Moreover, the commerce of other European nations, especially that with Mexico, could be greatly diminished, in favor of Spanish trade; and the proceeds of the latter would remain among the Spaniards, instead of being carried away to foreign lands and benefiting the enemies of Spain. Viana here, as in many other passages, laments the fatal indolence, negligence, and pride of his fellow-countrymen, which have prevented them from securing, as they might have done, the power and wealth which other nations have attained. He enumerates the valuable products of the islands, which ought to be developed and made available; chief among these are cinnamon and iron. Viana sets forth his project for retrieving the condition of the islands by establishing a Spanish trading company. He relates the great success, power, and wealth gained by the trading companies of the other nations; and urges that Spain follow their example, and thus obtain a share of those benefits and gains. Not least of these will be the awakening of the Spaniards, especially the upper classes, to a more active and useful mode of life, banishing the ignorance, idleness, and vice which are so prevalent among them. For this purpose, appeal is made to the king to encourage and favor the formation of a trading company. Viana advocates the establishment of shipyards in the islands, and enumerates the resources of Filipinas for supporting this industry. By establishing a Spanish company, many benefits could be enjoyed by the provinces of Filipinas, especially in developing their resources and furnishing employment to the natives; and many valuable products of the islands are enumerated which ought to be included in their commerce. An important advantage for Viana's proposed company is the friendly attitude of the peoples throughout India toward the Spaniards. He finds Manila's Asiatic commerce now reduced to that with the Chinese ports; but it should be reestablished with India, Siam, and other countries. Moreover, the proposed company can give new life to the Acapulco trade, and compel the Mexican traders to give fairer treatment and more advantageous sales to those of Manila. Viana remonstrates against the restrictions imposed on the commerce of the Spanish colonies, which really serve only to increase the gains of foreigners. These restrictions are caused largely by influences emanating from Cadiz and Acapulco; the arguments alleged in favor of them are vigorously refuted by Viana. In his opinion, it is the foreign merchants at Cadiz who are at the bottom of the opposition to Manila's commerce; and they are obtaining control of Spain's wealth, and causing much more injury to her industries than can the little competition of Manila. Far greater is the damage caused by the fraudulent dealings of foreign merchants who sell in Spain goods from China as if they were made in European countries; and by the commercial restrictions which prevent Spaniards from competing with those foreigners. These injuries could largely be prevented by the proposed Spanish trading company, which would also assure to Spain various positive advantages; and Viana suggests for that company free trade with Nueva España. No slight benefit resulting therefrom would be the great diminution of the illicit trade which the foreign nations are conducting in the Spanish-American dominions. Viana mentions the difficulties which that company will encounter, and proposes some measures to remedy these. One hindrance may be the jealousy of other nations; but they will not unite against Spain, and, in case of war, Holland and France would be inclined to side with her against the English. The greatest difficulty, however, will be the opposition of the Philippine officials of the crown to the company, which may be a check to its activities; Viana cleverly proposes to forestall this by entrusting to the company the government and management of the islands, the crown making over to it the tributes and customs duties. In the final chapter, he proposes to conduct the commerce of Manila with Nueva España via the Panama route, in case that by Cape Good Hope prove impracticable, and sets forth its advantages; he suggests that for this purpose that route be improved, and perhaps a canal be made between the two oceans; and closes with an appeal to the Spanish government for aid to this project.

The Editors

January, 1907.

DOCUMENTS OF 1751-1762

Sources: The first of these documents is obtained from *La Democracia* (Manila), November 25, 1901; the second, from a rare pamphlet published at Manila (1755), in the possession of Edward E. Ayer, Chicago; the third, from an original MS. in possession of Mr. Ayer; the fourth, from Mozo's *Noticia histórico natural* (Madrid, 1763), and a rare pamphlet by the Dominican Ustáriz, both from copies in the Library of Congress; the fifth, compiled from Zúñiga's *Historia* (Sampaloc, 1803), pp. 546–601, and Concepción's *Hist. de Philipinas*, xi, pp. 89–237, fully annotated from other writers.

Translations: That of the third document is made by James Alexander Robertson; all the rest, by Emma Helen Blair.

USURPATION OF INDIAN LANDS BY FRIARS

To the president and auditors of my royal Audiencia of the Filipinas Islands, resident in the city of Manila:1 Don Pedro Enriquez, an auditor of that same Audiencia, made a report, with sworn statements of his proceedings; of what he had done under the commission which was conferred on him by the government there for the pacification of the villages of Taguig, Hagonoy, Parañaque, Bacoor, Cavite el Viejo, and other places attached to them which lie near that capital, all which had revolted. [He reported that] they were pacified by merely the proclamation of a general pardon (except to the chief instigators of the revolt) which he published, and by the promise that their complaints should be heard and justice done to them; but the village of San Mateo also revolted, and he proceeded to its punishment and left it in ruins, because the people had not surrendered their arms; it was, however, already [re]peopled, with inhabitants who were more numerous and of more peaceable disposition. A similar insurrection or revolt occurred in most of the villages of the province of Bulacan, and these, like the former, by an agreement which they had formed by a public writing with the village of Silang protested, as they afterward made evident in their petitions, against the injuries which the Indians received from the managers of the estates which are owned by the religious of St. Dominic and those of St. Augustine, both calced and discalced — usurping the lands of the

Indians, without leaving them the freedom of the rivers for their fishing, or allowing them to cut wood for their necessary use, or even to collect the wild fruits; nor did they allow the natives to pasture on the hills near their villages the carabaos which they used for agriculture.2 Accordingly [the said auditor] determined to free them from these oppressions,3 and decided that they should not pay various unjust taxes which the managers exacted from them. Having proved to be capable in the other task assigned him, he received a commission as subdelegate judge of the adjustment of land-titles, in consequence of which he demanded from the aforesaid religious orders the titles of ownership for the lands which they possessed; and, notwithstanding the resistance that they made to him, repeatedly refusing [to obey], he distributed to the villages the lands which the orders had usurped, and all which they held without legitimate cause4 he declared to be crown lands [realengas] — as occurred with the convent of San Pablo, belonging to the calced religious of St. Augustine, assigning to it [i.e., the crown] a farm for horned cattle and two caballerías of land which were supposed to belong to it, according to the testimony of the village of San Mateo. He also took other measures which seemed to him proper for the investigation of the fraudulent proceedings in the measurement of the lands in the estate of Biñan, which is owned by the religious of St. Dominic — fraud which was committed in the year 1743 by the court clerk of that Audiencia [of Manila] with notable fraud and trickery, in which participated the two surveyors (appointed through ignorance or evil intent), to the grave injury of the village of Silang. This had caused the disturbances, revolts, and losses which had been experienced in the above-mentioned villages. The aforesaid proceedings [by the auditor] were considered and examined with the closest attention in my Council of the Indias, with the decrees that were also sent by the Audiencia there in the course of the proceedings in a second appeal interposed by the village of Silang — decrees obtained in that suit by the natives of that village against the college of Santo Tomas de Aquino, in regard to lands usurped [from them] and annexed to the estate of Biñan, which the religious own. On the subject of the disturbance among the aforesaid Indians, Governor Don Gaspar de la Torre, his successor the bishop of Nueva Segovia, and the provincials of the aforesaid religious orders set forth the allegations made in the name of the orders by father Fray Miguel Vivas as their procurator-general at this court, and by Father Pedro Altamirano, who acts in that capacity for the Society of Jesus for its provinces of the Indias (on the point that the province of San Ignacio in those islands had no share in the commotions in those villages, as was shown by various testimonies), and the explanations made by my fiscal, who was cognizant of the whole matter. It has therefore appeared expedient to me to advise you of the receipt of your letters of July 30, 1745, and July 17, 1746, and of the acts which accompany them; and to notify you that by a despatch of this date I approve, and regard as just and proper, all that was performed by the aforesaid Don Pedro Calderon Enriquez in virtue of the commission and appointment which was conferred upon him by Governor Don Gaspar de la Torre by the advice of the Audiencia there, in order that he might proceed to the pacification of the insurgent villages in the jurisdictions of Silang, Imus and San Nicolas, Cavite el Viejo, and the other districts which united on account of the controversy over the ownership of the lands which the religious—Dominicans, and both calced and discalced Augustinians—are endeavoring to keep. I also give him thanks for the judicious conduct and measures which he employed for the aforesaid pacification; and I likewise approve what he accomplished as subdelegate judge of the settlement of land-titles, in regard to the survey and boundaries of the estates which, in accordance with their legitimate titles, belong to each of those orders, in view of the more accurate and reliable information [obtained] from the interpretations of the four surveyors whom he appointed—the latter bearing in mind, to this end, the measures put into execution by the auditor Ozaeta in the year 1699, in accordance with the chart printed by the pilot Bueno, in his book entitled Navegación especulativa y practica5 [i.e., "Navigation, theoretical and practical"] (which chart serves in those islands as the standard for the surveys)—assigning to the aforesaid religious that which belongs to them by their [legal] titles, which is the same that was ordained in the executory decree despatched by the Audiencia there. I also approve what he did in adjudging to my royal crown the lands which the aforesaid religious orders had usurped, and in allotting lands to the Indians for the sum of two thousand pesos, at times and terms stipulated with them.

From the aforesaid investigations charges resulted against Don Juan Monroy, court clerk of that Audiencia, who was engaged in the survey and adjustment of boundaries made in those same lands of Biñan in the year 1743—in which, by the declaration of the two surveyors who took part in it, is evident their ignorance of such work, and of the rules and measures [to be used]. Although [sc., after?] the lands had been measured and a chart of the estates had been drawn, the computations were made by the said Monroy, and the surveyors signed it, supposing that it was correct; but it was acknowledged that in that same year, later, another survey and adjustment of boundaries was made by the aforesaid court clerk and one of the said surveyors on some lands over which there were lawsuits— some, in particular, with the religious of St. Augustine—in which survey there was assigned to each cattle-farm 3,024,574 square brazas of land, this being different from the previous survey, which was computed at 8,695,652 brazas. In this was proved the fraud with which the said Monroy acted, in giving to the said religious more than half of the land which belonged to Silang. Accordingly, it has appeared to me proper to condemn him to two years' suspension from his office, and to lay upon him a fine of two thousand pesos, applied to the fund of fines paid into the royal treasury; and for this exaction there is issued, on this same date, the proper despatch to the Marqués de Regalía, a minister of the said my Council and tribunal of the Indias, and exclusive judge of rents, settlement of land-titles, and collection of fines and condemnations. By another despatch of the same date, the government of those islands is commanded to exercise hereafter the utmost vigilance in order that the Indians of the said villages may not be molested by the religious, and that the latter shall be kept in check in the unjust acts which they may in future attempt against not only those Indians but other natives of those islands. In this, the government must always bear in mind the reiterated commands given in the laws [of the empire], and the frequent royal decrees that have been issued, to the end that the Indians shall be well treated and shall not suffer oppression or extortion; and shall direct that my fiscal there shall appear as their representative and in their defense on every occasion which shall present itself in this regard. Considering how important it is that the Indians shall know of the recourse which they can have when they are oppressed or ill-treated, and in their controversies, it would be very expedient that the government give them information of this, so that they may not be ignorant thereof, and that they may use these [peaceable] means without going to the extreme, as they did on this occasion, by employing armed force. For this time, my royal charity and clemency overlooks their proceedings, considering their heedless disposition; but when they shall have been advised of what they ought to do in such cases, and in others of a different nature, if they fail to use those means they shall be chastised with the utmost severity. I have resolved to notify you of this, in order that you may be acquainted with this my royal decision, and in order that, so far as you are concerned, you may make known my decree; and I command the most prompt and effective measures, to the end that it may be fully and duly carried into effect; for such is my will. Dated at San Lorenzo, on November 7, 1751.

I the King

By command of the king our sovereign:

Doctor Josef Ignacio de Goyenechea

[Farther down on this decree were three rubricas of the lords of the royal and supreme Council of the Indias.]

In the regular official session of the Audiencia of Manila, in September, 1753. The honorable president and auditors of the Audiencia, being in session in the royal halls of the said court, having officially considered a royal decree dated at San Lorenzo on November 7, 1751, by which his Majesty (whom may God preserve) was pleased to approve what was done by the auditor Don Pedro Calderon Enriquez in the pacification of the villages which had revolted, and to command him to execute what is expressed therein, with the other provisions of the said royal despatch and the claims of the fiscal, the said president and auditors declare: That they must command and did command that the orders given by his Majesty in his royal despatch be observed, fulfilled, and executed; and, in order that it may have due effect, the contents of the said royal decree shall be communicated to the reverend provincials of the holy orders of St. Dominic, St. Augustine, the Recollects, the Society of Jesus, and to the prior of the convent of St. John of God, in these islands. Attested copies of it shall be made, and sent to the alcaldes-mayor of the provinces of these islands, in order that, translating the decree into the language of the country, they may print it6 and make known its contents to the natives of the said provinces, so that the Indians may be informed of what is provided and ordered by his Majesty in the said royal decree — the alcaldes sending to the [proper] official of the court a sworn statement that they have thus executed the decree; and likewise notifying the clerk of court, in order that, in virtue thereof, he may fulfil what is herein ordered and forbear in the exercise of his office, and may appoint a notary approved to his satisfaction so that he may be responsible for the deposit of those papers and the record of these proceedings. Such were the orders and commands of the said honorable members, and they signed their names.7

Obando
Licentiate Arzadun
Calderon Enriquez
Before me:
Manuel de Antiquia, notary and secretary.
[This is a copy.]

1 This document was printed in the Manila newspaper La Democracia (the organ of the Federal party), on November 25, 1901; it was furnished to that paper by Hugo Salazar, a young Filipino — a native of Luzón, educated as a pharmacist, prominent in the Federal party during 1901-04, and in 1903-04 governor of Surigao province, Mindanao — under the pen-name of "Ambut." It was printed with accompanying comments written by him, which here appear as foot-notes, signed "Ambut." We are indebted to the courtesy of James A. LeRoy (now [1906] U. S. consul at Durango, Mexico) for a copy of the above issue of La Democracia, and for the above information.

2 Cf. pp. 141–143, post, note 63.

3 In view of these abuses which occurred in the middle of the eighteenth century, which have been repeated in our own time (up to the year '97) with an outcome favorable to the friars because the latter found support in the venality or the pliancy of the authorities, will it be possible still to deny the justice and good reason with which the Filipinos reject the friars, demanding the suppression of the religious corporations, which always and everywhere have had pernicious consequences? Libertas, in its No. 686, shows bad faith and shamelessness in addressing to a co-religionist of ours these questions in its editorial columns: "Can Don Leocadio inform us whether these popular tumults which keep him so preoccupied were known in Filipinas before the year '96? Is it not public and notorious that certain conspicuous attorneys, resident in Manila, are the ones who are deceiving the people, promising them impossible things, and obtaining from them beforehand enormous sums of money?" Don Leocadio does not answer, in order not to waste his time; but he recommends the reading of this royal decree, in which all the friar-lovers will find a complete answer if they will reason with their brains. As the organ of the friars, it is natural that Libertas should speak thus, displaying the blessing of his Holiness Leo XIII as a banner for concealing error and falsehood; it is likewise natural that those who reason with the stomach should form a chorus for that sort of scribbling; but it is truly regrettable that our women and other persons should aid, through their lack of instruction, through the influence of the confessional, and through religious fanaticism, in falsifying historical truth. — "Ambut."

4 It results, then, that the friars usurped not only the lands of individuals, but those of the State; this is called "filling both sides of the mouth with food" [comer á dos carrillos] — which they were doing, receiving salaries from the State and collecting dues from their parishioners. — "Ambut."

5 This work was composed by Joseph González Cabrera Bueno, a native of Teneriffe, and at the time of its publication (Manila, 1734) the chief pilot for the Manila-Acapulco line of galleons. He was a sailor of great ability and long experience, which, with this book, gave him a very high rank among the mariners of his day. He dedicated the book to Governor Valdés y Tamón; its censura (or examination by the censor) was made by Murillo Velarde; and its illustrations were engraved by the native Filipino artist Nicolás de la Cruz Bagay. (Vindel, Catálogo biblioteca filipina, no. 819.)

6 This direction to the alcaldes-mayor naturally suggests the query, "How many of the provinces were supplied with

printing-offices in 1753?" and reminds one of Dickens's "Circumlocution Office," and its efforts "how not to do it."

7 The pernicious character of the religious corporations, as an evil to society, is sufficiently proved; for even Catholic France is expelling them from her bosom. It only remains, then, to decide whether the prohibition of their existence is opposed to the principle of the separation of Church and State. To conform to the principle that the welfare of the people is a supreme law, and in virtue of that to deny legal existence to such associations as are hostile to the said principle, is not to fail in [loyalty to] the separation of the Church and the State, inasmuch as the prohibition has nothing to do with religious dogmas or ecclesiastical discipline; and, in order to be just and thoroughly impartial, it does not oppose itself to any specified community or sect, for it entirely sets aside the religious character of the corporations, considering them simply as groups of human beings in their relation to the general good. The State, in this case, legislates without passing beyond the bounds of its proper and exclusive jurisdiction, and does not invade the attributes of the ecclesiastical power.

Some will say that by prohibiting the existence of religious corporations liberties are restricted. To this I answer, that that liberty which causes harm to society ought not to be understood as liberty; and, [using the term] in this sense, the United States would not be disloyal to their Constitution in adopting restrictive measures in regard to the "trust," Chinese immigration, and the association of persons dangerous to peace, order, and the sanctity of the home.

As for the estates of the friars, Señor Sumulong was quite right, to judge from the facts in this royal decree, in asking for an ample and complete investigation of the legality of the titles to property which the friars could bring forward. It is to be observed that there was no opportunity here for [ascertaining] the real right of prescription, for it was impossible to protest against usurpations if one did not wish to be deported or shot as an anti-Spaniard or a filibuster. — "Ambut."

An interesting commentary on the above opinions is found in the recent action (December, 1906) of the French government in regard to the Roman Catholic church in France, the separation of Church and State there, and foreign interference with the proceedings of that government. — Eds.

MORO RAIDS REPULSED BY VISAYANS

Relation of the valorous defense of the Bisayan natives of the village of Palompong, in the island of Leyte, of the province of Catbalogan, in the Philipinas Islands, which they made against the Mahometan forces of Ylanos and Malanaos, in the month of June, 1754.

On the ninth day of the above month, about five o'clock in the afternoon, twenty-five Moro joangas came into this port of Palompong, with another small vessel, and entered the harbor with so little fear of being attacked by any armada that during the entire siege they left their vessels [sacayanes], high and dry, as if they were in their own land and enjoying an Octavian peace. At their arrival their vessels displayed a great number of banners, streamers and pennons, all of red silk; but they did not land until the following day, at seven o'clock in the morning. So many of them landed that they numbered more than a thousand, and so boldly that they immediately surrounded and encompassed the church; and at the first attack they succeeded in burning the sacristy (over which was the dwelling of the father minister), notwithstanding it was defended with two bulwarks, and fortified by two rows of palma brava and two other rows of wooden palisades with a rampart. In this conflagration were destroyed all the furniture of the church and the house there, as also the goods of the people who had gone into the church; and the fire was so fierce that it gave no opportunity to save two lantacas, two versos, and the supplies that were stored there — gunpowder and balls, and rice for the food of the people. These took refuge in the church in great confusion and fear, at seeing themselves surrounded by so many enemies, and trying to prevent the fire — which, notwithstanding that the church was unroofed, had already caught on the ridgepole and other timbers — from going further.

At the time when they burned the sacristy, the Moros made five trenches very near the church, and immediately began to fire their artillery; this consisted in lantacas of various sizes, and other pieces up to the caliber of three-libra balls, as far as we could judge by the balls which were picked up. Besides this, there were among them many musketeers that were very skilful, and the rest occupied themselves in hurling sumbilins and stones; and others threw a sort of wooden bar, sharp at one end, and with fire on the other; this caused much annoyance to the people, who, on account of the danger of fire, were manifestly without any protection by day or by night.

On this first day there were three killed and five wounded on our side, and all by balls, for there was no special harm done by the rest of their missiles. Since the Moros were so numerous that they could renew their forces, they fought so continuously that they gave us no opportunity to rest night or day, so that some of our dead could not be buried until after several days. At last the women, besides providing some little food for the men, were continually occupied in drawing water to extinguish the fire, and even putting it out themselves, and in making wadding, cartouches, etc.

On the second day, which was Tuesday, we had two killed and five wounded; for the balls rained on us, so that in some planks which were placed on the parapet I counted as many as ten holes in each one. Besides the continual fire from their trenches, the Moros made two covers resembling tortoises, with two rows of planks, and under these they steadily approached the two gates which communicate with the sacristy. From the mouths of these they continually hurled fire, pieces of wood, etc., in order to burn the repairs which were made by those within, so that they could burn down the doors, in order to fire afterward a cannon from under the said tortoises, and carry away with it the entire church; but those inside frustrated the intention of the enemy by continually throwing water and dirt [on the fire].

The Moros also made a bulwark, or cavalier, which overtopped the walls of the church, and through Wednesday night and Thursday morning they were pushing this close up to the church; but those inside, who by this time had recovered from their fear and consternation, in the midst of their total lack [of defenses], contrived to make a shelter of planks on top of the church, from which to fire a lantaca. When this was seen by the Moros, they desisted from pushing their machine close to the church, but they began another piece of work which was worse; for, as the side of the church was undefended after the burning of the two bulwarks, and no one could put his head out of the window on account of the furious rain of balls and bullets, the Moros stationed themselves at the foot of the wall and began to place against it a great quantity of wood, and whatever [fuel] the houses of the Indians supplied them, and set fire to this at a time when a very brisk wind was blowing; this carried the flames even within the church, and, notwithstanding they incessantly threw water on the fire, many timbers were burned, and the stone sills of the church were reduced to lime and ashes.

About this time they tried to scale the church on both sides, and a Moro ascended up to a window; but he was thrown down by a blow in the face which was given him, and his companions who were beneath were put to flight by throwing at them pieces of stone. At this the Moros were somewhat checked; and, seeing that on the side where they had made their greatest efforts to possess themselves of the church, repairs in proportion had been made within, they erected on the other side of the church two more bulwarks or cavaliers, which were higher than the first one. As fast as this was done, those within topped their walls with a parapet of molave planks; when they saw this the courage of the Moros fell somewhat, and the

Christians were so much encouraged that on the following day (the fifteenth of the month and the fifth of the blockade) they made a sally, scorning the firearms of the enemies, especially the guns, of which those within were entirely destitute.

In this sally the captain of the village killed a Moro with a lance-thrust, and the rest took to flight. A drum and three shields were captured from them, but the Christians did not dare to go very far for fear of some ambush. On retreating, and trying to enter by a very narrow gate, the Moros charged upon them with a shower of sumbilins, and a shot from a lantaca at a distance of four brazas, when the unconquerable St. Xavier so well defended his children that not even one of them was wounded. On another day those within again made a sally, and the Moros did not dare to face them; consequently the Christians were able to destroy their machines. They again made a sally on Monday, but not only did the Moros refuse to fight, but even in haste dragged out their boats, which were still on dry land; and vigorously rowing, with some of their boats flying a black flag, they quietly left the harbor, directing their course toward Carigara.

As for the Moros, it is known with certainty that those slain in this siege are forty-six who were shot, and three killed with sumbilins; and one from a lance-thrust. The number wounded is not known, nor is that of those who were killed at night, but certainly it would be a great number, because their fiercest attacks were always made at night; and as there were so many of them, and on our side a continual fire of lantacas with almost marvelous success in their shots, we do not doubt that a much greater number would be killed by night than by day. It is certain that after the Moros had gone all these shores were full of corpses; and it is known by captives who made their escape that the Moros, after they had gone away, proceeded to throw many of the wounded into the waters of the bay. It is also known through the captives that the Moros, astonished at such destruction, asked not only each other but the captives how it could be that in Hilongos, which is a large village, they had lost so few men, and in Palompong, so small a village, they had lost so many. Besides those who were killed and wounded by the gunshots, it is known that many were wounded by certain poisoned darts which they call borot,1 and doubtless many were rendered useless by their wounds.

Throughout this siege has been manifestly visible the power and protection of St. Francis Xavier, the patron of the village; it is not the least argument for this with me that this people in the absence of the father minister — who everywhere is usually the soul of the community, and whose presence is more necessary here on account of the disunited condition of the natives, who, as forming a new village, are of various factions, with continual jealousies—nevertheless could be encouraged to enter the church, when it is a fact that, left to themselves, they have a sort of aversion and horror of being shut in. Another evidence is, that in the burning of the sacristy God in His lofty judgments permitted that the fire, although so fierce, was not communicated to the church; nor did it cause in those people the horror which usually impels them irresistibly to flee even from less dangerous fires. The third, that inside the church water was obtained with such facility that throughout the blockade it was not lacking, although they were continually drawing it in order to put out the fire; while in the deepest old wells, on an occasion when they were making repairs, I have noticed that the water failed many times. And for stronger evidence that it did not fail in the time of the siege (although it was a time of drought), after the siege, although it rained heavily, I did not see any water in the five wells which they made inside the church. Fourth, that although in the fire there were hardly saved, in the judgment of all, some twenty cavans of rice, that scanty provision was sufficient for one hundred and thirty-five men, and some two hundred women and children, during the nine days of the siege. Fifth, that although in the said fire hardly four gantas, or zelemins, of gunpowder were saved, and the fire of the lantacas was continual by day and night, that supply was enough for the same number of days; for several persons have assured me that on three successive days there was not in their opinion more powder than enough for one day, and on the next day the amount that had been used was not missed. The sixth, that the Bisayans, who when left to themselves are so given to sleep, did not sleep an instant throughout the time of the siege. Seventh, that although they saw the wounded and dead beside them it made no greater impression on them than if it were a representation in a comedy. Eighth, when many of those who talked most valiantly had decided, in view of the lack of provisions and gunpowder, to leave the place and flee to the woods, on three successive nights, when they tried after prayers to open a door, they could never succeed in opening it before daylight. In this determination to go away many of the women were ready to die rather than surrender themselves to such a rabble, and on this account they had been armed in order that, by defending themselves, they might more easily meet death; and there was a man who had determined to kill his wife and children rather than see them in the power of enemies so cruel to soul and body. Notwithstanding all this, they never failed in the strong hope that their illustrious patron, St. Francis Xavier, would not abandon them. He was continually invoked, and his image was carried in procession by those who were not occupied with the defense; and this confidence increased on Friday (a day which so belonged to that saint), because on that day the face of St. Xavier's image was seen to be very smiling and joyous, a certain omen of victory. Greater than ever was their confidence in the saint's protection on Sunday, when, although their provisions were so short and the enemy was seen in every direction, all believed that on the next day before noon they would find themselves free from the siege, for the very reason that it seemed impossible for them to maintain their position any longer. They asked this from their glorious patron with a promise of a novenary; and the saint made full response to their confidence, delivering his children from the siege on Monday morning.

With the departure of the Moros, the people were left in great anxiety whether they would come back, as they were wont to do; for there was absolutely nothing to eat, and no place in which to find food, because the Moros had gone about ravaging and destroying all the grain-fields that they found. The people therefore are entirely destitute, suffering terribly from hunger, and without having any means with which to find food. For neither cotton, nor abaca, nor woven cloth were left for the women; and the men, besides seeing their grain-fields and boats destroyed, had no implements with which to cultivate the earth, or to fish in the sea.

Of those who fled to the hills there were seventeen captured and nine slain, and there was one Moro killed. The Moros were on the march and went as far as the vicinity of Ogmuc, following the Christians who were retreating. Finally, it is known by the captives who escaped that the chief dato went away from here wounded in the face with a ball, and their chief pandita was dying from a wound in his bowels.

Particular relation should be made of this valorous defense for being distinguished and aided, as is evident from its occurrences, by the powerful arm of the Highest; and therefore the glorious defenses of other villages which, with warning to the Moros, are celebrating the triumph of their bravery, I will reduce to a brief summary, which will thus make the memory of these eternal, without wearying the public with a diffuse account of their circumstances.

In the month of February of this year, the Moros, elated at the destruction of some little villages on that coast of the island [of Leyte] opposite Carigara, attacked the important village of Hilongos. There were some two thousand of them, and they besieged the place for eleven days; but the natives of the village, encouraged by the presence and advice of their father minister, who was with them, made various sallies to hinder the formation of the enemy's trenches; and they repulsed his assaults with the death of many Mahometans, without losing even one of our men in so frequent encounters.

In the month of May of the same year, four joangas made port at the island of Marinduque, with more than two thousand Moros, and for a week they besieged the little fort of the village of Gazang, which was defended by its natives from repeated assaults, under the judicious management of their courageous father minister; and the Mahometans, not carrying out their depraved intentions, smothered their fury, ravaging and sacking whatever they found outside the precincts of the said fort. During the continual fighting of those days, the Moros had more than ninety killed, and many more were wounded; while on our side there was no more than one killed, and another one wounded.

The Moros who went away unsuccessful from Marinduque sent eight joangas to the island of Luban, where they landed thinking that they would find very little resistance; but the father cura and the alcalde-mayor, with a few people who hastily gathered about them, defended themselves from behind a palisade which they had formed, with so notable intrepidity that with only the firearms of the alcalde-mayor they killed seven Moros; and, sallying from the trenches, they fell upon the enemies until they compelled them to a shameful flight.

A squadron of more than twenty joangas of the Mahometans almost at the same time attacked the village of Antiqui in the island of Panay; but they experienced a vigorous resistance from its inhabitants, which originated from the fiery spirit and persuasions of their father prior. The same thing happened to another squadron of the same or greater number in the island of Cuyo, the natives of which, with their father prior, not only defended themselves in their fort, but in a glorious sortie on the Moros—who were terrified, as was proved by the weapons and armor which the Indians secured as spoil.

Twice was the village of Ylog, the chief town on the island of Negros, attacked by thirty joangas of Moros, but on both occasions their designs were frustrated, with notable loss to their hosts; this was attained through the noble intrepidity of the natives, urged on by the fiery courage and direction of their father minister; and the Moros, seeing themselves attacked by the besieged, left several of their companions lying on the ground in the haste and confusion with which they embarked in their joangas, the moorings of which they cut in order to hasten their flight.

On the twenty-fifth of July, the day of the illustrious patron of the Spains, St. James the apostle, fifty boat-loads of Moros arrived at the important village of Catbalogan, and, divided into two bands, attacked the village on both sides. One of these parties gained possession of a high hill from which their lantacas dominated the fort, in which was enclosed the house and church of the [Jesuit] college; the other party attacked on the side of the village, and for a week the rest of the Moros hurled on it continual attacks; but all these were repelled with singular courage. The Moros therefore, many of them having perished with their dato, the chief in command of the squadron, withdrew the rest of their forces, making the boast that they would return with a stronger force to avenge their injuries.

The Moros then proceeded to the village of Calviga, which is situated on the same coast up the river, about half a legua from the shore, where some three hundred of them landed. These, on leaving their vessels, marched toward the village, regarding themselves as certain of taking it; but the natives, by the instruction of their father minister, waited for the enemy until they came within range of a cannon-shot. Thus they secured the effective fire of their lantacas, with which they killed fifteen Moros; and this alone was enough to make the enemy turn in precipitate flight. From here they went to the village of Boad, which was on an island near by called Palasan; and although they besieged it for three days, with redoubled efforts in their assaults, when they saw the vigorous resistance that was made by the natives and their father minister they retreated, balked in their intentions.

About the month of September, in the province of Albay the Moros found their arrogance defeated by the union which was formed among the natives in three villages, under the conduct of an ardent Franciscan; and by main force the natives compelled the enemy to go away from the province, rebuffed. Last of all, the two villages Ynitao and Lubungan, on the northern coast of the island Mindanao, especially experienced the fierce attacks of the Mahometans on four occasions, when they sustained continuous assaults, repulsing them with vigorous sallies, and inflicting heavy punishment, with evident losses, on the Moros.2

By this brief narration it is clearly proved that, although these favorable results have not preserved the villages from the ravaging of their fields and other injuries, at least their inhabitants were delivered from slavery;3 while, on the contrary, those who through cowardice did not make valorous resistance to the Mahometan enemy have not only lost their goods, but they groan in captivity, unless they have been delivered by the victorious arms of his Majesty. And thus the natives of this archipelago, arousing their own courage by the fortunate successes of their countrymen, can take example therefrom in order to avoid misfortunes in the future.4

1 Bolot (borot): an arrow with a hook or barb (Noceda and Sanlucar's Vocab. Tagal).

2 The year 1754 was especially disastrous to the Philippines on account of the Moro raids; thousands of people were slain,

and other thousands carried away captive; even the coasts of Luzón were ravaged, and the population of the Visayas suffered a notable diminution. See account of these losses in Concepción's Hist. de Philipinas, xiii, pp. 190–250; and Montero y Vidal's Hist. de pirateria, i, pp. 309–317. In July of that year, Ovando was succeeded in the government of the islands by Arandía, who at once instituted reforms in the military service, and did what he could to defend the islands from their enemies; he died on May 31, 1759, worn out with the cares and fatigues of government.

3 Forrest says (Voyage to New Guinea, p. 302) in describing the pirate raids by the Moros: "The Spaniards not allowing the Bisayans fire-arms, the latter prove less able to defend themselves." Also (p. 303): "On Celebes, they take, if in Dutch territory, even those of their own religion: a decent musselman, with his wife and four children were brought to Mindanao, by this very prow." "The Sooloos have in their families many Bisayan, some Spanish slaves, whom they purchase from the Illanon and Magindano cruisers. Sometimes they purchase whole cargoes, which they carry to Passir, on Borneo; where, if the females are handsome, they are bought up for the Batavia market. The masters sometimes use their slaves cruelly, assuming the power of life and death over them. Many are put to death for trifling offences, and their bodies left above ground." (Ut supra, p. 330.)

4 The archbishop of Manila, Don Miguel Garcia Serrano, wrote to his Majesty that in the period of thirty years during which there was no fortified post in Mindanao, twenty thousand Christians had been made captive by the Moros. (Torrubia, Dissertacion, p. 49.)

This relation was evidently written by some one of the Jesuit missionaries in Leyte, and perhaps even an eyewitness to the events related. The villages which he names as having repulsed the enemy seem to have been largely those in charge of the Jesuits. Some mention of the raids made in 1752–53 against the Recollect missions may be found on pp. 163, 164, post, note 88.

AUGUSTINIAN PARISHES AND MISSIONS, 1760

Report of the villages, tributes, those exempted by age and sickness, unmarried men and girls, schools for boys and girls, infants, missions, catechumens, and those newly baptized, of the provinces and ministries of the Order of our father St. Augustine, in these Philipinas Islands, this present year of 1760.

Provinces	Villages	Tributes of men and women	Exempt	Young men	Young women	Escolapios1	Young children	Spaniards, men and women
Tondo	Tondo	1,810	500	450	868	1,400	1,904	35
	Passig	1,520	490	400	600	1,310	1,450	0
	Taguiig	700	308	204	310	600	702	3
	Parañaque	1,025	330	300	400	820	1,090	6
	Malate	512	162	135	200	416	640	2
	Tambobong	1,650	500	510	650	1,130	1,710	12
	Total	7,217	2,290	1,999	3,028	5,676	7,496	58
Bulacan	Bulacan	1,250	380	450	580	1,000	1,150	12
	Guiguintô	300	52	80	100	125	280	0
	Bigaa	450	146	162	200	350	600	0
	Angat	622	160	220	316	502	916	2
	Baliuag	1,000	317	372	500	910	1,320	0
	Quingua	800	290	310	346	614	1,192	1
	Calumpit	550	140	150	210	300	718	0
	Hagonoy	750	240	300	390	630	1,030	0
	Paombong	250	70	60	90	110	250	0
	Malolos	1,300	425	520	625	1,000	1,154	0
	Total	7,272	2,220	2,624	3,357	5,541	8,610	15
Balayan	Taal	800	106	250	410	612	1,025	0
	Bauang	1,225	150	310	600	1,010	1,212	0
	Batangas	1,200	150	350	600	1,100	1,210	6
	Lipa	650	150	200	300	525	680	0
	Tiyauong	350	134	120	118	200	230	0
	San Pablo	850	140	200	420	750	892	0
	Tanauan	420	70	100	190	300	512	6
	Total	5,495	900	1,630	2,638	4,497	5,761	12
Pampanga	Macabebe	855	322	150	200	550	810	4
	Minalin	760	300	200	351	563	850	0
	Sesmoan	254	62	70	85	80	270	0
	Lubao	520	160	130	210	400	525	9
	Uauâ	680	250	160	302	550	560	18
	Betis	260	61	80	88	90	270	0
	Santa Rita y Porac	420	80	91	102	150	370	0
	Bacolor	1,150	400	504	510	220	1,300	40
	San Fernando	525	150	128	200	350	625	2
	Mexico	1,100	315	230	504	1,006	1,500	4
	Pinpin	500	140	120	200	312	532	0
	Arayat	800	309	200	290	525	850	0
	Magalang	300	70	90	100	105	312	1
	Tarlac	410	60	116	134	220	513	1
	San Joseph	150	20	32	44	80	200	0
	Tayug	62	16	20	25	30	64	0
	Santor	555	106	100	130	258	340	0
	Gapang	660	202	140	180	465	684	0
Ylocos	Namacpacan	1,020	230	211	358	590	1,114	0
	Bangar	700	212	130	254	307	595	0

Provinces	Villages	Tributes of men and women	Exempt	Young men	Young women	Escolapios1	Young children	Spaniards, men and women
	Candong	600	162	124	214	368	585	0
	Narbacan	1,150	260	110	326	515	1,119	0
	Santa Catharina	818	210	162	228	480	910	0
	Bantay	830	208	162	300	500	930	0
	Magsingal	855	183	154	257	483	663	4
	Cabugao	1,125	332	246	359	754	1,140	0
	Sinait	495	110	115	200	398	612	0
	Badoc	558	120	140	204	390	589	0
	Pauay	1,560	418	500	690	1,004	1,515	0
	Batac	1,780	506	512	790	1,102	1,655	35
	San Nicolas	825	208	180	400	610	920	0
	Ylauag	2,250	400	710	1,125	1,550	2,310	0
	Sarrat	480	75	102	224	237	508	0
	Dingras	800	240	196	248	25	801	0
	Bacarra	1,125	251	203	401	892	1,151	2
	Bangui	312	36	46	74	102	347	0
	Total	17,283	4,151	4,001	6,652	7,707	17,464	41
Zebu	San Nicolas	700	56	103	154	392	726	0
	Argao	225	300	325	506	925	1,136	0
	Bolohon	650	90	170	214	354	630	0
	Opon	790	104	164	259	448	770	0
	Cabcar	500	75	100	190	301	532	0
	Total	2,865	625	862	1,323	2,420	3,794	0
Yloylo	Oton	1,000	164	203	298	998	1,000	0
	Alimodian	1,490	125	656	780	1,309	1,050	0
	Maasin	1,390	380	268	340	1,100	1,200	0
	Matagub	825	108	203	260	752	834	0
	Tigbauan	1,260	398	360	594	916	1,300	0
	Guimbal	1,280	209	230	386	910	1,050	0
	Miagao	1,325	309	400	602	932	1,125	0
	Antique	990	180	295	358	510	890	0
	Sibalon	930	260	239	420	519	990	0
	Bugason	1,200	302	410	660	925	1,150	0
	Xaro	1,271	320	410	625	1,004	1,261	14
	Dumangas	724	142	157	209	604	767	4
	Anilao	430	75	90	130	140	344	0
	Camando	1,230	465	274	446	750	922	0
	Cabatuan	1,780	502	750	1,050	1,213	1,942	0
	Pototan	1,050	280	310	518	861	1,200	0
	Laglag	800	200	284	391	500	709	0
	Lambunao	772	182	204	310	435	719	0
	Passi	622	128	193	248	301	583	0
	Ygbaras	550	103	155	243	258	495	0
	Total2	20,889	5,132	5,991	8,868	14,937	19,976	18
Panay	Panay	1,019	350	375	496	784	847	3
	Capis	730	182	200	343	402	654	16
	Dumalag	1,080	223	350	589	703	994	3

Provinces	Villages	Tributes of men and women	Exempt	Young men	Young women	Escolapios1	Young children	Spaniards, men and women
	Dumarao	750	220	266	422	451	730	0
	Total	3,579	975	1,191	1,850	2,340	3,225	22

General summary of all the classes contained in this table

The above provinces	Tributes of men and women	Exempted, by age and infirmity	Young men	Young women	Escolapios	Young children	Spaniards, men and women
Tondo	7,217	2,290	1,999	3,028	5,676	7,296	58
Bulacan	7,272	2,220	2,624	3,357	4,541	8,610	15
Balayan	5,495	900	1,630	2,638	4,497	5,761	12
Pampanga	10,451	7,615	3,087	4,399	8,361	13,297	100
Pangasinan	3,064	725	541	843	1,568	3,001	0
Ylocos	17,283	4,151	4,001	6,652	7,707	17,464	41
Zebu	2,865	625	862	1,323	2,420	3,794	0
Ylo/lo	20,889	5,132	5,991	8,868	14,937	19,976	18
Panay	3,579	975	1,191	1,850	2,340	3,225	22
Total	78,115	24,633	21,926	32,958	52,047	82,424	266

Missions of various nations belonging to the province of Pampanga

Villages	Tribes	New Christians of both sexes	Catechumens
Mission of Magalang y Tarlac	Zambals	85	82
Mission of Tayug	Igorrots	343	60
Visita of Lupao	Balugas	62	20
Mission of Santor	Balugas	24	40
	Total	514	202

Missions of Igorrots and Tingyans belonging to the province of Ylocos

Villages	Tribes	New Christians of both sexes	Catechumens
Village of Santiago	Tingyans	352	200
Village of San Augustin de Bana	Tingyans	85	50
Territory of Batac	Tingyans	11	20
Territory of Narbacan	Igorrots	5	12
Territory of Candon	Igorrots	35	39
Territory of Bangar	Igorrots	79	33
Territory of Namacpacan	Igorrots	12	30
Territory of Agoo	Igorrots	12	9
Territory of Iringay	Igorrots	0	20
Territory of Bauan	Igorrots	3	5

Territory of Magsingal	Tingyans	6	4
Territory of Bacarra	Apayos	5	4
	Total	605	426

[Missions in] China

	New Christians of both sexes	Catechumens
Missions of China in various villages of that extensive empire	680	800

Total summary of the classes included in this table reduced to persons

[Notice is given that in the total of tributes it must be understood that each single whole tribute means two persons; and thus it will be noted in the figures. The total is as set forth below.]

Tributes	156,230
Exempt	24,633
Young men	21,926
Young women	32,958
Escolapios	52,047
Young children	82,424
Spaniards, men and women	266
Missions of these islands	1,693
Missions of China	1,480
Total	373,663

I, Master Fray Pedro Velasco, provincial of this province of Santísimo Nombre de Jesus of Philipinas of the Order of the Hermits of our father St. Augustine, certify that the lists of villages and souls contained in this table and which are administered by the religious of this said province, are set forth truly; and in order that this may be suitably evident, I have affixed my signature in this convent of Tondo, on April sixteenth, one thousand seven hundred and sixty.

Fray Pedro Velasco, provincial of St. Augustine.

1 Escolapios: regular clergy of the Order of Escuelas Pías (or "religious schools"), founded early in the seventeenth century by St. Joseph of Calasanz (1556–1648), an Aragonese priest. (See VOL. XLVI, pp. 114, 115, note 49.) Besides the usual three vows, they took another one, to consecrate themselves to the instruction of children. They soon attained great reputation,

and their order extended to many countries. So highly were their educational services appreciated in Spain that when the religious orders there were secularized (1835) that of Escuelas Pías was exempted therefrom by special grant, which was extended also to the Philippines. "Nevertheless, it is argued that they do not accept any salutary innovation or judicious reform, even when it is guaranteed by the experience of accredited instructors; and it is said that they walk on leaden feet, as if tied down to a stale routine." (Dominguez.)

Echegaray also gives to the word *Escolapios* the meaning of "students attending the Escuelas Pías," in which sense the word is evidently used here—except that the schools are simply the parish schools conducted by the friars among the Filipino natives.

2 totals given in these tables are in some cases incorrect, but have been left as in original.

LATER AUGUSTINIAN AND DOMINICAN MISSIONS

AUGUSTINIAN MISSIONS

[The following account of Augustinian missions in the first half of the eighteenth century is translated from Antonio Mozo's Noticia histórico natural (Madrid, 1763).1 It is presented partly in full, and partly in synopsis, preferring for the former such parts as are of ethnological interest.]

CHAPTER I-*In which account is given of the progress of the mission to the Italons, from the year 1700 to the present time*

After we had been able to reduce to our holy faith two tribes who dwelt at the summits of the most rugged mountains in the province of Pampanga, the Caraclans and Buquids, and from them had been formed three villages—Santor and Bongabon, quite populous; and Pantabangan, of smaller numbers, and lying more within the mountains2—this gate being now opened so that we could proceed further, it only needed that we should have the courage to do so. For at the first step were encountered two contiguous tribes: the Italons, a people fierce, brave, and bold; and the Abacas, who are somewhat less so. The religious therefore feared that those people, to judge from their ferocious natures, would without doubt tear them to pieces at the very outset, without even listening to them; and for this very reason they greatly dreaded to set foot within the territory of those tribes. While we were in these straits, our provincial then being our father reader Fray Francisco Zamora, about the year 1702 he selected for this purpose father Fray Antolin de Arzaga,3 whose virtue and ardor he knew well from experience, and entrusted to him this enterprise, as dangerous as difficult. [This gospel pioneer went out, equipped with what was necessary for administering the sacraments and with some trinkets to give the natives, "and with no other arms than his confidence in God."]

[On August 16, 1702, a letter from Father Arzaga to his superior gave account of his progress thus far; it was written from Pantabangan, which is "distant from Santor eight leguas by a very difficult road." From the latter village he sent a message, by the hands of four chiefs, to the chief of Lublub, who came out to meet him with forty infidels; but the father finally persuaded them to let him enter their village, where he exhorted and instructed them, receiving an attentive hearing. "This village [i.e., Lublub] has about one hundred and fifty persons; it is distant from this one [of Pantabangan] four leguas to the east, by an uneven road. This Italon tribe consists of fifty-six villages (so far as I have yet ascertained), which lie on the shores of two deep rivers, toward the north. They have a general language which is entirely separate from those of Tagalos and Pampanga; they have well-kept villages, with high houses. They take great care of their fields, and keep their grain in tambobos, or granaries, thus anticipating times of sterility and sickness. The fishing, as also the hunting, is abundant and good; the climate is temperate; and there are many open plains, beautiful to see. The people are kindly, but very warlike and of courageous dispositions; they are quite ingenious, and are hospitable. They understand that there is a God, and that He is in heaven, caring for all whom He creates — to whom they offer sacrifices, only when they make agreements of peace — and that there is no other God than He. They say that He rewards the good and punishes the bad, but they do not know in what manner; and they admit that they have immortal souls. They make a contract of marriage with one wife only, which lasts until death; they do not allow concubinage; and they do not marry their relatives. They observe the truth well; and, what is more, they desire to be Christians."4 Certain "bad Christians" have told these Italons that the Spaniards are trying to load them with tributes and take away their liberty; therefore they are waiting to make their decision, and fifteen of them, accompanied by an Augustinian religious, are carrying Arzaga's letter to Manila. He continues:]

"The Abaca tribe consists of ten villages, divided into two jurisdictions, one of which belongs to this village and contains six villages toward the north, extending, as they have told me, to the boundaries of the Igorrots. Twenty-two persons in the first village, called Diama, came to visit me as soon as I arrived here; having explained to them some mysteries of our holy faith, they returned to their own village. I visited them there, and they received me thus: They had placed a tall cross at the entrance of their jurisdiction, and from that place to the village they had cleared the roads, which are very bad, adorning them with arches up to the front of the house in which they lodged me; and there they had built another cross, even taller. This village is distant a legua and a half [from Pantabangan], and from it the gate is open for the entire Italon and Abaca tribes; it has wars with the Italons in regard to certain murders. I conferred with them about their making peace [with those villages], and their learning the truth which our holy faith teaches. They listened attentively to what I said to them; and, in conclusion, we made an agreement that they will at once become Christians and make peace. They ask that I catechize them, build a church, and baptize them. They are almost of the same type as the Italons; but some of them have several wives, and this is not so liberal a people as the former one. This village [of Diama] contains over a hundred persons; they speak a different language, for which reason it is necessary that there be a minister who can learn it, and devote himself to their instruction, for I am studying the Italon tongue. What I state to your Reverence is, that a minister is needed whom we can consult about some cases which are presenting themselves here; for it is very discouraging to act in the midst of scruples, in matters of conscience. What your Reverence shall ordain will be in every way most just.

"The second jurisdiction of this people pertains to Caranglan, to which I went with the determination to visit the four remaining villages; for father Fray Francisco de la Maza wrote to me from Itui that two of those villages desired to be converted, and were asking for a minister of our order, on account of being in our jurisdiction. I asked about this in Caranglan, and they said that it was true as regards one of them, which is an important village and is already Christian; and in the other village there are many persons who are Christians, although for lack of a minister they are going without administration. These two villages are a half-day's journey from Caranglan, by a bad road, and one is contiguous to Itui, on the western side. There are many rivers to be crossed; and, as these were filled by a storm which caught me at Caranglan, I could not cross them, although I waited a week. One Abaca has continued forty years in apostasy; he asks that I will reconcile him with the church, and baptize his wife and three children, and I am instructing them in order to do this. I am sending away the Italons [with this letter], and tomorrow the Indian who went to Manila will come, to go with me to the Abaca villages; we will do what is possible there, until the coming of another minister. When he shall come, I will go on to the Italons who are further up [the river]; they tell me that it will require two months, only to go to the villages. I have information that they desire to see a father, and to be Christians; this was furnished to me by Nicolàs de los Santos, who has been among these people; and he has done and is doing much good to their souls. He is my constant companion in my journeys, and serves me in everything; I earnestly commend him to your Reverence."

[The Italons who carried this letter to Manila were received with great kindness by Governor Zabalburu; and on their return they were accompanied by the minister for whom Arzaga had asked, for which post was selected his uncle, Fray Balthasar de Santa Maria Isisigana,5 who went as superior of that mission. The two entered upon its labors with indefatigable zeal and energy, and on December 28, 1702, Isisigana sent in an encouraging report of what they had accomplished. Arzaga had already built a church at a place four leguas from Pantabangan, which he dedicated to St. Thomas de Villanueva; and Isisigana writes that they have just erected another at San Agustin, and built a house for the minister, while at Santo Christo de Burgos, about six leguas distant from this, the timber is already being cut for another church and convent. Most of the people, whether adults or children, desire to embrace the Catholic faith; and the missionaries go about, surrounded by the children, who sing and dance with joy. In building the church of San Agustin, the fathers were aided by thirty infidels from another village, one and one-half leguas distant, who came of their own accord, simply because they had heard that a church was being erected there. Fray Arzaga went to the upper Italons, by wretched roads; he went on foot from Pantabangan to Tablayàn, the first Italon village, about eighteen leguas. Many natives visited him there; he desired to go farther, but was attacked with an illness which almost proved mortal, and was obliged to return to Pantabangan. The chief of Tablayan, with his family, accompanied him thither; and they were ready to build him a church and house at once, if he could have remained with them. The missionaries asked for cattle from Manila, and the provincial sent them two hundred and twenty. As they grew skilled in the native dialects, they were able to extend their labors further, and they baptized many people from the tribes in that region, Abaca, Italon, and Irapi; and by 1704 they had formed several villages and erected five churches. The fruits of their zeal, and those gathered by other Augustinian missionaries in the islands, are shown by a certificate given to the governor in that year by the provincial of the order, which reads as follows:]

"I, Fray Juan Bautista de Olarte, pensioned lecturer in sacred theology, provincial of the province of Santissimo Nombre de Jesus of the hermits of our father St. Augustine, do certify that, from the eighth day of October, 1702, until the twentieth of May in this present year, the two missionary religious of the said my order who were employed in the conversion of the natives in the Italon and Abaca tribes, who dwell in the mountains of Pantabangàn and Caranglàn,6 have founded five villages, to wit: Santo Tomàs de Villanueva, which is composed of eighty families; Santo Christo de Burgos, one hundred families; San Agustin, one hundred and sixty; San Pablo, one hundred and forty; San Joseph, seventy families. They all have accepted the faith of our Lord Jesus Christ, and the holy sacrament of baptism has been administered to four hundred and seventy-nine persons, all adults, who are instructed and taught in the Christian doctrine and the mysteries of our holy faith; and those who at present are being catechized and instructed for baptism number more than eight hundred persons.

"I also certify that in the said mountains of Pantabangàn and Caranglàn dwell the tribes called Igorrots, Irapis, and Sinay, and others, which contain a great number of natives who live in their pagan state; and that the Italon tribe alone contains fifty-six villages, all infidels, who have offered to become Christians when they shall have ministers who can teach them and preach the religion of our Lord Jesus Christ; and that the said missionaries of my order are employed in this ministry.

"I also certify that the minister of my order who serves in the villages of Tarlac, Magalan, and Bucsi, Zambal villages in the province of Pampanga, has catechized and baptized, from the year 1702 up to May 20 of this present year, fifty-eight adults, all of whom have come down from the mountains of the said villages.

"I also certify that the minister who serves in the village of Pórac in the said province of Pampanga has catechized, instructed, and baptized, in the missions which he has carried on in the mountains of the said village during the said two years, twenty-six natives among the blacks who dwell in that neighborhood.

"I also certify that the religious of the said my order who serve in the villages of Agoò, Bavang, and Bacnotan in the province of Pangasinan have converted to our holy faith, and instructed and baptized, in the period of two years twenty-six natives from the tribe called Igorrots, who dwell in the said mountains.

"I also certify that the ministers who serve in the province of Ilocos have in the period of two years converted to our holy faith and baptized one hundred and fifty-six natives from the infidel Tinguians who are in and belong to the said province, and live in its mountains and hills.

"I also certify that the minister for the village of Antique in the province of Octong has in his charge and care the islets which are called Cagayàn, and has labored for seven years to convert the natives inhabiting them to our holy faith. Having gone thither to visit the Christians, in the past year of 1703, he gave instruction in the Christian doctrine and the mysteries of our holy faith to forty-four adults, and baptized them, with others, who were the children of Christian parents; and he heard the confessions of all the old Christians, for he remained in that mission four months. In the said province of Ogtòn, the religious who are ministers at Guimbal, Tigbavan, and Xaro have converted to our holy faith and baptized thirty-six adults, on various occasions when they have gone into the mountains in their respective jurisdictions. That there has not been a greater increase [in the number of conversions] not only in this province, but in those of Pampanga, Pangasinan, and Ilocos, is [due to] the lack of religious ministers; for those in my province are not enough for even the maintenance of the villages and Christians who are in their charge. And in order that these things may be evident in the proper place, I give the present at the demand and order of the captain-general of these islands, and president of the royal Audiencia, Don Domingo Zabalburu; it is dated at this royal convent of San Pablo at Manila, on the twenty-sixth day of May, in the year one thousand seven hundred and four.

Fray Juan Bautista Olarte, provincial."

[So great was the zeal of Arzaga and Isisigana that they devoted themselves to seeking out the heathen among those wild mountains, enduring privations, exposure, and sufferings, until the health of both was broken down. Arzaga was again attacked by a sickness which prostrated him, and died in 1707; his uncle held out three years longer, and was then called in from the field, in order to recruit his strength, but he was never able to return to his labors, and died in 1716, in the convent of Vava.7 In their place was sent to this mission field Fray Alexandro Cacho,8 in zeal and courage a worthy successor to them. He succeeded in converting a chief named Dinalavang, dreaded as well as renowned for his fierce and warlike disposition and for his skill in all military exercises; also a sister of this man, as valiant and dextrous as he, baptized as Doña Maria. Mozo gives an interesting account of the fierce and cruel practices of these savage tribes (whom he compares to the Huns), "which more than once I have rebuked, when I have been among those people." "If they succeed in killing a person they try to drink his blood; and, cutting off pieces of his lungs, together with the testicles9 and other parts, they also draw out the entrails, and then divide these among themselves and eat them raw—not only to make themselves terrible, but also because they say it is a powerful medicine for exciting courage, fierceness, and fortitude in their battles. They also cut off the head, and carry it away in order to celebrate their festivals, with great gluttony and carousing, [filling the skull] with a sort of wine which they make from sugarcane and call ilang. Afterward, they take the grinders and teeth and set these in the hilts of their cutlasses; and, as a consequence, there is hardly any one in this tribe or in the Ibilaos whose cutlass is not adorned with many teeth of those whom he has killed, or who has not in his hut a collection of the skulls from human heads—this very thing inspiring them with greater courage when they fight, in the same way as it happened, as Virgil sings, to Æneas when he saw on his antagonist Turnus the scarf of his beloved Pallas. So these people, when they see the teeth of their own tribesmen on the sword-hilts of their opponents, fling themselves upon the latter like mad dogs; and from this may be readily inferred what degree of ferocity and barbarism theirs must be, and what sort of hardships and labors it will cost to free them from the power of the demon…. They greatly dislike arrogance in their neighbors; and they likewise abhor every sorcerer and wizard, a motive which makes them treat without mercy any one of these whom they seize, cutting him to pieces with their knives; and even at their feasts, and in the superstitious rites which they practice, they utter a thousand execrations against such persons, hurling at them a thousand curses, and swearing that they will not spare any one of them who may fall into their hands, [an oath] which they fulfil exactly." Mozo describes the secret raids made by these people against their enemies, marching at night and attacking a defenseless village at daybreak; and he accuses them of aiding their ordinary weapons with a diabolical practice—"they throw into a hole in some creek a root and herbs which they carry, provided [for this purpose], and, by their using various magic spells which the demon has taught to them, so violent a wind is raised, and a tempest of rain, that with the noise thus caused they are not observed, and likewise are better protected from the villages against which they march." He adds, "I do not relate fables;" and states that he has several times endeavored to restrain them from this devilish proceeding. Sometimes, he says, the proceedings are reversed, and the aggressors are, in their turn, surprised by those whom they have attacked, who then take revenge upon them. Mozo relates how, on one occasion, a hostile band of heathen attacked some Christians, and captured a loaded musket, its match still lighted; they examined it carefully, and, while handling it, incautiously let the match fall on the priming. The gun was discharged, killing some and crippling others of the group crowded around it; the survivors fled in terror, but afterward returned to the spot, and with a cord dragged the gun to their village and buried it in the ground. Learning that its owner lived in Bongabon, they immediately rated the people of that village as sorcerers, who had placed a powerful magic in the gun; and for more than fifty years they taught their children, as soon as the latter could speak, to avoid the dwellers in Bongabon as dangerous sorcerers.]

CHAPTER II-*The glorious triumphs among the Isinay and adjoining tribes are related*

In the wild and impenetrable mountain ranges which extend to the northeast and north, and separate the provinces of Pampanga and Nueva Segovia, there are various tribes who have almost the same customs as those of the Abaca and Ibilaos; one of these is the one called Isinay.10 To them, and to the adjacent tribes, the fervent zeal of the fathers belonging to the illustrious Order of St. Dominic11 had been directed, years before; but they found so much stubbornness, violence, and cruelty that—after immense labors, and having been in danger of losing their lives—they were not able to secure the conversion of one of those people to our holy faith. For this reason the fathers were obliged to withdraw from them, seeing that they were wasting time without having any result, or even the hope of it. [The Augustinian Cacho took up this task, and went on foot among those wild mountains and wilder savages; at first they repulsed him, and even tried to kill him, but finally his perseverance and patience softened their hard hearts, and they were willing to listen to him.] From the year 1715 until 1723, he was able to found four new villages of the Isinay people, not to mention many others besides, from other tribes, whom he baptized, and who united themselves with the other villages previously mentioned. Finally, continuing unweariedly in his holy task, and enduring the hardships which may be guessed, by the year 1738 he had come to the end of baptizing and converting the entire Isinay tribe, with a large part of other tribes, whom he settled in different villages. All these, thoroughly subdued and tamed, baptized, and established in a well civilized mode of life, the [Augustinian] province surrendered to the holy Order of St. Dominic, with churches, dwellings for the religious, the sacred vessels, and the other ornaments of the sacristy, because that of our father St. Augustine found that it had many missions for which to care, and not religious enough for all. This surrender was made in the year 174012 preceding the permission of the governor and examination by the judge whom he appointed for that task. The latter recorded a judicial inventory of everything that was surrendered, and even copied from the baptismal registers the numbers of the persons baptized, that these matters might be evident for all time; and at the same time he made a judicial investigation, showing who those were who began to evangelize the said tribes—from which it appeared that when our religious began their labors there, there was not any Christian in those places. This surrender being accomplished, then, our religious withdrew to their other missions, in which there are fifteen villages which have been formed since the year 1702, at which time that mission was commenced for the aforesaid places. In these glorious triumphs, those who attained greatest eminence and were most fortunate in winning souls, next to the three religious [already named], sons of this province of Castilla, were: our father Fray Vicente Ibarra,13 who afterward was provincial; the father definitor Fray Juan Velloxin, a most guileless man, full of virtue, and unwearied in labors; the father Fray Diego Nogueròl, who is still living, and has been definitor—all these three from this province of Castilla—and the father commissary Fray Joseph Gonzalez, a son of the province of Philipinas; also others, whom, in order not to be tedious, I omit.

[News of this change reached Spain in 1742, and the general public impression was that the aforesaid conversions had been accomplished by the Dominican fathers. At the representations of the Augustinian procurator at Madrid, the king issued a decree (dated December 19, 1742), approving and confirming the transfer made to the Dominicans, setting forth the facts in the case and giving the credit for these labors to the Augustinians. In the rehearsal of their achievements various interesting facts are stated. The people of Ituy were formerly called Isinay, a name given to them by the Italons. The first three Augustinian missionaries baptized, from the year 1715 to 1723, six hundred and ninety-five persons of all ages among these Ituis, not counting many others who were being prepared for baptism. Of these converts they formed four villages with their churches: Bujay (the chief village), Pigpig, Marian, and Canan. In this and the Italon mission they baptized in that period three thousand, four hundred and thirteen persons. In 1723 the order applied to the governor for further aid; he sent Auditor Pabón to inspect the missions, whose report led to the appointment of three more missionaries there, their stipends paid from the royal treasury. The eighteen Isinay villages had been reduced to nine14 by the missionaries; all of these contained church buildings, and most of them convents; and the people were considerably civilized. The missionaries had provided them with beasts of burden, and with "all the rest that was necessary for the cultivation of their grain-fields." Through the efforts of these missionaries, in conjunction with the Dominicans, a road was constructed from Pampanga to Cagayan;15 and another, from Pangasinan to Paniqui, was opened by the Dominicans, in which they were aided greatly by the Augustinians. The eighteen Italon villages, with two others, were reduced to fifteen: within the mountains, Puncàn, Caranglan, San Miguèl, Santa Rita, Bolo, Pantabangan, San Juan, and Santo Thomàs; in the valleys, Tayog, Umingan, Lupào, San Joseph, Palosapes (or Urorin), San Agustin, and Santa Monica. Perhaps the greatest among the Augustinian missionaries was Alexandro Cacho, who died in 1745. After him came Fray Agustin Barriocanal,16 a man of great zeal, who formed a village called Ambayavan; in the flower of his youth he was drowned while trying to ford a swollen stream (June 5, 1747). Another noted missionary was Pedro Freyre; he converted eighty families in the Jumangi tribe, and gathered them into a village, with their own church; and he converted great numbers from the Italon, Abaca, Ibilao,

Irapi, and Ilongot tribes, and even some of the blacks (Negritos). Mozo cites their labors in order to show that the missionary spirit was then even more active and aspiring than in the early days of the conquest; and confirms it by describing the mode of life of these mountain tribes, and the consequent difficulties in missionary labor among them, saying:]

The tribes converted by the early missionaries were more civilized, dwelt on the plains, and had a more orderly mode of life, sowing grain and gathering enough for their support; but these of whom we speak, besides being rough in their behavior, hardly know any tillage of the soil, living generally by hunting. Their mode of cultivating what little they plant is as follows: They first clear some little piece of ground from the brush and weeds on it, with their knives (which resemble those which the butchers use); then with the point of the knife they make holes in the ground, in rows, and throw into each a few grains of seed; they know no other plow, or any other thing which might serve as one, for which reason the harvest that they gather is always very small. They do the same for any planting of sugarcane which they make—from which, when the cane is mature, they press out the juice and make wine for drinking at their feasts; after cutting out of the soil the grass to the roots, they make little holes in it, and then thrust into these the shoots from the mature canes which they had cut. For this reason, and because it is necessary to provide means by which those who are converted may obtain a suitable support, so that for lack of this they may not go wandering about, as soon as we begin to confer baptism we endeavor to find animals and other necessaries for the cultivation of the land—the religious being often the first one who begins to plow and sow, directing them in this way, so that they may learn how to do it. The same thing occurs with reaping. They do not use sickles, but go on picking the grain spike by spike; and, as there is so little of it, they soon end their task. But, now that they are taught to plow, it is also necessary to teach them to cut and winnow the grain; and this is done, the religious being the ones who commence it, in order that the people may imitate them—in which the work alone is for them, as they give up all the fruit of it for the benefit of the said barbarians. [The missionaries also had to contend with the attachment of the savages to their mountains, for they abhorred the life on the plains. One reason was, their dread of the smallpox, which never entered the mountains, because these savage dwellers there instituted a strict quarantine—closing up the roads and paths with logs and brushwood, and sending out the declaration that they would immediately kill any one who dared to enter their territory. Another reason was, that the hotter climate of the plains did not agree with them. Accordingly, in order not to exasperate them, no further effort was made to change their dwellings, and the religious continued to labor among them in the midst of a thousand trials and hardships.]

CHAPTER III-*Missions of the provinces of Ilocos and Pangasinan in general*

[Mozo states that the two provinces of Pampanga and Pangasinan were so populous that, "of those whom our forefathers converted in these two provinces alone are counted more than one hundred and fifty thousand souls—who, settled in villages, and maintained in a very civilized and Christian society, hold their own on the frontier of the infidels; for their territory allows them no alternative, shut in on one side by the sea, and on the other by very rugged mountains."]

Four very noted tribes, three of them very extensive and populous, the fourth of more restricted territory and containing fewer souls—in which last the enemy [of souls], strongly fortified, has resisted for long ages— have been the aim to which the zeal and fervor of the evangelical ministers have been directed. The said tribes dwell among mountain ranges that are very extensive, lofty, and rugged—which, stretching from the province of Pampanga and bordering that of Pangasinan, run throughout Ilocos, through a space, with bends and turns, of about a hundred leguas.17 The first of these tribes is called Igolot, and, corrupting the letters, they are wont to call it Igorrot; their territory occupies about thirty leguas, from the confines of Pampanga to those of the province of Ilocos. Contiguous to this tribe is another which is called Tinggian, not less numerous; and it extends for a distance of about forty leguas along the same mountains, even trenching upon the province of Ilocos. Then comes another, called Apayao,18 extending about thirty leguas, which consists of many thousands of souls; and at one side dwell another tribe, called Adang, which has fewer people, but, for the very reason that they find themselves less powerful, they have their dwellings in places almost inaccessible—maintaining (as do the three others) their own different dialect. Of the said four tribes, the first and third are to a great degree cruel and barbarous; but the second and third, although sufficiently obstinate, are more tractable. It is said that the Igolot tribe are a caste of those Chinese who had come over with the pirate Limahon to conquer those islands; and, being conquered, he escaped with those whom he could gather, those who could taking refuge in these mountains, in which they have multiplied exceedingly. Besides the reasons which favor this opinion, it is apparently confirmed by their appearance; for, although they go about naked, and are subjected to every inclemency of the weather, they nevertheless greatly resemble the Chinese in the light color and gracefulness of their bodies, especially in the eyes, in which there is a close likeness between them. Their fierceness and cruelty is unequaled; their only desire is to take captives, in order to have slaves for their service, and, when they have enough of these, to kill whomever they encounter. For this reason, without a strong escort one cannot pass, except with great danger, through the upper part of those mountains; and even the villages are so infested with them that as a precaution they always keep some men armed to resist these marauders — at night stationing a sentinel with his drum, who is changed during the daytime — throughout that mountain range. And because in every place our natives (especially if they are away from the village) are so harassed by the Igolots, therefore when they go to sow their grain or gather their crops they erect high sentry-posts, from which they can see if the enemy are coming; and those who work keep the sickle in one hand and a weapon in the other — as we are told of the Israelites when in the time of Esdras they were building the walls of Jerusalem…. And even when they do this, they are not safe from the fury of these savages. Such was the ferocity of this tribe, in which they continued until the past year of 1755, and in such manner did they try the patience of all those villages.

The tribe adjoining this one, called Tingguian, are more gentle and more industrious, and maintain a much more civilized condition, because they have much intercourse with the Christians in whose vicinity they live; and for the same reason they are more open to the teachings of the religious. And although so far as concerns the acceptance of baptism they have continued very obstinate, for many years refusing to allow a religious to live among them, yet always it has been a very satisfactory harvest [of souls] which annually has been gathered and united with the Christians, as may be seen by the certificate of the reverend father provincial which is presented above; speaking of the Tingguians, he states that in only two years one hundred and fifty-six infidels had been converted to our holy faith by the religious of the villages near by — which has always been the fact, sometimes more and sometimes fewer. With such a drop of comfort as this, the ministers were consoled — who, not finding any hindrance in going from time to time to visit those savages, went in and out, carried away by their holy zeal. And although, when the fathers talked to them about our holy law, they would reply that the time for it had not yet come for them, nor was it possible to overcome their caprices by any arguments, nevertheless there was always one person here, or another there, who was made ready to receive the heavenly influences.

The third tribe, which is the one called Apayao, not only does not remain behind the Igolot in cruelty, bloodthirstiness, and barbarism, but in a great degree surpasses it. For not only are its men continually going about, placing a thousand ambushes in the roads, in order to exercise their rage on the wretches who have the misfortune to fall into their hands, without sparing any person, no matter of what rank or condition he may be; but they have, besides, a specially barbaric custom and cruel superstition at the funerals and obsequies of their chiefs and other persons whom they respect, in every way very similar to that which for many centuries the Greeks practiced at the death of their heroes, and other persons of rank, before and after the so celebrated destruction of Troya. [Here Mozo makes a long digression regarding the customs of the ancient Greeks and Romans in killing slaves or other people at the death of a prominent person.] These [Apayao] barbarians, then, are wont to celebrate the funerals and obsequies of their dead, although not promiscuously of all, but only those of their chiefs and other persons to whom they pay respect; and because they believe that the shades [manes] of the deceased take delight in human blood, they endeavor to give them this pleasure by killing people—a greater or less number, according to the station of the dead man. To do so, they avail themselves only of those whom they capture for this purpose, and these they go out to seek with great diligence, as soon as the dying man has ceased to breathe. In order that they may not lack these captives, they assemble a considerable number of men, and, some taking one road and some another, they go down from the mountains well armed, and, hiding in the brushwood near the roads, they wait very silently for some passers-by; and, as soon as they discover such persons, they attack them with great fury, and kill them with their javelins on the very spot. This done, the assailants cut off their heads, and laden with these (leaving the bodies there) they carry them to their own dead, and place the heads about him. After this they celebrate their sort of banquet, at which they eat and drink like beasts; and when this is finished they complete the burial. Placing in the tomb some portion of food and drink, they bury the corpse with those heads, being greatly pleased and satisfied at having pleased the shades of their dead, and believing that through this whatever they may undertake will have a prosperous issue.

[Mozo recalls the scanty results of missionary work among these savage tribes in the early days. "In the year 1660, when Don Diego de Salcedo was governor of these islands, two religious escorted by some soldiers entered the territory of the Igorrots, and in a place called Cayam19 they established a small military post with a church, which they dedicated to the archangel St. Michael; and from this place they began with apostolic zeal to preach to those tribes the holy name of God, but the harvest of souls which they could obtain was exceedingly small...." A little while after the said religious had made this entrance, the soldiers became sick through the insalubrity of the region, and the barbarians threatened to cut them into pieces if they did not immediately go away from that place. Accordingly, not having sufficient force to resist, the fathers were obliged to yield to this opposition, and retired with much sadness, taking with them such persons as they had baptized. From that time until recent years, none of the various attempts to found a mission there had been successful, although occasional converts were made among those tribes. Among the Apayaos and Tingguians also this experience was repeated; only within recent years had they allowed the religious to labor among them, a few, however, being converted by missionaries in villages near them.]

CHAPTER IV-The missions of Ilocos, in especial

[The missionaries who most zealously and successfully labored in this field were: Fray Joseph Herice, Fray Jacinto Rivera, Fray Nicolàs Fabro, and Fray Manuel Madariaga.20 The first-named established this mission in 1720; he formed a village of his converts, the first thus established among the Adang tribe, another having been made among the Apayaos, which was called Vera [i.e., Vira?]. The infidels named Father Herice "the hunter of souls." He labored among them twenty-two years, dying in 1742; and three years later Father Rivera followed him, after gaining considerable extension for this mission.]

CHAPTER V-The mission to the Tingguians

[Father Fabro labored in this mission also, and formed a village of converts which he called San Juan; by the year 1750, it contained more than a thousand souls. This missionary labored indefatigably, and much exposure and hardship finally crippled him; Fray Madariaga came to his aid, and, although his health was not good, he accomplished wonders. In 1736 he formed a village at Dingras, naming it Santiago; his death occurred in 1744. In 1753 two other Tingguian villages were newly formed—one three leguas from Santiago, further within the mountains; and another, four leguas from this. In that same year, Father Juan Solorzano was sent to this mission; he was most zealous and useful, and forgetful of self, so much so that within the first year he contracted a fever, as the result of exposure, which ended his life in four days.]

CHAPTER VI-The mission to the Igolot tribe in especial

[Mozo refers to what he has already mentioned, that these barbarians would not allow the missionaries to settle in their country, but that some of them became converted through the labors of outside missionaries. They were not disturbed by this, however, but rather were pleased, because their relatives or friends who had removed to Christian villages were thus able to supply them with articles of comfort or luxury which they themselves had not—"blankets, which they wrap around them when there is some cold weather, in the time of north winds; wine; hogs and cattle, of whose flesh they are very fond, and use it continually in their feasts and banquets." Through this commerce, also, the missionaries find opportunity to reach some of the heathen, and thus secure occasional conversions. Mozo describes a barbarous custom of theirs: "It is a usage among these people not to give burial to any of their dead, especially if he was a chief, until whatever he may have left has been consumed in gluttony and carousing among his relatives and others belonging to him; with some chiefs this is commonly no small amount, because in the rivers there some gold is found, and all the people endeavor to obtain it for their chiefs. For, expending for cattle, hogs, rice, and wine whatever the dead man possessed of this sort, they make enormous bonfires about the corpse, which they lay in the ground; and having killed the animals, they thrust them just as they are—with hair, hides, and entrails—into the said bonfires, and thus prepare barbecues[21] which are savory to their taste. Afterward, beginning to dance around the corpse, they keep this up night and day, one set giving place to another.[22] They eat and drink frequently; and if any one is inclined to sleep he squats on his haunches, with his head resting on his knees, and needs no other bed. Thus they remain, ten, fifteen, or twenty days with the corpse, without interring it; and, even when it emits a stench and swarms with maggots, it does not drive them away. They reserve some gold and some food, which afterward they inter with the deceased, so that he may have it, as they say, for his journey." In 1747 the Augustinian Fray Francisco Cordova (who had been the associate of Cacho) was sent to Agoo, on the frontier of the Igolots, and soon secured their good-will, although they long refused to allow him to live among them. Finally, after seven years of this apparently unfruitful labor, a miraculous change occurred. During the visitation of the provincial—then Fray Manuel Carrillo, accompanied by Mozo as his secretary—while he was conferring with Cordova at Aringay, five chiefs came down from the mountains, and asked Carrillo to send missionaries among them. He sent a deputation of them to Manila to ask this favor from the governor; who received them most graciously, and granted whatever they asked; they were instructed in the faith and baptized while in Manila, and returned to their tribe, who eagerly sought baptism also. Cordova[23] was made superior of the new mission, with Fray Francisco Romero and Fray Pedro Vivar as his assistants; they built two churches, and baptized many hundreds of the people. In other Igolot villages, missions were also conducted by Fray Carlos de Horta, Fray Joseph Torres, and Fray Juan Sanchez.]

CHAPTER VII-Missions to the Zambals

Along the provinces of Pangasinan and Pampanga, fronting their western side, there dwells another tribe, which they call Zambal, no less fierce than those already mentioned, and exceeding them in boldness. They are continually assaulting travelers, and they take their greatest pleasure in killing. So continual are their descents from the mountains to infest the said roads that it is only with great peril that one can cross from one province to the other without an escort; and even then many mishaps occur frequently; for these bandits lie hidden in the thickets and ravines at the sides of the road, and, when one of them gives a yell, all discharge their arrows, in the management of which they are very skilful; and, felling to the ground those whom they can reach, they cut off the heads of these, and carry them away in order to celebrate their feasts. They are also wont to approach the villages by night, and in hiding to wait for any person who strays from the rest and leaves the village early; then they do the same with him, be his rank what it may; afterward they take the skull of the slain man's head and use it for a drinking-vessel, in the same manner as did the Scythians, as Ravisius Textor and Plinius relate.

This tribe obtain their living generally from the hunting of deer, wild swine and buffaloes, and from the honey produced by the innumerable bees which are in those extensive forests and shut-in mountains. They are accustomed also to plant certain potatoes, which here we call Malagan potatoes, and there are named camote, the seed of which, with the name, was carried [thither] from Nueva España; but they care little for the said planting, because without any work of their own the Author of Nature provides them with a kind of wild palm, so useful and profitable that this tree alone admirably displays the wisdom of its Creator—for what it spontaneously yields is a thing to cause astonishment, and would even be incredible to one who did not see it. [Mozo here cites several authors regarding the uses of the palm in other countries, but says, "all this is nothing compared to the palms which we are going to describe; accordingly, for the praise of the Creator, I am going to give a full account of the said tree," which he accordingly does. The palm referred to is the buri,24 or sago-palm; its farinaceous product is called yoro in Pampangan, and in Tagálog sagu. He describes the native method of fire-making among these people, as follows: "They take two splinters of a kind of bamboo, very thick and tall, which grows in abundance throughout the forests there, and along the creeks; and, scraping the outer surface of one of these a little with a knife, they make tinder of the shavings. Then they make a notch in the splinter with which they must rub the other one; and, placing on its outside that which serves for tinder, they make the other splinter firm, placing it on edge against some tree, first paring its upper edge thin, like a knife-blade. This done, with the other and notched splinter (and the tinder filling the notch) they begin, holding it flat, to rub the lower one very hard. In less than two minutes it begins to smoke, and is fully kindled; they breathe upon it to raise a flame, and, feeding this with dry leaves, grass, and little sticks, in a very short time they make a fierce blaze."25 Mozo also describes some vegetable medicines used by the natives. Among these wild people were sent missionaries, Fray Gonzalo de Salazar and others; these form villages with their converts— "Magalang, Tarlac, Bucsic, and Panlinlan, in which there are more than seven hundred families, as appears from the original register, made in the past year of 1759, of which I have a legal copy." In 1728, Fray Juan Velloxin formed the village of Tunàs; and in 1755 Fray Sebastian Morono established those of Pandolan, Garlit, San Miguèl, and another one. Besides these, many converts removed their residence to other Christian villages. Mozo notices, as a curious phenomenon, that among these Zambals are certain persons who are immune to the bites of poisonous animals and insects—as he thinks, because of some quality of their "humors," or of their physical conditions; he cites therefor Pliny and other writers, and various instances of which he has known personally. He also describes the cure of these poisonous bites by sucking out the poison, which act (as also the person who does it) is called, in Pampangan, tavac; but the ability to accomplish this he ascribes to some peculiarity of temperament or physique on the part of the healer.]

CHAPTER VIII-*Missions to the Balugas,26 or Aetas*

Besides the aforesaid missions, the province maintains another, scattered through all the islands, to a class of people who, it is believed (and with no small reason), were in olden times the masters of the entire land. One of the grounds for this belief is, that in all the islands (which are very many) these people maintain an identical language, and different from those of all the other peoples among whom they live; while the other natives of each island have a language different [from those spoken in other islands], and even in some places (as is evident throughout all this treatise) are encountered at every turn different dialects in the same island. Another argument is drawn from the similarity which there is between the peoples of those islands and the Malayos, and even in their respective languages—these Malayos are natives of Maluco, and are quite energetic and warlike—excepting the people of whom we now speak. From this it has been inferred that these blacks ruled that country; and that the said Malayos, coming to it and subduing its former masters, compelled them to retire to the bush and the mountain heights, abandoning the rest of the country to the conquerors.

These people of whom we speak are very dark in color, not black like those of Angola; neither have they thick lips, or curly and short hair, like them. But their color is a brownish or pallid [descolorido] black, their hair like that of a mulatto; their lips are not thick; many of them are very corpulent, and all have large abdomens, and generally both men and women appear feeble. All go naked, with no other covering than a long strip like a narrow sash, with which, tied round the waist and drawn between the legs, the men cover their private parts; while the women wear a sort of apron, which covers them behind and before as far as the knees. Both sexes make these coverings from the bark of a tree which they call balete; stripping off its bark, which is very smooth and flexible, they place it in water, afterward beating it in order to loosen the outer layer; then washing and drying it, it remains of the color and softness of a chamois-skin, although it is thin. They keep this on until it wears out, and when they can no longer use it they repair to the shop in the grove, to look for another in their storehouse.

The nature and peculiarities of these Balugas are described by the reverend father, former provincial of the Philipinas, our father Fray Vicente Ibarra, in the report of the missions which he made to the governor of those islands, Don Fernando Valdés Tamon, in the year 1738. He says, then, speaking of these people: "The third mission which is in these mountains is very arduous, not so much on account of the toilsome roads as because the people have less intellect than [any other that] is known in these islands; for this reason it has not been possible to introduce them into any civilization, although those who are baptized are numerous. Their maintenance in the faith is so difficult that it cannot easily be explained after the no small expenses that are incurred; for all the time while the ministers are devoting themselves to their instruction it is necessary to support the fathers, furnishing to them rice, meat, wine, and tobacco, along with some trinkets for the women and children. For those people have neither house nor fields, nor any furniture save the bow and arrow and some heavy knives [machetes], with which they are continually seeking their food, without reserving anything for another day."

[Mozo adds other information, acquired during his residence of three years among the Negritos; but precedes it by various citations from learned authors. Returning to his subject, he says:]

They have their own territory, within which they go about in bands and from which they never go out; but they do not have any fixed dwelling-place in it, for they remain a short time in one place hunting, and afterward they remove therefrom four or five leguas away. In whatever place they arrive, they make their hut in an instant with four rough sticks, and with a sort of grass, very long and flexible, with which the country abounds, which they call ilib,27 or with the leaves of palms—with which and with the stakes they form their huts (which resemble those of the vineyard-keepers), in which with a piece of wood and some dry grass,28 which they are sure to find about the entrance, they forthwith have bed and pillows, and all that they need for sleep. They live entirely in common, and therefore when they capture any deer or wild swine (by hunting which they live) they immediately share it equally—except the head and neck, which parts they set aside for the dogs that they have, who start the said game.

Each band, usually containing twenty-five to thirty persons, goes by itself, with one man to whom the rest pay respect, generally the one who is most daring and valiant. In the summer they go down to live on the banks of the streams, seeking the fresh air; but in times of rain, or when the north winds blow hard, they huddle together in the thickets, so dense that the wind hardly enters them. If one of them dies, as soon as he expires they bury him in a very shallow grave; and then they take to flight, in order that death may not seize another person and carry him away, as they say. When the time for [gathering] honeycombs arrives—and the stores of honey which the bees29 gather in those dense forests are without limit—they are busy in searching for these; and if they come across a honey-tree the person who finds it immediately makes a mark on the trunk of the tree, and possesses it as securely as if he had it in his own house. For, even if another person goes there and finds it, when he sees the mark he says: "This tree already has an owner," and therefore he goes on. Afterward, they go at a convenient time, and, waiting until there is no wind, so that the smoke may not be prevented from rising perpendicularly, they make a fire [under the tree]; and, the bees being scared away, men climb the tree, carrying a sort of sling, strongly made from a palm-leaf, very broad, [from the tree] which they call anao.30 They take out the comb entire, with wax and all, placing it in this receptacle; and then tie it together and carry it down. They eat the honey, and sell the wax in order to buy tobacco for smoking, without which they cannot pass the time. So long as such people have their tobacco, their bows and arrows, their half-cutlass, and their outfit for striking fire, they do not desire anything else—money, or clothing, or lands—neither do they envy any person for anything. They shoot arrows with the greatest dexterity, and will pierce a deer with one from side to side in his most rapid flight. When they have food they eat it in a barbarous manner; but if on account of bad weather they have not been able to obtain any game, they boil water and drink it, and compress their bellies with cords. They are also accustomed to dig in the ground and search for a root called sucbao,31 with which, when it is roasted, they can subsist, although in summer they never lack fruits in the woods. They are always happy, and keep themselves plump and contented; and among them are persons who are quite old.

I frankly confess that, in the midst of the sorrow that was occasioned in me by the extreme barbarism and mental stupidity of this people when I knew by experience their mode of life, at the same time not only were presented before me those golden ages, so celebrated, of which Ovid treats at length in his Metamorphoses, Cicero in his Aratus, Lactantius Firmianus in his Institutiones, and Seneca in his Epistolæ, but I also saw how true is that Epicurean maxim, which, distinguishing human necessities, says, Naturales necessitates satiari pene nihilo. To which Pythocles adds, Si vis hominem divitem facere, non pecuniæ adjice, sed cupiditatibus detrahe.32 It is worth while to see the said people going about naked, without house or shelter, without land, and even without desire for it, yet living contented, happy, plump, and satisfied; without having any anxieties beyond that of searching for enough to get through the day with — which, as it is but little, they soon provide from what is yielded by nature in those mountains…. Again I say that their mode of life arouses my admiration, and that if they were enlightened by our holy faith, and were enduring for God's sake the sufferings that they experience, I believe that not even the most austere monk of the Thebaid could equal them. It is, however, true that they avail themselves of the "bill of divorce," although before marriage a false step is hardly heard of among them; and that in some districts they are cruel and murderous.

[Mozo here makes observations on various medicinal plants, which he found by actual experience or observation to be highly efficacious. Among these are two roots which these natives used in cases of parturition — one to facilitate the birth, the other to cleanse and strengthen the mother's system; the woman was able to go out from her hut, carrying her infant, within one day, or even a few hours. Seeing the great virtue of this treatment, Mozo obtained a quantity of these remedies and prescribed them successfully in many similar cases, after he left the Negritos. They poisoned their arrows with a decoction of the bark of the camandag,33 and of some other plants, in order to kill large game — so powerful a poison that even a buffalo would die within two minutes if one of these arrows hit even its hoof.]

It is a fact, however, that they do not use the said poisoned arrows against any save animals, considering it an inexpiable crime to shoot rational beings with them; but for hunting those animals — "the great game," as they call them — they use these arrows continually, and with them kill innumerable beasts. When one of these falls to the ground, they immediately cut off its head; and, having thoroughly washed the flesh, they eat it without any misgivings. I baptized the man who chiefly made this poison, who was already past the age of ninety years, who never was willing to leave me until he died; and on various occasions he explained to me the method of making the said poison, naming to me the separate ingredients, although I never was acquainted with them. These same people have other plants, the use of which I tried, in my religious instructions, to banish among them—not only because some persons make use of them for evil purposes, but also because they lead one to suspect some diabolical aid, for those people accomplish with them things which are truly amazing. But since information of this may be of great assistance in explaining some things which, written by the ancients, give the moderns material for many and various curious inquiries, I will briefly describe what those barbarians are accustomed to do with the said plants. They use, then, I was told, certain herbs that are amatory, or adapted for philters, if thus they should be called (which I do not dispute), in order to captivate the love of those whom they desire to win. For instance, do they desire to marry some woman who does not love them? Then, obtaining their herbs (which they know very well), they carry these with them, endeavoring at the same time to carry them in the mouth when they talk with the woman; and the attraction is usually such that in a short time they succeed in gaining the affection of women who before were very averse to loving them. They do the same when they enter the presence of some person whom they have offended and whom they fear. They take the said herbs in their mouths, and, armed with this antidote, they are not afraid to be seen by him and to talk with him; and such are the results that they experience that, even when that person is greatly offended, he feels for that time so changed that, far from showing his anger, he receives them with great kindness, and with indications of special affection. They are also wont to use the aforesaid herbs in order to succeed in committing their lewd acts with women; and the women do the same in order to make themselves beloved by the men, very often, but not always, succeeding in this. [Mozo relates an instance of this: a convert of his own, a most virtuous, modest, and exemplary widow, at first refused to marry another man, an infidel; but with the odor of these plants he overcame her opposition and carried her away with him. "Never since then have I been able to see them again, although I tried to do so that I might convert that barbarian, and marry them afterward." He also relates how sometimes the natives would try this spell on him, if they feared that he was offended with them; after careful examination, he was satisfied that it caused not the slightest change in his feelings. He argues that any effect produced by the use of these herbs must, after all, be a natural one, and not caused by diabolical influences—a conclusion which he enforces by quoting various learned doctors. He and other missionaries made vigorous efforts to prevent the natives from such use of these herbs, on account of their bad results—as also in another custom, thus described:]

In order to enable them to kill some deer quickly, they take some herbs which they call in their own language panarongusa, which signifies the same as to say in Spanish, aliciente para venados [i.e., "a lure for deer"]. They distinguish the said herb into male and female, and therefore they make two small bundles of them, the male plants in one and the female in another. This done, they stick an arrow into the ground, and, placing at the top of it the herbs tied together, they begin to call the deer, imitating its voice, which they do to perfection. If in that vicinity there is any deer that hears the said sound, it infallibly sets out at once, and, beginning to scent, steadily approaches the fixed arrow, without taking fright at the men who are stationed near it. They allow the deer to approach, and, when it is in the place which suits them, they shoot an arrow at whichever part of its body they wish, and bring it down without difficulty. When I heard these things, I endeavored with those very persons, after they were baptized, to make a more than minute investigation, to ascertain whether the devil was giving them any instruction in it, whether they used any superstitious words, or performed [like] acts, so that I could form some opinion regarding these; but the unanimous reply of all was, that there was nothing of this sort, but that their ancestors had known that the said herbs possessed this virtue, and that they simply made use of them. There was, consequently, nothing more for me to do, except to declare that these were among the frauds of which the enemy [of souls] avails himself, in order by these baits to ruin their souls, and so much the more as he more secretly endeavored to introduce such things [as these among them]; and that on this account they ought to abstain from this mode of hunting, using only the common one, and trusting in the Lord who gives food to all living creatures, without despising the raven's nestlings who cry unto Him, that He would furnish what they might need for their support. I think that I succeeded, and that other religious will succeed in gradually banishing much of this abuse.

[In Ilocos Fray Alexandra Cacho formed a village of converts, under the name of San Juan de Sahagun; and Fray Velloxin greatly enlarged the village of Santa Monica, "although in past years there came a pest of smallpox, which in a short time swept away a great number of the inhabitants." Fray Francisco Alvarez, a son of the province of Philipinas, in 1740 formed two other small villages in the mountains of Santor; this was removed to another site by Mozo himself in 1747, and in the period of three years he secured more than a hundred and fifty conversions, and even the attendance of their children at school. The harvest among those people, Mozo says, is great, and many more might be saved if there were more missionaries; those who are among them are overworked, and in a few years are worn out or killed by their labors.]

CHAPTER IX-Missions to the apostates and infidels intermixed

Another mission, in my judgment more arduous than any of those I have mentioned, according to what I myself have experienced—and this is the general opinion of all those who are engaged in its cultivation—is the mission which the province maintains in a place which is called the Marangley. This is composed of some very extensive and close forests, with various mountains, so covered with thickets and lofty trees that the sunlight can hardly enter there—although at intervals the natives have their clearings, of land which is so fertile that it seems incredible; and for this very reason, thinking that it would be considered fabulous, I omit an account of the abundance with which the land responds to whatever handful of seed they are accustomed to cast into it.

In the said forests and hills dwell many people of various tribes, mingled together, Christians and infidels. Some are there, attracted by the hills from which they went out [in former times]; others, in flight from the officers of justice, who are seeking them. Many also go there in order to live in idleness, and to free themselves from the payment of tribute and the fulfilment of other obligations; and many, because it is the region in which they were born, and where they have lived as infidels. There they dwell intermingled, infidels and Christians being married together, and mingling a thousand superstitions with the law of Jesus Christ. From this results a hydra more fierce and more difficult to conquer than the celebrated one with which Hercules fought; for the apostates, as being entirely corrupt, are most difficult to reclaim, and they with their corruption, persuasions, and evil customs, to a great degree pervert the simple nature of the infidels, just as St. Paul tells us. Their sustenance is like that which I related of the Zambals, that is, [obtained] from the chase and from the innumerable wild palms which I have already mentioned; but they also sow their scanty bit of rice, the land responding to them with an incredible harvest, although they cultivate it wretchedly and take very little care of their fields. As many of them are Christians and had learned the mysteries of our holy faith, while the infidels among whom they live have a thousand superstitions, omens, and foolish observances, they make a medley of Jesus Christ and Baal, which is not even that of those Samaritans of whom it is related that they desired at the same time to serve the God of Israel and not to cast out their [false] gods. And because among these peoples are generally encountered not only the superstitions which those infidel communities maintain, but also the frivolous beliefs in which the peoples of Philipinas were living before they could receive our holy faith, I have thought it well to reserve this information for this place — observing, moreover, that among the Christian communities hardly a trace of these things is now encountered. This is the result of the labors, past and present, of the religious in extirpating them, and even in so short a time they have been able to banish them; while in our Europa, and even in our España, after so many centuries remnants of the ancient paganism are still frequently encountered.... Those of whom we are speaking believe that every forest, every mountain, every river, and every grove has a powerful spirit who rules in those places; they call him Nono, which signifies "grandfather" — by which name I understand they call him, partly because they think that the said spirit is that of some one of the powerful ones who once lived there, and also partly on account of the extreme veneration which those people have for their old men. It is also very credible that this foolish belief among them comes from their neighbors the Chinese, who likewise attribute to every river, forest, field, and grove these Penates and fauns, giving them a name which signifies the ruler and master of those places. They believe, then, that this spirit which they say rules there has his dwelling in some one of those trees which are most distinguished for size and for abundance of leaves, as likewise in some great heaps of earth, shaped like a sugar-loaf, which are made by a kind of ants, very destructive, which they call anay,34 of which many are found in the open country there. Accordingly, not only do they regard it as a religious duty not to pick fruit or take anything from the said hills without first asking permission from the nono, with words of great reverence, but likewise, whenever they pass before the said tree or hillock, they pay their respects, saying in their language, Tabipo, which means, "By your permission," and then they go on their way. They are so fearful that, if they fail in doing this, they imagine that the said spirit will send upon them some sickness which will deprive them of life; this notion they confirm with some irrelevant casualties — some persons having failed to perform this ceremony, and afterward by accident having fallen ill — from which they conclude that this was a punishment from the nono; and therefore they try afterward to appease his anger by various gifts, which they offer to him after their fashion. Moreover, in the said trees there is often heard some loud noise, which, although it is frequently made by some great serpent which has its abode in some hole that may be in the tree, they attribute to its nono — although it is true that the demon, in order to blind them more and thus to inspire them with greater terror, is wont to appear to them often in the said trees. The sacrifices which they are wont to offer to him in case of sickness, as likewise several times in the year, are reduced to burning certain herbs in front of the said tree, and placing there some little portion of food, drink, leaf tobacco, and an herb which they are accustomed to chew when combined with the small fruit of a palm, which they call luyos in the Pampanga tongue, and bonga in the Tagal (and that fruit and the herb all together they call in the former language mama, and in the latter buyo), all which things, after having thus offered them, they themselves eat, having made their prayers, such as they are. [Mozo here stops to recall how like superstitions and heathen sacrifices lingered for a long time in Africa and even in Europe, and the efforts made by the Christian fathers to extirpate them. He says that in Filipinas the heathen do not "adore the trees as gods; but the aforesaid tree they regard as the dwelling in which the spirit who rules that grove or forest has his abode, and therefore they offer before it what we have described, and perform the said acts of prayer and veneration; but these are not directed to the tree, but to the spirit or nono who resides in it."]

Besides this, they have another and exceedingly foolish superstition and belief, which is also found among the Chinese (and the Romans had it, as we read in our father St. Augustine and others); this is the belief that there is an evil spirit who is hostile to the birth of children, and who, they say, in the form of a bird approaches the house where the woman lies in childbirth, and kills the child by tearing out its bowels. This spirit they call in their language usuang (and it is the same that the Romans call Silvanus), which, they say, shines by night. In order to free themselves from this spirit, they do a ridiculous thing. As soon as the woman begins her travail, the husband, attended by other persons, strips off his clothes, and, taking his naked cutlass, climbs to the ridge-pole of the house, his companions remaining below with their lances; and he does not cease making cuts at the air until the infant is born. They believe that the said usuang is frightened away by this, and dares not return. At other times they do the same thing, [except that] they are stationed below the house. They also fear greatly two other genii or spirits, of whom they tell a thousand stories. One they call tigbalang, which they say has the body of a giant and the legs of a horse; and the other, which they say resembles a pigmy they call patianac.35 It is certain that the demon thus appears to them, to terrify them with threats if they fail to serve him.

They also use auguries, which they obtain from a bird that they call *batala*, in the manner of which Virgilius sings, and which his commentator Servius explains; upon this Gellius, Pompeius, Cicero, Tiraquellus, and other humanists expatiate at length. And it is not surprising that they should be prepossessed by this error; for, if we believe Luis Vives, it passed from Assia to Grecia, and thence to Italia and Roma. Their belief is of that sort in this particular, that, if they set out on any expedition against another people, and on encountering them this bird should appear, singing in what they think is a melancholy tone, they immediately turn back and abandon their purpose, fearing to be entirely destroyed. On the other hand, if the bird sings to them agreeably, they at once regard their success as certain.

When they make peace with their opponents, they use a thousand execrations and imprecations with which they sign their treaties; and in order to divine whether there is any insecurity in the decision they catch a hog, and having stretched it on the ground, with its feet fastened thereto, they thrust into the midst of its body a knife, very broad and sharply pointed, and, quickly drawing this out, they carefully look for the blood on both sides. If on the side which faces either of the two parties there is no blood, or if it is there but not running, they conclude that the people on that side are deceiving them; but if the blood runs on both sides they shake hands, together they feast on the hog, and they swallow powerful draughts [of palm-wine?] — forming the same opinion from the blood as did the ancients from the entrails of the animals which they sacrificed, Cicero's statement being verified that there is hardly a nation which does not find auguries in these things.

In the eclipses they display great sadness, believing that some dragon will carry away the sun or the moon, and therefore they call upon it in terms which express that idea. Accordingly, in order to succor those heavenly bodies they raise loud yells, and shooting arrows upward, they make a thousand demonstrations of grief, as did the Romans, according to Tacitus and Livius.... To this the Chinese add still more; for, besides the said shouting, they bring out some copper instruments, a sort of timbrel, having a very loud and disagreeable sound; and striking these all at the same time, they make a frightful and horrible sound. This, they say, is to aid the sun not to be carried away by the dragon, which they think is frightened by this noise, and thus lets the sun go free.

These and other superstitions and idle beliefs are generally held by the infidels of these islands, and among the peoples of whom we are speaking not only are these ideas found complete, but also, since among those people dwell apostates, who have some knowledge of the mysteries of our holy faith and of Christian observances, they introduce among the multitude of such notions others from Christianity — with the mixture which they make of these, bending one knee to Christ and the other to the demon, and believing all these things equally. But it is not surprising that they do this, when even over here after six hundred years there still were left relics of the ancient heathenism, like to these, as appears from the Councils, and from the saints above cited, who rebuke in terminis these very things — to which may be added the Council of Agde,36 and other writings of the saints. [Mozo here relates some incidents to show how the devil holds these poor people in bondage, and terrifies them with threats and horrible sights.]

[In these missions, from the year 1718, multitudes of infidels were baptized and hundreds of apostates reclaimed. Prominent among the laborers therein were Fray Juan Velloxin, Fray Antonio Leon and a brother of his (who died worn out by the fatigues of his work), Fray Manuel Calvo, and Fray Francisco Alvarez.37 During that time four villages of converts were formed—Ururin, Lupao, Umingan, and Tayog, in which the natives lived in very Christian fashion, their numbers increasing with new conversions. Mozo relates several instances of the opposition made by the devil to this work.]

CHAPTERS X, XI-Missions to Visayas

Having now made known the triumphs secured in this present century in the great island of Luzon, it is right that we say something of the missions which the province maintains in the various islands which are called Visayas; and, in order that the reader may better understand the pious labors which are being endured in the conversion of the infidels therein to our holy faith, it will be very proper to say something about the customs of the said peoples, and of the places where they dwell, even though it be without enlarging much thereon. Commencing with the latter point, I relate how in two islands, called Zebu and Panay, there are some exceedingly dense woodlands, and mountain districts more rugged than can be described; for they are so impenetrable, and so thick with undergrowth, that it is impossible to make a step forward without the utmost toil, and even danger, especially for those who are ignorant of the path, such as it is— which the natives know, and by which they go down, when it suits them, to look for some things which they need. In the said mountains dwell a people who are called Mundos;38 they have the same characteristics of fierceness and barbarism as those of whom we have spoken in preceding missions, but they have besides this a peculiarity which renders them intractable, for they have among them some fearful wizards, who by conversing with the demon do things which cause terror, and who are able to render credible much of what is regarded as fabulous. [Here our author cites various writers to show how prevalent was witchcraft in the ancient times.]

In this manner, then, instructed and misled by the demon, those barbarians do fearful things, especially to revenge themselves, to the continual terror of those about them. The natives say that these wizards, changed into crocodiles, follow them when in their canoes, and do not stop until they seize some person whom they hate; also that they change themselves into other animals, in order to commit other wicked acts—as likewise that, availing themselves of various enchantments, they commit horrible murders, with a thousand other diabolical acts which are attributed to them. For this reason, if any one having this reputation enters any village to settle there, or, when already resident there, some rumor arises that he may be such a person, they immediately summon him peremptorily to depart from the village within three days; and if he does not obey they burn his house, and even himself and his family, nor is it once only that they have killed such persons with their lances. I do not doubt that the vulgar herd invent much, but as little is it doubtful that there are many wizards, whc do a thousand evil things.

Among them a malady is apt to prevail which they call bungsol (which signifies "a sudden swoon"), which is apt to attack them as a result of swellings, as hard as a stone, which originate in their stomachs; this trouble is often caused by chills, which they experience from going barefoot in the water and in wet places, and is wont to cause them such pains that on occasion they will suddenly appear as if dead. At other times, this sickness is also caused by some magic of a sorcerer, which they call gavay, by which word they are accustomed to denote the witchcraft and the act of practicing it—in which they do not often make a mistake; for through their mouths, as well as through other conduits of the body, these sorcerers on occasion eject rice in the hull, and other things, which could not be done if they were not aided by something of the said magic. In order to cure the person bewitched in this manner, they endeavor to summon some other person who has the reputation of a sorcerer; and this person, performing various exercises of his powers, calls to the one who caused that sickness. If the sufferer does not improve, the sorcerer at once pretends that the first one must be very far away, and for this reason cannot hear him, but will return the next day; and by this means he keeps the people deceived, and eats and drinks at the cost of the poor sick man. It also sometimes happens that they are quickly cured, and therefore when they see these things they feel such fear that, when the sorcerer goes so far as to ask for anything, they immediately give it to him, fearing lest he may bewitch them—in the same way as occurs over here [in España] in some little villages, when those persons go through them whom they call loberos,39 and others of that stripe.

If on a journey they lose their way in some desert plain, they attribute this to the patianac of whom we spoke before; and in order that they may be able to find the road they strip off their clothing, and with this they say that they succeed in doing so because this proceeding frightens the patianac, and he takes flight and does not mislead them. In order to discover and know who it is that has taken from them any missing article, they employ a diabolical device, which they practice with a sort of sieve, which they call bilao—an act in which one plainly recognizes that it proceeds from the demon; for by simply shaking the said sieve while they name various persons the [name of the] thief comes into their minds. They also summon their manes, or [spirits of the] dead, when they are assembled in the house where some person has died; and in order to see whether or not those spirits come they lay down a sort of fine mat, and, scattering over it ashes in order that the marks of feet may be printed thereon, often there may be seen the traces of footsteps, and with this they remain well content. It is true, however, that even over here [in Europa] such things were wont to be seen in olden times, as we read in various writings which describe the sacrifices which were offered to such departed spirits; and our father St. Augustine points out this, citing Marcus Varro, while it is individually explained by Tiraquellus and others....

As for the missions which the [Augustinian] province has in the Visayas Islands, the toil with which they have been and are being cultivated is inexpressible, and very little, if anything, has been published or known about them—partly because, as this work is carried on more remote from sight, it has been less likely to attract applause; and likewise because the religious, content that God, for love of whom they are employed therein, should be cognizant of their labors, care little for the rest, thus avoiding the subtle vainglory which, under pretext of the glory of God and the honor of the religious order, often deceitfully seeks praise for oneself....

Let the first mission, then, to become known to the public be that of Bugasson, in the mountains of the province of Panay, in order that it may be known how great has been the labor in the conversion of those infidels. In the year 1704, father Fray Thomás Sanchez, a son of this province of Castilla, when he had finished baptizing the Indians who lived on the plains in that region, was assigned by his obedience to the said mountains, with two other fathers, as his associates. They obeyed the orders of their superior, and, after having conquered various difficulties, with a thousand risks of their lives, and having endured a thousand hardships of hunger, want, the fatigues of the wretched roads, and other inclemencies of the weather, amid the terrors of death they were able to secure the baptism of a number of barbarians, enough to establish a foothold in that region and erect a church. They continued in their task, reaping considerable fruit, although in a short time, worn out by fatigues, the said father and one of his companions died. Others were sent in their places by the province, who were able to imitate the zeal of the first missionaries so closely that in the year 1733 they were able to form a village of the recent converts alone, on a most favorable site, of more than two thousand five hundred souls; and, our Lord continuing His favors, so great a number have been added to the flock of Christ, by means of the continual preaching and industry of the missionary religious, that in the original chart of the said village which was sent to his Majesty in the past year of 1760, it is shown to have, counting women, men, and children, six thousand and eighty-nine souls, who are now baptized and reclaimed to civilization.

At the western side of the province of Panay, about twenty-five or thirty leguas out at sea, there are some little islets called the Cagayans; they are so low that they can hardly be seen, except when one is very near, and therefore when the Indians sailed thither they followed a star, by which they had marked the location of these islets. In them were many infidels, and even therein took refuge all the outlaws, and men who committed murders. There is no water in the said islands, but they contain so great an abundance of the palms called "cocoa" that, with the water of the said fruit, they do not feel the need of any other. [To go among these people was exceedingly dangerous, on account of their fierce natures; but it was accomplished (in 1703) by Fray Hypolito Casiano, who succeeded in winning their friendship and converting them to the Christian faith, so that in two years (as stated by the provincial Olarte, ante) he had "baptized all the infidels there, and induced all the criminals who had resorted thither to repent of their deeds and reform their lives." He continued these labors and these triumphs until his death, in 1726.]

The third mission of the Visayas Islands is that of which the reverend father provincial Fray Vicente Ibarra gave a particular and exact account to the governor of the islands in the year 1738, when he had finished his visitation of the missions, having received an urgent request that he should make report of their condition and progress (for with all this strictness are affairs examined in Philipinas, since such is the command of his Majesty, whom may God preserve); and because the said father provincial, as being an eyewitness and well acquainted with the religious who began that mission, can speak with more accuracy, I will set down his very words, as follows: "The third mission which my province maintains is in the mountains of Bosoc in the province of Ogtong, on the further coast of the province of Panay. This mission was established in the year 1728, an entrance being made in the rugged region of those mountains by father Fray Felix de Zuñiga40—a religious of the most religious habits and the gentlest demeanor; and so zealous for souls that, without heeding the inclemencies of those wild mountains, he went about on foot, unshod, in sun and in rain, crossing almost by a miracle swollen and rapid rivers, and, despising danger, made his way into the most secluded places, in which there are many apostates and Carib41 blacks, of which sort are all those who are in the mountains of these islands. Such power had his zeal and constancy that he gained no small number of souls, since from those who were converted he was able to form three small villages; but, while he was praying one day in the little house which he had made for his dwelling, some apostates killed him with their lances. At present the said mission is cared for, on account of the great deficiency of men that we experience, by two religious who are in the village of Bugasson."

[All these missions were still conducted, when Mozo wrote, and were saving many souls; but their work was greatly limited and hindered by the scarcity of workers. These missionaries displayed the same spirit of devotion, zeal for souls, and self-sacrifice as did the earlier ones, but "with this difference [in results], that our predecessors dealt with peoples who were gentler and more civilized, while those of the present time are handling people who are more fierce and barbarous; and for this reason their triumphs must be the more glorious, and their virtue and constancy most firmly grounded. Many other souls are caught for Heaven in these islands by those religious who serve in villages near the districts where there are infidels, of which there are many in the said islands. They penetrate further into the country when they are permitted to do so, and they lose no opportunity when those [infidels] go down to their villages to procure articles that they need, which occurs often; those [thus converted] amount to several hundred persons annually."]

[Mozo here describes certain remedies for sickness which are used by the natives. Among these are the gall and fat of the python (called *saua* and *biting*, in various dialects) and another similar species of serpent, which reach an enormous size in the forests of the interior. The gall is used both internally and externally by the natives, to cure chills and pains in the stomach — to which they are especially liable from going barefooted, and more or less naked, through mud and rain at all times; also for malignant fevers and any inflammation which causes them. Mozo relates how he had cured himself of a high fever, when the physicians had "sentenced him to death," by the use of this remedy, and had on other occasions been relieved or cured by it; "consequently, I guard what I have of it like a precious jewel." The fat of these serpents is equally efficient for swellings or pains in the muscles and sinews, especially those caused by chills and exposure to weather; also it relieves the pains of gout.]

[Those Indians used a small stone, resembling a nut, in order to facilitate childbirth; they said that it was found, although only in small quantities, in a mine somewhere; this stone, applied to the left thigh, would quickly relieve the most difficult case of parturition,42 and afterward, applied again, would bring away the placenta; but in both cases it must be removed as soon as the desired effect was accomplished, or else it would "cause even the bowels to be drawn out." They also made use of a certain root, called in the Pampanga tongue sugapa,43 to inflame their courage in battle; "he who eats it is made beside himself, and rendered so furious that while its effect lasts he cares not for dangers, nor even hesitates to rush into the midst of pikes and swords. On many occasions, therefore, when they go out to fight with any who are hostile to them they are wont to carry this root with them, and, by eating it at the time of the attack, they enter the battle like furious wild beasts, without turning back even when their force is cut to pieces; on the other hand, even when one of them is pierced from side to side with a lance, he will raise himself by that very lance in order to strike at him who had pierced him. Sometimes, also, when they wish to revenge themselves on some more powerful man, it occurs to them to eat the said root; and, with the fury which it arouses in them, they fling themselves upon him like rabid wolves, being carried away by that rage in the presence of the person whom they meet, whoever he may be. Therefore, on account of the pernicious effects which the said root causes, the Dutch have given peremptory orders in Batavia that any person who sees another, whoever he may be, in the said fury shall without fail shoot him or [otherwise] put him to death, in order that an end may be put to the fatal accidents which are daily seen in that city, on account of the natives there being very prone to this barbarous proceeding. The Malanao and Joloan Moros are accustomed to use this plant much. They are also acquainted with other herbs the use of which is no less pernicious, although in another way than is the root above referred to. I have forgotten their names, but in those regions there are many who know them, and are even acquainted with those plants (would that it were not so!). It is true, indeed, that among those who are now living in a civilized manner and are grounded in the faith, hardly any abuse is found in this respect; and even, except very seldom, any one who is acquainted with those plants; but among some infidel tribes there is often much of this, as I could confirm by cases which occurred to me while I was among those people." [Mozo here mentions certain herbs (unnamed) which produce a complete physical torpor in the person to whom they are administered, so that he can use neither voice nor limbs;44 the natives are apt to avail themselves of this for purposes of robbery, but "they do not use it in order to abuse women, which is an especial providence of our Lord." He relates an "amusing trick" played by the natives on another religious: this father had baptized some infants, on condition that they be surrendered to his care to be brought up as Christians; after a time, the parents came one night, and burned the above-mentioned herb under the house, thus producing its effect upon the inmates; "and in the sight of all, without any one having the power to move, they seized the infants and went away with them," nor was the father ever able to find either the children or their parents.]

[The rest of Mozo's work (pp. 152–234) is occupied with the relation of the Augustinian missions in China; at the end is a list of the baptisms solemnized by one missionary during the year 1760–61, giving the name, age, and residence of each; most of these persons are children, and one had been a priest of an idol.]

DOMINICAN MISSIONS IN PANIQUI AND ITUY

[In a rare pamphlet printed at Manila and dated 1745—of which the Library of Congress possesses a copy—Bernardo Ustáriz,45 then provincial of the Dominican order in Filipinas, wrote a sketch of the above missions, from which we make the following summary:]

[The missions of the order had reaped a rich harvest in central Luzón, but the fathers were not satisfied because the gospel had secured no stable footing "in Paniqui,46 which was hiding among the provinces of Cagayan, Pangasinan, and Pampanga." They succeeded in making an entrance therein in 1739, at the cost of the lives of four of their missionaries; but six years later they were maintaining four laborers in that region and making encouraging progress. In this enterprise they were liberally aided by Governor Gaspar de la Torre. In those remote and wild regions the missionaries suffered greatly from lack of suitable shelter and food, the inclemencies of the weather, and the hardships of traveling. As an illustration: "On one occasion, a missionary having set out from the village of Appiàt for the place called Cauayan, night came upon him when he reached a village named Làcab; he expected that he could find a lodging there, and thus pass the night less uncomfortably, under some roof. He uttered loud cries, calling to its inhabitants, but his only reply was a confused yelling from the women, who in anger cried out that the religious should not enter the village. At the time they were offering a public supplication, in order to obtain from their idols rain for making their fields fruitful; and, as they formed the opinion that the devil would not speak to them through fear of the religious, they would not consent that the father should lodge in any of their houses. Accordingly, he found himself obliged to sleep on the ground that night, exposed to any disagreeable change of weather that might arise." For some time the missionaries were derided, repelled, and threatened, and the natives endeavored to prevent them from entering the houses; but they persevered undauntedly, and the devil was often thwarted by their courageous resistance. Many persons desired baptism, but some were lured away by the devil, speaking through the priestesses (or aniteras), and others were intimidated by the opposition of their friends and relatives, who would even threaten a convert with death. Some fancied that to become a Christian would render one "a perpetual slave to the Spaniards." In 1743, a chief at Appiat came with his family to the missionaries to be baptized. In the aforesaid space of six years, they had "succeeded in erecting six churches, in the villages of Cauayàn, Appiàt, Bagabag, Lappàu, Darùyag, and Carìg. To these should be added that of Bayombong; for, although some Christians were there when it was received from the reverend Augustinian fathers, there were still many infidels, of whom some lived with the said Christians, and others had fled to a forest called Vàcal—from which they have gradually come out by dint of the visits which the missionaries have frequently made them, and with the baptisms among them an increase has been made in the number of the Christians who were in Bayombong when the Order of St. Dominic began its ministrations there. Thus, in the said seven churches there is the number of nine hundred and seventy souls, baptized in the said time—besides ten apostates, who after many years have returned to the Christian faith. The number of Christians would be greater, if the missionaries did not use especial care in administering baptism, and if they were willing to comply with the desires of many persons." Many of the requests for baptism were caused by the desire to escape from tyrannical lords, or from creditors, or from the penalty due to their crimes; and not a few imagined that they could thus gain some more influential position among their people. In those seven churches there were eight hundred and fifty-eight catechumens; and these would have been more numerous if there were missionaries. At the time of Ustáriz's writing, there has been a gratifying change in the feelings of those people, even among the infidels; they are more docile, and more friendly to the missionaries, and they even live more peaceably among themselves, committing fewer murders. Governor Torre granted to these fathers "extraordinary Indian guards, who even yet have not been able to complete the works in all the villages. In Cauayàn and Lappàu, they have built substantial houses and churches of planks; in Bagabag and Daruyag they have constructed houses of the same sort, and although [in those places] there are pavilions suitable for saying mass, they will proceed to build there substantial churches when they finish the wooden house and church in Appiàt (or Gàpat); they will also build a house in Carig, where a large church of planks has already been completed. In the village of Bayombong it has likewise been necessary to build a new house and church of planks, because the buildings which were there for both these were little more than hovels." These same Indian guards had been obliged to spend much time in opening and repairing roads, which had delayed their work on the church buildings; but those new roads had enabled the missionaries to secure an easy communication with the surrounding provinces, and to discover the lurking-places of the heathen natives. The work and maintenance of these Indian laborers are paid for by the government; but the fathers had to spend no small sum in other ways, to secure the spiritual conquest of the heathen about them. "It is necessary to influence them not only by fear but by love," and thus the missionary must give them gratuities and presents; he must also support some of them, even for several months, who came from a great distance to receive instruction and, being in a strange land, had no means of support. The fathers had furnished plows to all who asked for them, that the natives might better cultivate their lands.]

[In the villages of Bujay and Dupag, and still more in the district of Ytuy, they met many obstacles and afflictions, as those natives were not so docile as those of Paniqui. "Nevertheless, much fruit has been gathered, in baptizing many infidels of the neighboring tribes, Ygolot, Ylongot, and others; and in reclaiming some apostates who were hiding in the mountains." The missionaries were troubled not only with the obstinacy of those in Ytuy (or Ysinay), and the persistent efforts of the devil to render their labors vain, but with the hostilities committed on their converts by a tribe close by Ytuy, called Panoypuyes, who made head-hunting raids on their Christian neighbors. The Ysinays were a timid people, and these fierce marauders kept them in abject submission to their tyranny—killing them when found alone or unprotected on the road, killing or snaring their cattle, demanding from them contributions of produce, and even human beings whom the tyrants slew and then "offered in sacrifice to their false gods." The missionaries feared that they must abandon this mission; but, hearing that Auditor Arzadun was then making his official visitation in the province of Pangasinan, they appealed to him for aid. He sent a body of armed men from that province against the Panoypuyes, but they could not administer sufficient punishment; he then ordered troops from Cagayan, two hundred and eighty-two in number. To these were added fifty of the Indian guards from the mission of Santa Cruz of Paniqui, and some of the native converts there; and this expedition was able to check the insolence of those dreaded marauders. Ustáriz presents an extract from the report of this enterprise which was furnished to him by Fray Antonio del Campo, the vicar-provincial of the said missions. The expedition captured and burned the villages of Ajanàs (the principal village of the Panoypuyes), Masi, Taveng, Bangao, and others; and slew Sapàc—the chief who ruled that tribe, and had been most tyrannical toward "the poor Ysinay Christians"—with many of his followers. In Ajanàs was a large building, on higher ground than the rest, and surrounded by a wall of stones, which was their sole fortress; "it was destined only for the residence of the unmarried men, who, according to the custom of that tribe, are not allowed to cover the more shameful part of their bodies, nor sleep where the married people live; the said pavilion also served as a watch-tower the duty of sentinel service belonging to the unmarried men." Since this castigation, the missions and Christian Indians had enjoyed peace; and the natives, relieved from their terror of the enemy, had flocked to the missionaries for baptism. In Bujày there were baptized about two hundred persons of the Ygolots alone, and at this writing there were "more than seven hundred souls newly added to this mission; for, the report of the valor of the Cagayan Christians in this undertaking having spread abroad, it has penetrated into even the most remote part of the mountains, attracting even the most secluded of the Ylongots, a tribe who rival the Panoypuyes in valor and fierceness. The mission of Paniqui likewise felt these benign effects; for at the report of such an achievement more than six hundred persons came to enroll themselves for the [instruction in] catechism, from the Yogad and Gaddàng tribes—besides forty souls from the village of Ybana in the Ygolot tribe, who united themselves to the village of Bayombong. Nor was this blessing monopolized by these two missions, but, crossing the mountains, it went on to Pungcan—to which place many families, influenced by the rumor of this influx of people [to the missions], have come down from the Gumangi tribe, in whose instruction the reverend Augustinian fathers are occupied."]

[A pamphlet (Mexico? ca. 1740) by Fray Manuel del Rio, then provincial of the Dominicans in Filipinas, relates the "events in the mission of Santa Cruz in Ituy, in the" province of Paniqui: in the year 1739;" it is reprinted by Retana in his Archivo, ii, pp. 175–205. The following information is gleaned therefrom, space not permitting us to present more than the leading facts contained therein.]47

[The Dominican province of Filipinas had within the islands the following active missions: San Miguel de Oriong, in the mountains of Batan; Pantol and Asingan, in those of Pangasinan; in the islands48 which extend toward Hermosa Island, those of the Batanes and Calayàn; and in the mountains and hills of Cagayan, the missions of Santa Rosa of Cifun, Tumavini, Orag, Mavanan, Santa Cruz, Vangan, and Capitanan. The missionaries in the provinces of Pangasinan and Cagayan had long desired to extend their work into the inland region lying between those provinces; and this was begun in the year 1632, in the district of Ituy, or Isinay. This mission was founded by Fray Thomàs Gutierrez, who afterward died therein. The district of Paniqui was afterward chosen for missionary labors, but up to 1736 with only indifferent and occasional success; it "was founded in Zifun by Fray Pedro Ximenez, and afterward was transferred to the location which it now has, with the title of Santa Rosa." In 1735, the Augustinian fathers (who at the time of Río's writing were administering the Ituy mission) observed some indications that those hearts were becoming softened; of this they informed the Dominicans, who in the following year made the eighth attempt to establish a mission in that heathen district. On May 25, 1736, Fray Diego de la Torre went from his village of Ilagan (in Cagayan) to make a reconnaissance among the heathen people of Cagayan; at first they rebuffed him, but by dint of kind treatment and presents he won the confidence of some among them. These told him that the only obstacle in the way of his efforts was, the impassableness of the high-road from Cagayan to Pangasinan; if this were made passable, they would have no longer a barrier between themselves and Spanish influence. Fray Torre's report of his dealings with these heathen induced the Dominican provincial, Fray Geronymo Sanz Ortiz, to ask Valdés Tamón for government aid to their new enterprise; the governor granted the establishment of a mission in Paniqui, composed of four religious and the guard necessary for their protection, at the expense of the king; and the following religious were sent thither: Fray Manuel Molinér, Fray Joseph Thomás Marin, Fray Romualdo Molina, and Fray Pedro de Sierra. They began their labors in July, 1737, and encountered determined opposition from the natives, who, advised by the demon, would not admit them into the villages. The chiefs demanded, as the price of even allowing the missionaries to remain near the villages, gifts of beads, cattle and horses, and gold; and, finally, two men to slay as offerings to their demons. Fray Molinér died suddenly, it was suspected from poison given to him by some heathen; and in his stead Fray Torre was sent. About this time (1738) the fathers received protection and hospitality from an Indian woman of rank in that tribe; and this aid, with the presents given by the fathers and their persistent charity and gentleness, softened the hearts of the unbelievers until they consented to make a treaty of peace, some of the chiefs even going to Nueva Segovia to ratify it. Nevertheless, the fathers still experienced much opposition, especially from the people of Bayongbong, the most southern and the chief village of that heathen district; and often their lives were in danger, especially when their Indian guards became frightened and began to retreat to their homes. Indeed, Fathers Torre and Molina died suddenly, probably from poison, like Molinér. The Dominican provincial again appealed to the government for aid, asking that more guards be assigned to the missionaries, and that one or two military posts be established in that province—partly for the protection of the missionaries, partly to ensure the safety of the road which was to be built from Pangasinan to Cagayan;49 this was granted by the governor, and the necessary provisions made therefor. By the time when news of this came to Cagayan, Marin had so far advanced matters that "almost nothing remained to overcome;" he had secured the support of a powerful chief named Danao, and toleration from another named Ansimo; and Marin went to Pangasinan, taking with him Pyrán, Danao's grandson—who was so caressed and honored by the Spaniards that he returned home a firm friend to the missionaries, and did much to open his countrymen's hearts toward them. The Dominican father provincial determined to open a direct road from Paniqui to Pangasinan, at the expense of the province — a most arduous and difficult undertaking, on account of the rugged surface of the country and the hostility of the Igorrots, "a bloodthirsty and very treacherous people." Father Manuel del Río was sent out to make the necessary explorations for this road, in which he suffered great hardship. The Igorrots were greatly opposed to the intended road-making; but they were finally induced, by the father's arguments, but still more by his liberal distribution of presents, to give their consent. The treaty made with them was thus solemnized: "In the presence of all, a hog was killed, and, as soon as the knife was thrust into it, profound silence reigned — all watching the dying struggles of the animal, and the flowing of its blood, which seemed like a fountain gushing upward. After a long time, a Christian Indian who was experienced in their ceremonies came forward, and, collecting in his hand some of the animal's blood, went, with loud cries and a swaggering step, and smeared with the blood the feet of the Igorrot chiefs; at this they were well pleased, and began to talk vigorously in their own language, and with bold gestures, as a sign that they would fulfil their agreement. This done, they were given something to drink, and the cattle, carajays,50 salt, and other things at which the bargain had been settled were placed before them; and they returned to their villages contented, having remained from that time friends with the Christians. This road is two days' journey in length, from the most eastern village of Pangasinan, called Asingan, to the village of Buxay among the Isinay people, which is a mission of the Augustinian fathers. For the greater comfort of travelers, road-houses were built at regular distances, in the places called Colong, Malalapang, and Malionlion; and in the last-named, which is the last town on the border of Pangasinan, a religious was stationed — on account of some Igorrot Christians being there, with some others who, it was hoped, would become Christians — with the title of missionary to the infidels there; he was separate from the other four who were in the province of Paniqui, who were destined to the reduction and conversion of the infidels in that province. This was a great achievement to open this road for communication between the provinces; for this has been an undertaking often attempted but never carried out, and often the royal exchequer has incurred great costs in it, and always without any benefit — especially twenty years ago, when the unfortunate mariscal Don Fernando Bustillo, governor and captain-general of these islands, attempted to open this road. Many thousands of pesos were spent, many unlucky events occurred, and no result was attained; and now, without any expense to the royal exchequer, at the cost of the religious order, it was readily cut through and opened. It is hoped that this road will be of great utility, not only for the said communication and trade between the provinces, but also for the easier conversion of the infidels—who, through trade and communication with the Christians, will learn their civilization and excellent customs, and will after a time abandon the barbarous condition in which they lived before." In April of 1739, Father Río was accompanied to Manila by Danao and the other chiefs already mentioned; they were feasted and laden with presents, and the governor "granted freely whatever they asked." In this road-building and other matters pertaining to this mission, the Dominican province spent "almost three thousand eight-real pieces; although it is the poorest province in the Indias, it can liberally spend its treasure, as now it has done, in the service of God and for the good of souls, for which chiefly it was founded."]51

1 The title-page of this work reads thus in English: "A plain historical account of the glorious triumphs and fortunate progress gained during the present century by the religious of the order of our father St. Augustine, in the missions which are in their charge in the Philipinas Islands, and in the great empire of China. Information is given regarding each of those peoples, their usages, customs, superstitions, mode of life, and medicines which they use in their diseases, with other curious information. Composed by the reverend father Fray Antonio Mozo, of the same order, formerly secretary and definitor of the province of Philipinas, and now commissary and general definitor for the same, who dedicates it to this province of Castilla of the same order. With the necessary licenses. At Madrid, by Andrès Ortega, Las Infantas Street. The year 1763."

This book contains much information regarding the customs and superstitions of the natives, especially of the Negritos, which is valuable not only as being furnished by an educated man who lived among them, but on account of his kindly nature, comparative freedom from bigotry and prejudice, and his inclination to take an impartial and philosophical view of his subject. For this reason, a very full synopsis has been made of his work, and his observations on the natives have been mostly translated in full. He left the islands in 1759, as he states on p. 76 of his book.

2 This mission field was located in the eastern part of what is now the province of Nueva Ecija (formed at the beginning of the nineteenth century), on the Rio Grande of Pampanga and its tributary the Santor, nearly half-way from the source of the

former to its mouth; the peoples here mentioned evidently dwelt at first on the heights of the Caraballo de Baler—part of the Caraballo Sur range, from which flow northward the waters of the Magat and the Rio Grande of Cagayan; and southward the Rio Grande and the Rio Chico (respectively "great river" and "little river" of Pampanga). The name "Buquid" apparently simply designates them as dwellers in the mountain forests. The Italons—a name of the same signification, applied by the Gaddans to the Ilongots dwelling in the Caraballo mountains of Nueva Ecija and Príncipe (who are called Ibilao by their Isinay neighbors north of that range)—and Abacas lived on the headwaters of the Rio Grande and Rio Chico. Barrows says (Census of Philippines, i, p. 437): "The Ibilao who inhabit the mountains of Nueva Ecija are among the most persistent head hunters of northern Luzón. Their raids upon the Christian settlements of Nueva Ecija are incessant, and they have repeatedly taken lives in the vicinity of Carranglán and Pantabangán within the last two or three years." (See also ut supra, pp. 470, 471.)

3 In another place this name appears as Alzaga; but Pérez (Catálogo, p. 179) spells it Arziaga. This missionary was a native of Valladolid, and came to the islands in 1699; he died in 1707.

4 For a modern description of the Ilongots (or Italons), see that given in Census of the Philippines, i, pp. 545–547; the writer (L. E. Bennett, governor of Nueva Vizcaya) says: "The chiefs of all these settlements stated to me positively that adultery was unknown among these people, and that their family relations were very closely drawn. They further stated that they never knew of a case of a young woman giving birth before she had been married." "Fighting is never carried on in the open, but they depend entirely upon assassination and ambush. They set pointed bamboos and spring guns for each other in places known to be traveled, and use spears and bows and arrows with poisoned tips when they fight."

5 This name is spelled Isasigana by Pérez. He was born in Durango, Vizcaya, in 1665, and came to the islands in 1699. Three years later he was sent to Carranglán, where he remained until he was worn out with missionary labors. Recalled to Manila for his health's sake, he afterward held various offices in his order (1706–10), and was minister at Guagua and Apalit (1712, 1713). He died at Guagua (Vava, in Mozo), in 1717.

6 "The missions of Pantabangan were administered by the Augustinians until they surrendered them to the Franciscans in order that the latter might unite these to their missions of Baler, which lies on the further coast that is called by that name. They maintain in these missions two or three religious, who minister to Pantabangan, where there are 60 houses; Puncán, which has 56 houses; and Carranglán, 82. Very little progress is made in these missions, on account of the misgovernment among the Indians and the lack of policy on the part of the Spaniards." (Zúñiga's Estadismo, Retana's ed., i, p. 473.)

Vindel describes in his Catálogo, t. ii, no. 328, a rare pamphlet (apparently not mentioned elsewhere): Relación del descubrimiento y entrada de los religiosos de N. S. P. S. Francisco ... en los pueblos ó rancherías de los montes altos de Baler; it is undated, but was probably published at Manila, about 1755. In it, "Fathers Manuel de San Agustín and Manuel de Jesús María Fermoselle report to their provincial, Fray Alejandro Ferrer [who held that office during 1753–56], the condition in which they found those villages." San Agustín labored in Baler and neighboring villages during 1747–60. The mission of Baler was founded in 1609 by Franciscan missionaries, but half a century later was ceded, through scarcity of laborers, to the Recollects; the latter order abandoned that district in 1703, for the same reason, and the Franciscans resumed the charge of it. Baler was formerly situated on the right bank of the San José River, near the sea; but on December 27, 1735, it was utterly destroyed by a tidal wave, and the surviving inhabitants removed the village farther inland, to higher ground. (Huerta, Estado, pp. 280, 477.)

7 Pérez states that he died at Guagua, a town in southern Pampanga; for this name Vava is apparently a phonetic Spanish corruption.

8 Alejandro Cacho was a native of León, and came from a noble family; he arrived at Manila in the mission of 1690. He was a missionary to various tribes in upper Pampanga (now Nueva Écija), among whom he labored indefatigably for more than forty years. "He formed villages, opened roads, established schools, built churches, and felled groves; and what was but a little while before a gloomy and impenetrable forest afterward burst upon the sight of the astonished traveler as a broad plain, which the directing hand of the indefatigable Augustinian converted into a fertile field and beautiful province, the pride

and hope of the new converts. And he accomplished even more; assigned to the missions of Carranglán and Pantabangan (1707) he eagerly devoted himself to the study of the flora in those unknown regions, examining the medicinal virtues of each plant; and as a fruit of his laborious task, besides practicing successfully the art of the physician among his beloved parishioners he left us the works which we mention below." "He is one of the figures which most clearly illustrate what the religious in Filipinas was, in the double conception of priest and maintainer of the Spanish sovereignty in this archipelago." (Pérez.) He died in Carranglán in 1748. The works alluded to are: "A treatise on the medicinal herbs of the mountains of Buhay;" "Origin and customs of those barbarous peoples;" "History of the Augustinian missions among the Italon Ilongots, the Isinais, the Irulis, and the Igolots," during 1704–33; and three maps drawn by Cacho, giving valuable information regarding the habitat of those peoples in central Luzón. Besides these, he wrote catechisms in the languages of those tribes, directions for their government, etc.

9 Spanish, al testud; this word does not appear in the lexicons, and it is impossible to determine its meaning accurately from the text. Testud may be possibly a misprint for testuz, meaning "the hind part of the head;" but it is more probably the mistake of an amanuensis for testiculos, these glands being regarded as the source of virile power.

10 "Isinay is the language spoken by the Igorot of the hills in western Nueva Vizcaya, and by a part of the population of the towns of Aritao, Dupax, and Bambang, who are of Igorot origin, but whose ancestors were converted in the latter half of the eighteenth century." "The name Igorot (in Spanish form, Igorrote) means in several Malayan languages, 'people of the mountains.'... I have adopted it as a general designation for the whole body of primitive Malayan tribes of northern Luzón who are of the same physical type, speak closely allied languages, and present the same grade of culture." (Barrows, in Census of Philippines, i, pp. 471, 472.) See also VOL. XX of this series, pp. 269–279.

11 See account of Dominican missions, following this of Mozo's. Interesting accounts of the Dominican missions in Luzón and its dependent islands, in recent times, may be found in the Correo Sino-Annamita (a missionary publication issued from the college of Santo Tomás, Manila, during the period 1866–97), vols. i, iv, xiii–xv, xx, xxi, xxiii–xxx.

12 A royal decree (given in full by Mozo, pp. 48–51) states that the Augustinians informed the Dominicans, by a letter of September 8, 1739, of their decision to surrender the Ituy missions, contingent on the permission of the governor; and the actual formal surrender took place on April 8, 1740. This transfer was liberal and disinterested, the Augustinians asking no compensation for their property, which was of considerable value. The number of baptized persons included in these missions was 2,755; and the Augustinians had taught them to irrigate their lands, and had furnished them with animals and plows.

13 Fray Vicente Ibarra was born in Durango in 1694, and made his religious profession at the age of sixteen; he came to the islands in 1712. He was minister at Santor and other places (1720–28), and afterward held several offices in his order. In 1737 he was prior provincial, and made a visitation of all the Augustinian religious ministers there. The latter part of his life was spent mainly at Manila, where he died on December 24, 1760. He left various writings in the Pampanga dialect. (Pérez's Catálogo.)

Juan Belloxin was born in the province of Logroño in 1695, and made his profession at Salamanca when seventeen years old. He came to the islands in 1718, and spent ten years as missionary to the heathen Isinays, on whose dialect he left some MS. volumes. He was minister in various villages in other districts, and died at Manila in 1742.

Diego Noguerol was a native of the province of Coruña (1699), and professed at Compostela in 1716. Two years later he arrived at Manila, and went to the upper Pampanga mission; he was the first minister at Buhay (1728), where he remained seven years. He labored in other ministries and held offices in the order, dying at Manila in 1785.

14 These were Bujay (the mission center), Dupag, Meuba, Mayon, Diangan, Limanab, Batù, Paitan, and Bayongbong (this last located in Paniqui).

15 See description of trails in Igorot country, in Census of Philippines, i, p. 542.

16 Agustín Barrio Canal was born in the province of Burgos, and made profession in the Augustinian convent of Salamanca in 1733, at the age of nineteen. He came to the islands in 1737, and became a missionary in western and central Luzón, where he died as related in Mozo's text.

Pedro Freyre was born in the province of Lugo, and entered the Augustinian order at Burgos. He came to the Philippines in 1737, and labored among the tribes of central Luzón until 1753; he then became a minister in Pampanga, where he spent nearly twenty years. In 1771 he was removed by force from his post there, for refusing to accept the diocesan visit; the rest of his life was spent at Manila, where he died in 1790. (Pérez's *Catálogo*.)

17 Reference is here made to the great western mountain range of Luzón, the Caraballos Occidentales; it is nearly 200 miles long, and, including its subordinate ranges, one-third as broad. It is really a system of mountains, its central range forming the divide between the waters flowing to Cagayán River on the east and those flowing to the China Sea on the west. Its southern portion is called Cordillera Sur, which, bending eastward, under the name of Caraballos Sur joins the Sierra Madre or eastern coast range. This last range stretches along the eastern side of Luzón, from the northeastern point of the island to Laguna de Bay, a distance of 350 miles, and divides the waters of the Cagayán valley (which is about 50 miles wide, and 160 in length) from those of the Pacific slope. See Census of Philippines, i, pp. 60, 61.

18 Barrows classes the Apayaos as an Igorot division, located in the district of Ayangan; (cf. VOL. XLIII, p. 72, note 11). The Tinguians also are Igorot, and are the pagan people of Abra; "they have developed toward civilized life, being about on the same plane of culture as the Ilocano." "This word is derived from tingues, meaning 'mountain,' a Malayan word, archaic, and almost unused now in Tagálog, and the suffix an." Adang evidently means the Gaddans, or Gaddang, another Igorot branch in western Isabela; some of them, christianized in early days, occupy the northern towns of Nueva Vizcaya. (Census of Philippines, i, pp. 469, 471, 477.)

19 Cayán was formerly the capital of Lepanto; and is three miles from the present capital, Cervantes.

20 José Herice was born in 1691, in a town in Navarra, and made his religious profession at Pamplona at the age of twenty. He came to the islands in 1718, and was sent to the Ilocos missions. He was the pioneer evangelist among the Adang (or Gaddans), and consumed so much of his strength in that field that he was transferred to easier charges in Ilocos, from 1725 on. He died at Batác in 1742. (Pérez's Catálogo.) Rivera came to the islands in 1713, and was sent to the Tinguians, but for like cause was also transferred to the plains villages in 1719. Madariaga came over with Herice, whose associate he was among the Gaddans and

Apayaos, until 1729, when he too went down to the plains; he died in 1744.

21 Spanish, barbacoas: a word adopted from the Indians of Guiana, their name for the frames on which they roasted or smoke-dried any kind of meat or fish; it is also applied (in English, corrupted to "barbecue") to a hog or other large animal roasted whole, and to the open-air entertainment at which such roasts (now usually made in a pit dug in the earth) form part of the food.

22 See account of Igorot canaos (or feasts), and their dances at these, in Census of Philippines, i, pp. 535–537.

23 Francisco Javier Córdoba was born in Mexico in 1712, and entered the Augustinian order at the age of seventeen. He came to the islands in 1732, and spent the rest of his life in the missions of Pampanga and Ilocos; his death occurred there, about 1764.

Romero was a native of Cadiz, born in 1729, and entered the order in Mechoacán, Nueva España, in 1750. Two years later he came to the islands, and joined the Igorot mission, afterward being cura in Indian villages; finally he returned to America (soon after 1774).

Pedro Vivar was born at Logroño in 1737, and made his profession at Valladolid, at the age of fourteen; he came to Manila with the mission of 1752, and two years later was sent to the Igorot mission. After three years labor there, he took charge of the ministries in various native villages of Ilocos, where he died in 1771. In the revolt which occurred in that province during the British occupation, he and other missionaries were imprisoned by the insurgents, and narrowly escaped being slain by them. Vivar left several MSS., among them a history of the above rebellion, which was recently published (Manila, 1893), in vol. iv of Biblioteca historica Filipina. (Pérez's Catálogo.)

24 The Tagálog name of the sago-palm (in Pampanga called ebos, according to Mozo), or Corypha umbraculifera. C. minor is commonly called palma brava (Tagálog, anáhao or anáo); see VOL. XLVII, p. 181, note 27.

25 This is the fire-saw, a variant on the fire-drill so generally used by the North American Indians and other savage peoples. See description and illustration of the fire-saw used in Borneo, (similar to that of the Zambals), in Ling Roth's Natives of Sarawak, i, pp. 377, 378.

26 "'Baluga,' in the Pampango language, means half-breed or mixed blood. It has quite a wide use to indicate Negrito-Malayan roving savages." (Barrows, in Census of Philippines, i, p. 469.)

27 Ilib: a Pampango name of the cogon grass (Imperata arundinacea); see VOL. XXIX, p. 233, note 74.

28 Spanish, lumbre, meaning "fire," thence "light;" and by extension "tinder," used to produce fire. Evidently the allusion in the text is to material used for tinder—in such a region and for use as a bed, obviously meaning dry grass.

29 See Delgado's description of the bees in Filipinas (Historia, pp. 848, 849). He states that there are several different kinds of bees, which produce great quantities of wax and honey—especially in the Visayas, where two crops are gathered in the year.

30 See note on sago-palm, p. 91, ante.

31 Evidently the same as súcao, an Ilocan name for a kind of pond-lily, Nelumbium speciosum; its tubers (and Blanco says, its flowers) are edible—as is the case with those of other species of the same genus, in America and other regions, which are used for food to some extent by the savages.

32 That is, "Natural necessities are satisfied with almost nothing." The other saying is: "If you wish to make a man rich do not add to his wealth, but take away his desires."

33 The Visayan name for the shrub (Croton tiglium) which yields the croton oil of commerce; it belongs to the order Euphorbiaceæ.

34 "Termes monocerus (Koen), the common name for which is anay. The anay, or white ant, is a very remarkable insect, with a large head, on the upper part of which it has three small eyes; and it is armed with two hard teeth, shaped like a forceps, with which this creature destroys in a very short time the woodwork of a house, the best depository of papers, the largest library, or the finest wardrobe of clothing. The only wood that it does not attack is the molave, on account of its bitter taste and excessive hardness. The anay lives in families; it is found in all wet localities, and erects dwellings of clay which are two or three meters in height, and so solid that the passage of buffaloes over them is not sufficient to destroy them. The interior of these ant-hills contains a multitude of little cells, divided by thin partitions; and in these they deposit thousands of eggs (some 80,000 to each female) that are infinitely small. One [in each hill?] of these terrible insects is distinguished by its enormous proportions, and this one the Indian calls 'queen of the ants.' In the rainy season, wings grow on them, and they fly in fabulous numbers at sunset. The damage which these insects cause is incalculable." (Montero y Vidal, Archipiélago Filipino, p. 114.)

The same writer mentions, in the preface to the same work, as an instance of the prevalent ignorance in Spain of the nature and needs of that country's colonies in the East, that some member of the royal Council undertook to despatch a decree that the army in Filipinas should go in pursuit of the *anay*, believing it to be some terrible criminal.

Salazar makes an interesting reference (*Hist. Sant. Rosario*, p. 567) to some unnamed species of ant: "In that country [of the Mandayas] are certain ants which are called 'Dutchmen,' whose sting is so sharp that it becomes unendurable;" and he relates that this creature was used by a Dominican missionary as a new penance.

35 Cf. account of these superstitions as still believed in Batangas, in Census of Philippines, i, pp. 520, 521.

36 Agde (Latin, "Agatha") a city in southeastern France, was anciently the seat of a bishopric suffragan to Narbonne; it was suppressed in 1790. The council here referred to was held in the year 506, "in the time and with the authorization of Alaric, king of the Visigoths in Spain, although he was an Arian." (Chevin's Dictionnaire de noms de lieux, p. 5.)

37 Antonio Léon was born in 1702, in the province of Alicante, and made profession in the Augustinian convent at Salamanca at the age of sixteen. He came in the mission of 1724, and spent the rest of his life mainly in the missions of Pampanga, in which he died (1766). His younger brother Pablo came (being then a novice) to the islands at the same time; he was missionary in Puncán (1731) and Santor (1732) and died in 1733.

Manuel Calvo was born in Almagro in 1704, and when sixteen years old entered the Augustinian order at Toledo. He came to Manila with the foregoing brothers, and labored in Pampanga missions; he died at Ayárat in 1758.

Francisco Alvárez was a native of Oviedo province in Spain, and made profession at Madrid in 1727, at the age of twenty-two; he came to the islands in the mission of 1732. He also labored in the Pampanga missions, and died at Manila in 1769. (Pérez's *Catálogo*.)

38 "In the mountains [of Iloilo] there are many Indians whom they call Mundos; they should be called vagamundos [English, "vagabonds"], but the Indians bite off half from Castilian words when they are somewhat long. These Mundos are descendants of the Christians who, not being able to remain in the villages on account of their delinquencies, have fled to the mountains. They are not unwilling to become Christians, provided the fathers will go to their hamlets to live; but as this is impossible, on account of those places being inaccessible to civilized people, they continue in their infidelity. Some come down to the villages, and in their places others escape [to them] who

commit new crimes; and [thus] this caste of people is continually maintained, notwithstanding the efforts that have been made to reduce them. The Indians trade with them, and give them rice and cloth in exchange for the wax and pitch which they bring down from the hills; and, in order not to lose this advantage, the Indians have been opposed to the reduction of the Mundos to a civilized and Christian mode of life." (Zuñiga, Estadismo, ii, pp. 93–94.)

39 Loberos (from lobo, "wolf"): Dominguez calls it a synonym of espantanublados ("scare clouds"), an epithet of "the vagabond who, wearing long garments, goes through the hamlets begging from door to door; and the country folk believe that he has power over the clouds" (Diccionario of the Academy).

40 Félix de Rioja y Zúñiga was born at Cadiz in 1691, of a noble family, and made his profession there at the age of seventeen, renouncing an inherited title. He came to the islands in 1712, and seven years later was sent to the Bataan mission. He was sent to Guimbal (1722) and Bugason in 1728; in the latter place he was murdered in June, 1734.

41 Carib: the name of the Indian race who inhabited the Antilles and adjacent coasts when the New World was discovered; also applied in general to fierce (and especially to cannibal) savages.

42 Cf. Matilda C. Stevenson's account of a ceremony employed at childbirth by the Sia Indians of New Mexico, in which an ear of corn (which among them is the emblem of life) is passed up and down the body of the mother, accompanied with prayers to one of their divinities, to secure a safe and easy delivery. (Report of U. S. Bureau of Ethnology, 1889–90, pp. 134–141.)

43 This plant is evidently Datura alba (or perhaps in some places D. fastuosa, which has the same properties), commonly called "jimson weed" in the United States; it is called catchúbong or tachibong by the Visayans, and in Tagálog talamponay. (See Official Handbook of the Philippines, part i, pp. 377, 401; also Merrill's Dictionary of Plant Names, p. 142.)

44 It is possible that this plant is Euphorbia pilufera, a soporific; it is used, as are many other plants found in the islands, for poisoning fish.

45 Fray Bernardo Ustáriz was born in the archbishopric of Zaragoza, and entered the Dominican order at Calatayud; he came to the Philippines with the mission of 1730. In the following year he was minister at Binondo, and in 1739 at Abucay; with these exceptions he was engaged in high offices of his order— being the head, at various times, of the college of Letran and of the university of Santo Tomás; and twice (1743 and 1755) the

provincial of the order. He was afterward appointed bishop of Nueva Segovia, taking possession of that see in 1761. In the following year the capture of Manila by the English occasioned a revolt in Ilocos; the efforts of Ustáriz to oppose the insurgents were unsuccessful, and drew upon him their resentment. They kept him a prisoner for six months, and were on the point of killing him; but his life was saved by the opportune arrival of a Spanish force. He then accompanied the troops through their campaign for the pacification of Pangasinan, and the hardships which he underwent therein and in his previous captivity shortened his life; he died at the hospital of San Gabriel, near Manila, August 2, 1764. (Ferrando's Hist. PP. dominicos, v, pp. 6–9.)

46 Father Manuel del Río thus describes the district of Paniqui and its people (Retana's Archivo, ii, pp. 185–187): "This province of Paniqui extends from north to south; and its length, from the last Christian village of Cagayan, which is Itugug, to the last infidel village (but close to the mission of Isinay), called Bayongbong, is probably two and one-half or three days' journey. Its breadth thus far has not been ascertained; but I think that it includes more than fifteen leguas of plains, or level ground, from the mountains of the Igorrots to those of the Ilongots. These are two ranges of lofty peaks, which intersect this province in the middle, and likewise others in the center of this island; and in these mountains dwell these two and other barbarous tribes, whom hitherto it has been impossible to conquer, on account of the inaccessible character of the mountains. The land of this province of Paniqui is quite level, and good for cultivation. The villages are numerous, although not very large; for on the shores of the Maga River alone, which flows through the length of that province from south to north, are counted eighteen villages, including both large and small ones. The people of that tribe are distinct from those adjacent to them, and have a different language from the others. The men are accustomed from childhood to file their upper teeth into points, which often causes them to decay; and the teeth, after being dyed a sort of dark blue, are adorned (when the person is a chief) with small golden pegs. For persons of rank, it is considered very unsightly to have white teeth. They also pierce their ears, as women do; and some cleave them through. These people are barbarians in their customs, without any kind of civilization or government; and they pay respect only to some chiefs, who have acquired a reputation as such by their valorous deeds. They are not idolaters, nor are they given to religion or to worship; they have only some superstitions regarding the songs of birds, and similar things, founded on oracles which are given to them by the demon, through the agency of their aniteras, or

priestesses. These women, through a compact which they have with the demon, after taking a certain potion are possessed by that same demon; and through their mouths this enemy is able to declare his will to those wretched people. At other times, the demon speaks to them in his own person, in an aerial body; but never, or very seldom, does he allow himself to be seen by those who hear him. Through the counsel of this chief enemy of the human race, those heathen are wont to buy Indians from other provinces, in order to offer them in sacrifice, by killing them, to the demon. Of this class must have been a little boy four years old, apparently an Igorrot, who was seen by the said father commissary, Fray Diego de la Torre. Those infidels were buying the child, to kill him; and the father, not having with him any forces for preventing this, could only obtain from them that they should bring the child to him for baptism before the sacrifice. God chose that the bargain should not be settled, and that the father should buy the child for some trinkets and beads, which those people value; and accordingly he brought the lad to Cagayan, snatching him from the teeth and claws of the infernal wolf. The said father encountered among those infidels, another boy, about seven years old, who was white and ruddy, like a European—a very singular thing among people so swarthy as they. His mother had had other children, but dark, like herself; and she says that when she was pregnant with this boy she dreamed that they commanded her to give him the name of Adàn [i.e., Adam], and therefore did so, calling the boy Adàn. They regarded him as a little idol; and therefore, although the father urged them several times to give him the child, he was unable to obtain it."

47 See earlier accounts of these Dominican missions in Central Luzón, in VOL. XXXVII, pp. 98–101; and in VOL. XLIII, Salazar's history, book i, chap. xxxiii, and book ii, chaps. ii, xi, xxii, xxxv, xlix. Cf. Ferrando's Hist. PP. dominicos, passim, for detailed accounts from the beginnings of those missions down to 1830.

48 In Retana's printed text this word appears, by some error, as montes, when the context plainly indicates islas.

49 See account of this project, the explorations made for it, and its successful accomplishment, in Ferrando's Hist. PP. dominicos, iv, pp. 367–382.

50 Carajay is, according to Vidal y Soler (Viajes de Jagor, p. 138), an earthenware jar, used for cooking by the Bicol natives in Camarines.

51 According to an official report sent to the king in July, 1752, the Dominican province of Santisimo Rosario had then only 83 religious, who were in charge of 219,459 souls. Besides the missions of China and Tun-kin, the province conducted in the

Filipinas Islands seven missions in Cagayan, two in Pangasinan, six in Ituy, one in Cauayan, and eight in Paniqui; and one in the mountains of Oriong, in Bataan. "In all these missions, or villages of new converts, there were reckoned 8,917 Christians, with many catechumens who were being prepared to receive the holy sacrament of baptism. This number is not included in the general administration of the province previously mentioned. Some of these villages or missions were committed to religious appointed as vicars in other and older villages, to which the former were added, and considered as visitas or annexes—especially in Cagayan, where there has not been any religious with only the title of missionary. The number of souls who are today in charge of the province in the islands of Luzon and Batanes, according to the general report of 1870, is 560,911." (Ferrando, Hist. PP. dominicos, iv, pp. 560, 561.)

EVENTS IN FILIPINAS, 1739–1762

[A brief summary of events during the above period is here presented; it is taken, like similar abstracts in previous volumes, mainly from the histories of Zúñiga, Concepción, and Montero y Vidal.]

[The government of the islands by Valdés y Tamón ended in the summer of 1739, when he was succeeded by Gaspar de la Torre. Just before this time, the former ordered the royal fiscal, Christoval Perez de Arroyo,1 to be sent to prison for refusing to give up certain documents in his possession; the fiscal then took refuge in the Recollect convent, and his property was seized. After Torre's coming, the archbishop (Fray Juan Angel Rodriguez), at the instance of the Recollects, made arrangements with him for Arroyo's restitution to office; but the governor, instead, imprisoned the fiscal. The suit against him could not be decided at Manila, and was therefore referred to the court at Madrid, Arroyo meanwhile remaining a prisoner, and harshly treated. The archbishop was so grieved at this, and at his having been the cause (although innocent) of Arroyo's imprisonment, by inducing him to leave his asylum in the convent, that he became seriously ill; and the heroic remedies prescribed by the physicians so reduced his strength that he soon died. Among the accusations made against Arroyo was that he had married (in 1738) Doña Maria Luisa Josepha de Morales y Santistevan without the knowledge and consent of her 'guardian; but this was apparently settled by the proof afterward adduced that the marriage took place on August 12, 1742, and was performed by the guardian himself, Juan de la Fuente y Yepes, dean of the cathedral. In the following December Arroyo died; his widow was summoned to take his place in the legal proceedings then pending against him, but asked the authorities to release her from this requirement; nevertheless, her property was seized, and the case was referred to Madrid for settlement. The court censured both Valdés y Tamón and Torre for their proceedings in the matter, and ordered that Arroyo be restored to his office, with pay for the time which he had spent in prison; but this decision reached Manila (April, 1743) only after his death. (Concepción, Hist. de Philipinas, xi, pp. 89–121.)]

[In January of 1743 the bishop-elect of Nueva Caceres, the master Don Isidoro de Arevalo, asked from the Manila government permission to go to Macao to receive his consecration, there being no bishop in the islands to confer it. But the governor had received letters from China which told of the expedition of the English commander Anson (see VOL. XLVII, p. 231, note 48), his depredations on the South American coast, and his presence in the harbor of Canton for the purpose of repairing his vessel; and he therefore asked the bishop to defer his voyage for a time, in order to avert the danger of his capture by the English "pirate." In the following May, news came to Manila that Anson had sailed from Canton, and gone toward the Embocadero to lie in wait for the Acapulco galleon "Cobadonga;" the ship "Pilar," which Anson had been previously foiled in capturing, was despatched (June 3) to aid the galleon, but its commander seems to have been timorous, and took refuge in the port of Ticao at the news of a strange warship being seen (June 22) in those waters. Finally, his ship began to leak, and he returned to Manila without accomplishing anything. On June 30 the "Cobadonga" was captured by Anson, after a brave resistance by the Spaniards. The residencia of the officers of the "Pilar" was delayed for two years, and, although the charges of delay and negligence brought against them were serious, they were finally exonerated from blame; those of the expedition which endeavored, but unsuccessfully, to find and punish Anson after his capture of the "Cobadonga" were also justified. As for the commander (Don Geronimo Montero) and officers of the latter vessel, severe charges were brought against them by the royal fiscal for surrendering the ship; they were arrested, and a special investigation of the matter was made by the royal Audiencia. The fiscal demanded that they be punished; but after examination of the testimony, the governor decided that they were not to blame for the surrender; but they were condemned to pay the costs of their trial. In this voyage the "Cobadonga" had not brought from Mexico the returns on the investments made for that year by the Misericordia2 and other administrators of obras pías; these returns, amounting to 1,200,000 pesos, were left behind at Acapulco, either through fear of the English cruisers or for more profitable investment in Mexico. Hence arose a controversy as to the restitution of these funds, and the Misericordia brought suit for their recovery from the agents who had withheld them; but it was decided by the Council of Indias that the latter were not bound and could not be compelled to repay the money. "In the outer court of justice this went very well, but in the inner court it was quite otherwise; for we have knowledge of actual restitutions of the property thus withheld being made to the obras pías, by those persons who had more healthy consciences." (Concepción, Hist. de Philipinas, xi, pp. 121–237.)]

[The remainder of this summary is taken from Zúñiga's *Historia de Philipinas*, pp. 546–601.]

Señor Don Gaspar de la Torre made a bad beginning of his government; the violent proceedings which he instituted against the fiscal Arroyo began to make him odious to the community, the misfortunes which occurred during his term of office exasperated the minds of the citizens, and all his conduct was directed more toward pacifying this hatred than to gaining the esteem of the subjects whom he ruled. Seeing that he was disliked in the city, he began to be affected with melancholy, from which resulted a dysentery, a disease from which one seldom recovers in Philipinas. His illness was aggravated by the news which reached him that the village of Balayan in the province of Batangas had revolted;3 and finally a supposed revolt of the Sangleys ended his life. There was a rumor that the Chinese were going to come into the city, and, notwithstanding his illness, he tried to go out against them; his friends would not permit this, and soon ascertained that it was all a fabrication;4 but he became so feverish from the shock that he died a few days afterward, September 21, 1745…. In his place began to rule, conformably to the directions given by his Majesty, Señor Arrechedera of the Order of St. Dominic, the bishop-elect of Ylocos. He made investigations in regard to the uprising of the Chinese, and found that they had no such intention, nor had they given any cause for suspecting them of rebellion; it was therefore believed that this report had been circulated in order to vex the governor. No long time was spent in quelling the uprising in Balayan; for the sargento-mayor went out with a hundred men of the regular troops and many Indians, encountered the insurgents, and, although he could not conquer them, because the Indians who accompanied him all fled immediately, checked the onset of the enemy, without his having suffered any mishap, save that he received a musket-shot from one of his own men, a raw recruit. He asked for aid from Manila, and they sent him two hundred men, with whom he conquered the enemies and punished them as they deserved—shooting some, and banishing others, according to the influence that they had exercised in the sedition, which vanished like smoke. He left behind a small detachment in that province, in order to inspire some respect [for the Spanish power] in the seditious who might remain in hiding; and the rest of the troops were sent to Cavite, because, besides the information which he received that the English were at Batavia with a squadron, the alcalde of Ilocos gave warning that two ships had been seen from that coast, with two smaller vessels, which were believed to be enemies. The most illustrious governor put the town in a condition for defense, erected various works, purchased arms through the agency of foreigners, and cast some cannons. All these preparations were not necessary, for the English did not come, although they resented our having taken from them a brigantine and a balandra…. In Philipinas, Manila found some consolation in the arrival of two ships,5 which had returned from Acapulco and brought some funds to relieve the necessities of the commonwealth. In one of them came Don Fray Pedro de la Santisima Trinidad,6 who, while a member of the Council of Indias, had taken the Franciscan habit in the Recollect convent of Pomasque; and his Majesty presented him for the archbishopric of Manila, asking the pope to compel him to accept that dignity. Fray Pedro, not being able to oppose the mandate of his Holiness, was consecrated in España; he came to Philipinas, and took possession of his office [mitra] on August 27, 1747. It appeared that he ought to have begun at the same time to rule as governor [of the islands]; for the king's decree appointed for the vacancies [in that office] the archbishop of Manila, and in default of him the nearest bishop — through which arrangement the office had been assumed by Señor Arrechedera, who ought to have surrendered the authority to the archbishop as soon as the latter took possession of his see. His most illustrious Lordship did not choose to stir up this question, and contented himself with reporting the matter to the court; answer was made to him that orders had already been previously despatched that he should take charge of the government ad interim, but this royal order did not arrive [at Manila] until after the arrival of the proprietary governor. [His most illustrious Lordship] also brought a decree in which his Majesty committed to him the expulsion of the Chinese — which had not yet been effected, on account of the personal interests of the governors, although it had been repeatedly commanded; but he thought it well not to make the decree known until a better opportunity, because he found Señor Arrechedera greatly devoted to the Chinese."7 This was the only defect that was observed in this most illustrious prelate and governor; in other matters his most illustrious Lordship carried himself with much honor in his government. He quelled the revolt in the island of Bohol, sending Commander Lechuga with a suitable force; this officer punished some of the rebels, and reduced all the fishermen's villages of that island to obedience to the king of España; but in the hill-country the insurgents remain until this day.8

The Jesuits had been urging our Catholic monarch Phelipe V, and constrained him to the inglorious act of writing to the kings of Joló and Mindanao; the governor sent ambassadors to deliver his letters and make an alliance with the Moros.9 Those petty kings were greatly delighted at the honor thus done them by a king so great as that of España, and, in order to gratify him by complying with his requests to them, consented to receive missionaries into their countries. A Jesuit father went to Mindanao, but, seeing that the chiefs were restless and the king had little power to restrain them, he feared that they would take his life, and abandoned his mission; and he fled for refuge to the fort of Zamboanga. In Joló two Jesuits began to sow the seed of the gospel,10 but gathered little fruit because the panditas of the Moro religion raised a fierce opposition to them, and the leading men of the kingdom were not willing that the missionaries should preach a different faith from that which they had inherited from their ancestors. In these circumstances the king of Joló, Mahomad Alimudin, desired to go to visit the governor of Manila; but the Jesuit fathers were displeased at this resolution, because they feared that the king's brother Bantilan, an enemy to the Christians, would be left in command. From this resulted jealousies and disturbances in the court, and the minds of men became so inflamed that some one gave the sultan, or king, a lance-thrust.11 Affairs were thrown into so bad condition that the fathers of the Society, not considering themselves safe in Joló, precipitately retreated to Zamboanga. The sultan Alimudin likewise fled from his kingdom in order to go to Manila, to seek aid from the governor in order to punish the rebels who had given him the lance-thrust and conspired against his person.12 He reached Zamboanga,13 and there the Spaniards furnished him with means to proceed to Manila; he entered that city with a retinue of seventy persons, with whom he was lodged in a house in the suburb of Binondo, which was kept at his disposal at the cost of the royal treasury. Afterward he made his public entry [into Manila], and was received with great ostentation; the leading persons in Manila visited him, and presented to him gold chains, robes, diamond rings, sashes, and gold-headed canes—so that he was astonished at so much magnificence, and at the generosity of the Spaniards, for whatever he needed for the support of his household was supplied to him from the royal treasury.14

The governor desired that the sultan should become a Christian, and spoke to him about it; and the latter did not delay to pretend to embrace our religion. He was entrusted to two Jesuit fathers for instruction in the faith, and very soon he was instructed in the Christian doctrine, and gave signs of being truly converted, by the urgent requests which he made to the archbishop to baptize him. Nevertheless, his conversion was somewhat uncertain. Some said that he became a Christian only that the Spaniards might place him on the throne from which he saw himself ousted, and that we ought not to trust in his conversion; others were of opinion that in his conforming to the usage of the church we ought to believe that his intention was sincere, and that he should be baptized, so long as he did not in his outward actions give cause for thinking otherwise. In view of this diversity of opinions, his illustrious Lordship thought it expedient to delay the baptism, and to wait until the sultan should give stronger proofs of his resolution. This delay vexed the bishop-governor, who desired to see him a Christian as soon as possible; and, as he could not change the archbishop's mind, he sent Alimudin to the village of Panique,15 which is the nearest one [to Manila] in his bishopric of Ylocos, in order that he might be baptized there; and he sent a Spaniard to appear in his name as sponsor. Besides the guard of his own people, the sultan was accompanied by another guard of Spaniards; and in all places through which he passed a ceremonious reception was given to him. In Panique he was baptized by a Dominican religious, on April 29, 1750, with great solemnity and the assistance of other religious of the same order. On his return to Manila, the governor received him with a general salvo from the plaza, and ordered that festivities should be celebrated with comedies, dances, fireworks, and bull-fights, in sign of rejoicing.

In Joló the brother of the sultan, named Bantilan, had continued in the government of the kingdom; it was he who had ordered that his brother be assaulted, and had stirred up the rebellion among the chiefs which compelled his brother to take refuge among the Spaniards. Bantilan was the greatest enemy that the Spaniards and Christians had, and gave orders that many boats should go out to infest our seas. The Joloans—who were rebels against their own king, and pirates by office—equipped many pancos, joined with them other Moros, whom they call Tirones, and began plundering raids through all the islands. The most illustrious governor gave his commands against them, and commanded some small fleets to set sail; this did not fail to cause in the Moros some respect [for our power], and to restrain them; but no injury was inflicted on them, nor were their insolent acts punished, because there were in Manila few troops. For this reason it was impossible to restore the throne to the king of Joló, who was now, since becoming a Christian, named Don Fernando de Alimudin; the proprietary governor, who arrived in the same year when he was baptized, met him in Manila with the greatest ostentation.

CHAPTER XXXI

Don Francisco Joseph de Obando, a native of Caceres in Extramadura, went with a squadron to the Southern Sea, and was in Lima at the time when that great earthquake occurred in which Callao was submerged.16 There the favor of the king was extended to him, in appointing him governor of Manila; he went to Mexico, and in that kingdom married Doña Barbara Ribadeneyra; and, accompanied by his wife, he embarked for Philipinas to render service in the government, of which he took possession in July, 1750. As soon as he arrived, the archbishop presented to him the royal decree in which his Majesty charged him with the expulsion of the Sangleys. The governor held a council for the discussion of this subject, and in it was stirred up a controversy over a seat, which frustrated the excellent intention of his Majesty to expel the Chinese, who are so injurious to these his dominions. The archbishop attempted to seat himself on a chair at the left of the governor, at the head of the table [en la testera]; the latter would not allow this, nor that the guards should form in ranks when the archbishop entered the palace or passed through the gates of the city; and these points of etiquette were sufficient to prevent the execution of the order to expel the Sangleys from Philipinas. Information of this controversy was sent to the court, and on both points came decisions in favor of the archbishop. The royal Audiencia had a dispute with the governor on another point, because he had by his own authority appointed Don Domingo Nebra temporary warden of Cavite, when he should have conferred this post after consulting the royal Audiencia, as his Majesty had commanded. The governor did not gainsay this royal order, but he said that there was no person competent for the building of the vessels which it was necessary to construct for the commerce of Acapulco and the defense of the islands against the Moros, except Nebra; that the latter was seventy years old, and could not be compelled to take charge of the construction of boats unless he wished; and that in no case would he accept the post under consultation of the royal Audiencia, because in that case he would be subject to residencia. The governor concluded that, in an extraordinary case like this, he ought not to adhere to the usual rules, but decide what was most expedient for the royal service.17 The royal Audiencia made their remonstrances and protests, but, seeing that the governor was the stronger, they yielded, and appealed to his Majesty. In spite of the knowledge which the governor so highly extolled in Nebra, the fragata "Pilar," which he careened and which was despatched to Acapulco, perished at sea, without any news about her having come here.

Another and very noisy controversy occurred in Manila about this time. A lady who had made profession in the beaterio of Santa Cathalina, where she was called Mother Cecilia, became enamored of Don Francisco Figueroa;18 and presented herself before [the ordinary, during] the vacant see (Señor Arrechedera being then the governor), alleging that her profession was null. The provisor, who did not desire controversies with the Dominican fathers (to which order the governor belonged), pacified her, [arguing] that she should be silent for the time, and wait for a better opportunity to press her claim. As soon as Señor Obando arrived, seeing that the difficulties had ceased which until then had made her keep silent, she presented herself before the archbishop, asking, as she had done before with the provisor, that he would annul her profession. His illustrious Lordship commanded that the beata should be placed [for the time] in Santa Potenciana, but this was vigorously opposed by the Dominican fathers. They had recourse to the superior government, but, not finding support in that tribunal, they gave way and surrendered the lady to the provisor, to whom was entrusted this sequestration. The lawsuit followed, and the archbishop decided that, in view of the fact that his Majesty had forbidden that the beaterio of Santa Cathalina should be erected into a convent, Mother Cecilia, who had made profession in it, could not be truly a religious, and therefore her profession was null.19 The Dominican fathers lodged an appeal before the [papal] delegate, who was the bishop of Zebú;20 and the appeal was admitted to allow another trial in the former court, but not to suspend its decrees [en lo devolutivo, y no en lo suspensivo]. In order to follow up their appeal with vigor they sent a religious who might carry on active judicial proceedings against the beata, because they thought that to do otherwise was a disgrace to the beaterio; but that bishop declined to hear so vexatious a lawsuit, under pretext of his poor health. There was no other bishop in Philipinas to whom they could have recourse, for which reason they carried the suit to the archbishop of Mexico; and he summoned Mother Cecilia before his tribunal, demanding that she be sent to Mexico in order that he might hear and decide the case there. As the appeal had not been admitted for the suspension [of the first sentence], the beata contracted matrimony, and with her husband embarked for Mexico, where the marriage was considered valid and her profession as null.21 The documents in the case [el espediente] having been carried to the Council of Indias, orders were given that the beaterio of Santa Cathalina should be extinguished with the death of the beatas who [then] were its inmates—which has not been done, because the Dominican fathers have obtained the revocation of this order.22

The governor, being informed of the ravages which the Moros were committing in the provinces of Bisayas, determined to attack them with a powerful squadron, which could at the same time reëstablish Don Fernando Alimudin (whom, now become a Christian, Señor Obando had found in Manila) on the throne of Joló, of which he had unjustly been despoiled. There was a diversity of opinions on this latter point, because many persons believed that no confidence could be placed in his fidelity, and suspected that on the first occasion that might arise he would practice some treachery, as his fathers had done. But the decision was made in favor of the exiled king, and he was carried to Joló in the almiranta of the armada, which sailed from Cavite under command of the master-of-camp of the royal regiment, who bore commissions for both these offices. The armada reached Zamboanga, but the almiranta did not make its appearance; and, in order not to lose the monsoon, and not to give the Moros time to fortify themselves, the fleet, without waiting for the almiranta, sailed from that port on June 13, 1751, and on the twenty-sixth anchored in the cove of Joló, at a mile distant from the forts of the enemy. They began to fire the cannons at these, and those who were in command were so intimidated that they began negotiations for peace; and they signed a letter in which they bound themselves to obey their king and receive him as faithful vassals, and to surrender to the Spaniards all the captive Christians who might be in the island. With this compact the master-of-camp returned, much elated, to Zamboanga in nine days; and carried with him two champans of Chinese23 whom he found trading there, seizing them under the pretext that they had sold a cannon to our enemies the Joloans, with whom treaties of peace had just been made.

The almiranta had been delayed because it had met some damage, and had remained at Calapan repairing its rudder, for which reason it did not arrive at Zamboanga until July 25; but the king of Joló, impatient at waiting so long, had embarked with two caracoas and arrived there twelve days before. In spite of his activity, the governor of Zamboanga was very doubtful of his fidelity; and, having found two letters which Alimudin wrote to the king of Mindanao — one in the vulgar tongue, [written] by order of the governor of Manila, and the other in the Arabic language, which he had learned in Batavia, where he had spent some time — the commandant became curious to know what he was saying in this language, [now] obsolete in our islands. He sought for someone to translate the letter, and found that Alimudin said that what he wrote in the other was in obedience to the governor of Manila and to his commands; and he could not avoid obeying him, or excuse himself, because he was in a foreign dominion. To this suspicion was added the fact that a brother of his named Asin, and the chiefs of Joló who had made the compact with the master-of-camp to receive their king and surrender the captive Christians, came to Zamboanga to visit him; and they not only brought no captive, but it was said that, under pretext of this visit, they were bringing in arms, in order to gain possession of the fort. The governor, influenced by these reports, arrested the sultan with all his following,24 and searched the house in which they lived, but he found only a few arms, which gave no indication of an uprising; but other faults were discovered, which gave plausible ground for their arrest. Various despatches and presents which he had sent to the Moros were considered as suspicious; and the commander and two passengers of the almiranta declared that he was on very bad terms with the people in Manila, from whom he had received many kindnesses, to whom on all occasions he showed himself ungrateful; that he said the new governor had kept him like a prisoner; that he gave no sign of being a Christian, since he went every night to sleep with his concubines, did not hear mass, and had taken away the crosses from the rosaries belonging to the people of his household; and, finally, that he had apostatized from the faith by offering a Mahometan sacrifice at Calapan, where he killed a goat, divided it into twelve parts, with many superstitious ceremonies, and gave them to his followers to eat, in order to celebrate Easter.

The governor of Zamboanga made report to Manila regarding these charges and his arrest of the sultan and his household; and answer was made to him that he should send Alimudin and all his people to Manila as prisoners, and that war should be declared on the Joloans25 — giving authority to every one who wished to equip his vessel as a privateer, and allowing him to keep for himself whatever he should seize as plunder; and any persons who should thus be seized should remain captives,26 since the Moros of Joló had been declared not only enemies to the Spaniards, but pirates, who ought to suffer captivity, just as they imposed this lot on the Christians whom they seized. The extermination of the Moros was undertaken with so much ardor that pardon [indulto] for their crimes was granted to those who should present themselves to serve against the enemy. The armada which the master-of-camp had at Zamboanga was reënforced,27 and a second expedition was made to Joló, more unfortunate than the first — for the Spaniards attempted to land in that island, and the Moros received them with such valor that they compelled our people to retreat, with heavy loss and great disgrace to the Spanish arms, to the fort of Zamboanga.

The haughty Bantilan, who ruled the kingdom of Joló in the absence of his brother, undertook to induce, by the victory which he had gained over the Spaniards, the men of Mindanao to break the peace which they were observing with us, and to harry us as much as they could; and he urged all the pirates who were in those islands to take up arms against the Spaniards, whom he represented as conquered, and in fear of their arms. Then the seas of Bisayas were seen covered with little fleets of Moros, who carried desolation everywhere. Nothing was heard of save plundering, the burning of villages, the seizing of vessels, captivities, and [other] acts of violence, which the Moros committed in our territories28 — so that Señor

Obando wished to go forth in person to restrain them, and to repair the many injuries which they were inflicting on us. His Majesty had commanded that a fortified post should be established in the island of Paragua, in order to shut off the pirates from entrance [into Bisayan waters] on that side, just as it was closed on the other side by the post of Zamboanga. In order to proceed in all respects with moderation, the governor sent an ambassador to the king of Borney, in order that the latter should cede to us the territory that he possessed in that island; and when it was ceded he made ready a squadron to build the fortified post, and from that place to follow up the Moros who were plundering our islands. He intended to go out in person at the head of this armada, and consulted the royal Audiencia on this point; but the auditors were of opinion that it was not expedient to hazard his person, and that he could entrust this expedition to another person, who by carrying an engineer to draw plans for the fort which it was necessary to build on the island of Paragua could accomplish all that was expected from the expedition. In accordance with this advice, the governor appointed, as its commander, Don Antonio Fabea, [sc. Faveau] who sailed from Cavite with eleven vessels; he took with him Don Manuel Aguirre, who went with an appointment as commandant of the military post which was to be established, and bore orders to go to Igolote, in the same island [of Paragua], to dislodge the Moros, who usually took refuge in that place. Here his men fell sick, to such an extent that, without doing more than to take possession of that district, they went back to Manila, leaving behind two hundred and seventy dead, and carrying home many sick men in the squadron.29

The king of Joló had already reached Manila, and was imprisoned in the fort of Santiago,30 to the great satisfaction of those who had been opposed to his baptism and had always doubted his fidelity; but he obtained from the governor permission that his daughter the princess Faatima, who was imprisoned with him, might go to Joló with letters from him for his brother and other chiefs, in order [to urge them] to make a stable peace with the Spaniards; and for this permission he bound himself to surrender fifty Christian captives.31 The princess accomplished the return of the captives, and obtained from her uncle Bantilan the despatch of an ambassador to Manila, to attend to her father's affairs. The envoy carried authority to conduct, jointly with Bantilan's brother the king, negotiations for peace with the governor, and to solemnize the treaties which they should regard as expedient, [the chiefs] binding themselves to obey whatever the two should sign. It was stipulated with the king and the ambassador that the Moros of Joló should surrender all the Christian captives who were in their island, and send back all the arms which they had taken from the Spaniards, and the ornaments which they had plundered from the churches; and, in order to make these treaties effective, permission was granted to one of the chiefs who were prisoners with the king to go to Joló in company with the ambassador whom Bantilan had sent.

The governor had very little confidence in the promises of the Moros or in their treaties, because they had always broken them with the same facility with which they had made them; and he prepared a strong squadron [to go] against them, in order to compel them by force to observe the treaties which he did not expect they would keep of their own accord. Nor did his suspicions prove to be groundless, for in that year (which was 1754) occurred the worst inroad which those islanders had made into Philipinas. In all districts they made raids with blood and fire, killing religious, Indians, and Spaniards, burning and plundering villages; and taking captive thousands of Christians, not only in the islands near Joló, but throughout our territories, even in the provinces nearest to the capital Manila.32 The fleet which the governor had made ready went out against them, but, before they could do anything, his successor came, at the end of his four years' term of office; for this reason, he left the islands in the most deplorable condition that had ever been known, the cause of these evils being either his own misconduct or the unfitness of those to whom he gave appointments, or perhaps his misfortune. What is certain is, that he experienced a very grievous residencia, and many charges against him resulted; and in the following year he embarked in the galleon "Santisima Trinidad" for Acapulco, and died on the way, without reaching España.

CHAPTER XXXII

Don Pedro Manuel de Arandia,33 a native of Ceuta and of Vizcayan ancestry, took possession of his government in July, 1754. As soon as he arrived in Manila, he undertook to organize the troops, and to place the military force on a regular footing and in conformity with the ordinances which are observed in España. From the royal troops that were in the islands he formed the "king's regiment" of two battalions; he reorganized the body of artillerists, placing it in the condition in which we now see it; and he assigned to both the soldiers and the officers pay with which they could decently support themselves and meet their obligations, without being harassed to seek in some other way what was necessary for life. He was very diligent to put in order the arsenal at Cavite, and whatever depended upon the royal officials — in which he did not fail to suffer annoyances, and to incur the dislike of many persons who did not enjoy so much reform and so great zeal.34 At the beginning of his government, in the month of

December, occurred the terrible eruption of the volcano of Taal, which lies in the middle of Lake Bombon, in the province of Batangas. So heavy was the shower of ashes that it destroyed four villages which were on the shore of the lake, and it was necessary to remove them a legua inland. There were many and severe earthquake shocks, and a noise as of squadrons engaged in battle; and the atmosphere was darkened with the quantities of sand and ashes which issued from the volcano—so that in Manila, which is distant twenty leguas, but little could be seen at noonday; and in Cavite, which is somewhat nearer, that time of day seemed like a dark night.35 I have ascended with Señor Alava36 to the summit of this volcano, and only a lake was seen, about half a legua in diameter; it was very deep, and its waters were dark green.

The armada which Señor Obando had sent against the Moros met so poor success that the governor was obliged to take away its command from Don Miguel Valdés, who had been sent as its chief officer; and it was conferred on Father Ducos, a Jesuit, from whom he expected better results. In fact, that father was fitted for the post, and acted with such valor and discretion that he took from the enemies more than a hundred and fifty vessels, destroyed three of their villages, killed their inhabitants, and made captive innumerable people; and he checked the onset of those barbarians, who were devastating everything.37 These happy tidings arrived at Manila in January, 1755; Señor Arandia gave orders that the Te Deum should be sung by way of thanksgiving, and confirmed Father Ducos in his command of the naval squadron; he had great esteem for the father because the latter was the son of a colonel who was the governor's intimate friend, and because he seemed to have inherited his father's valor.

Señor Arandia treated the king of Joló with much kindness, and allowed him his liberty, although the king voluntarily continued to live in the fort of Santiago; the governor gave him a monthly allowance of fifty pesos and six cavans of rice for his support, and prevailed upon the archbishop to grant him permission to hear mass and receive the sacraments, of which he had been deprived. The king desired to marry as his second wife a woman who had been his concubine but was now a Christian;38 the archbishop would not permit this, and Señor Arandia not only smoothed away all the difficulties, but gave the king the use of his palace in order that in it he might celebrate the marriage with more pomp and solemnity. He did not gain these dispensations without some dispute with his most illustrious Lordship, to which was added another, which, although of less importance, was sufficient to alienate feeling and cause resentment in Philipinas. The governor complained of the archbishop because the bells were not rung for the former when he entered or left any church, as ought to be done on account of his being vice-patron, especially when he went [thither] as president of the [ecclesiastical] tribunals. His most illustrious Lordship declared that he had no order from the king for doing so; but these formalities, together with the attacks of illness which the most illustrious Señor Trinidad suffered, caused his death; this occurred on May 29, 1755. Señor Arandia continued to favor the king of Joló, for he thought that by this means he could end the war with the Moros. He sent to Joló all the princes and princesses, the datos, and all the women, who were detained in Manila, leaving the king alone—who acknowledged his vassalage [hizo pleito homenaje] and took the oath of fidelity, until a decision [of his case] should arrive from the court of España, which had been informed of his detention. The princes and princesses arrived at Joló on October 5 of this year; they were graciously received by Bantilan, who, grateful for the generosity of the governor, promised to observe faithfully the treaty of peace which his ambassador and his brother had signed at Manila. It was necessary, in order to extricate ourselves entirely from the war, to make an agreement with the men of Mindanao; the governor undertook this, and sent ambassadors to them; but the petty rulers who are in that island are so numerous and so treacherous that it is impossible to establish a permanent peace with them. Even assuming that all the petty kings of the Moros may desire to observe the peace with the Spaniards, they will never succeed in it, because they possess so little authority over their vassals that they have never been able to restrain them,39 and they will prevent them from going out to plunder and to seize captives throughout our islands, for they have given themselves up to this kind of life; and only the spiritual conquest of their provinces is adequate to deliver us from these troublesome enemies.

During this government was undertaken the reëstablishment of the missions in the islands of Batanes, which lie to the north of Cagayan. From early times the Dominican fathers maintained in the islands of Babuyanes religious ministers, who gave instruction to their inhabitants; but in the year 1690 they removed these people to Cagayan. The king having decreed that they should go back to their own land, the religious who directed them established a mission in the islands of the Batanes,40 distant some thirty leguas from Cagayan; and after his death his companion withdrew, leaving the mission abandoned until the year 1718. It was then reëstablished by another Dominican religious, who fixed his headquarters in the island of Calayan, in which place he attempted to make the Indians in the other islands settle, in order that, brought together there, they might be instructed in the Christian religion. Great as was the desire of the Batanes to enter the bosom of the church, only a hundred and fifty persons took the resolution to change their place of abode; and half of these died in a short time. That island offered few means of comfort, for which reason the father missionary became sick; and, although he had a successor, the mission was entirely abandoned.41

In the year 1754, two religious were sent, of whom one died and the other retired to Cagayan, seriously ill; but he returned in the following year with another companion. In order to ameliorate the destitution which they had suffered in the preceding year, they determined to take with them a carpenter, a lay brother of their order, in order that he might, as soon as they reached the place, put together a house, which was to go in the vessel, in pieces. Their zeal did not permit them to wait until the work was finished; and, fearing that the monsoon would pass away, they embarked without their little house. Hardly had they reached Calayan when the two fell sick; other fathers went to succor them, and all became sick; accordingly, they returned [to the mainland] one after another, and it was necessary to abandon the mission after the Dominican fathers had incurred large expenses for it. Afterward, this conquest was again undertaken, by Señor Basco in 1783; and this effort has been successful in maintaining there the Dominican fathers, converting those islanders to the faith. A commandant was stationed there with his garrison, which caused much expense, because it was necessary to send them all their supplies from Philipinas; for in all those islands the only produce is camotes and such other eatable things as grow in the country itself. There is no doubt that other articles would be produced, but so numerous are the rats, which consume everything, and so frequent the baguios or hurricanes, that one may rest assured that these plagues would devastate the fields before the crops could mature. Every year a bark was sent to carry succor to the islands, but, as the baguios are so frequent in those seas, many of these vessels were wrecked; it has therefore been recognized that the maintenance of that post is impossible, and the result is, that only the Dominican fathers remain there with a small guard, who must be succored from Cagayan. For this enterprise Señor Basco was granted the title of Conde de la Conquista; but I assert that if half of what he spent in Batanes had been expended in placing missionaries in Ylocos, Pangasinan, and Cagayan, he would have gained more vassals for the king of España, and with less risk.

I am astonished that we should have left the beaten track of the conquest or pacification of the Indians, and taken up another which is more dangerous and more costly, only because it makes more noise and a more showy appearance, that is, [the conquest] by arms, which always has produced bad effects—as occurred at this time, in the hill-country of the Igorrots. In the year of 1740, the Augustinian fathers handed over to the Dominicans the missions of Ytuy, or Ysinay, in order that, these being joined to the missions of Panique which they had established in the preceding year, the provinces of Pangasinan and Cagayan might be united on their southern borders.42 The Indians, both Christians and unbelievers, resented this change of missionaries, from which resulted a species of civil wars among them; and it was necessary for the auditor Don Ygnacio Arzadun y Rebolledo, who was then making official visitation of the province of Pangasinan, to send troops [to Ytuy] to silence the malcontents. Our men fought a battle with them, in which the natives were defeated and pacified; but a few years later they again became restless, and finally, in the year 1756, many Christians apostatized; and these, united with the unbelievers, raised a furious tempest. They burned some churches, slew many of the people who remained faithful, and, losing reverence for the missionary fathers, searched for them to take their lives. On account of this, Señor Arandia despatched an expedition to this mission and to the hill-country of the Ygorrots, which had very little effect; for it accomplished nothing save to frighten the Indians and make them flee to the hills, to come down again as soon as the soldiers should go away.

In order to know how to pacify the Indians, it is necessary to understand their character. Whether because of their naturally superstitious disposition, or because God has thus ordained it, they are very affectionate to the missionary fathers, and have much reverence for them; but there are not lacking some who dare to plan some perfidy against the fathers, and for this reason they need escorts to protect them from audacious attempts of that sort. At times the natives become heated and rise against authority, and the multitude come out against the fathers, unless there is some check to restrain them; such a check, is in the military posts, which ought to be near the missions, so that the Indians may have respect for these, and fear lest they will be immediately punished if they commit any insolent act. With these measures of precaution the islands were conquered, and the same are observed at the present time; but the missionaries are very few, from which it results that they are so widely separated that they have to make a day's journey to visit one another, when they need to be confessed or on other occasions, and they are very poorly paid. For what is a hundred pesos and two hundred cavans of rice for a Spaniard to maintain himself with decency in the missions? [Even] this small stipend they sometimes cannot collect without a thousand annoyances and vexations which are occasioned to them by the alcaldes-mayor, who seek various pretexts for not paying them, and compel them to go from the mission to the [provincial] capital to collect it, as I have seen. So wretchedly do these poor religious live that there are occasions in which they find themselves obliged to use for their own support what was given to them for their guards; and they live without these, preferring to remain exposed to the affronts of the heathens rather than perish with hunger. The military posts are also few in number, and the Indians in them are unable to impose respect on their countrymen. If the money that has been spent in useless expeditions could have been employed in these sure means of pacification, that undertaking would have made much greater progress. It is true, we shall never see the rapid advances made by our ancestors in the conquest [of the islands], because the Indians have their eyes more open; the Christians themselves persuade the others not to be baptized, in order that the tribute and other taxes may not be imposed on them. Moreover, they themselves have a custom which greatly hinders their civilization, and consequently their conversion. If any one commits a murder in another village, its people do not rest until they have avenged the crime; the consequence is, that the weaker villages are obliged to remove from the district, or to league themselves with other villages. In either case, the Christian church suffers much, because those who are baptized must follow the infidels of their own village and separate themselves from the [missionary] fathers, or else must enter into the general hostilities. Nevertheless, gradually they would all be converted; for if in the neighboring villages many unbelievers are continually being baptized, who leave their own lands and are held in less regard than are the oldtime Christians, how many more would not be baptized if they could remain in their own homes, honored and courted by their old acquaintances? Christian morality is very holy, and attracts all hearts in which vice has not become deeply rooted.

On May 15, 1757, the holy Congregation [i.e., of Propaganda] at Rome issued the decree which put an end to the controversies which the discalced Augustinians (or Recollects) sent out by the Propaganda had in the kingdom of Tungquin with the Dominican missionary fathers from Philipinas over the administration of certain districts, and in regard to the [association called the] "Lovers of the Cross" [Amatrices de la Cruz].43 The Dominicans had received into their missions various priests sent out by the Propaganda, who — for lack of ministers, or on account of the persecutions — had ministered to some villages in the Dominican territory. On this account his Lordship Fray Hilario de Jesus, bishop of Coriza, asked from the Dominicans a residence for a Recollect (as the latter belonged to his own order); and soon after that he asked for the entire district, which was granted to him during the lifetime of that religious. When the bishop saw the Dominicans so compliant, he did not delay in demanding another district for his discalced fathers. The Dominicans did not accede to this demand, and his illustrious Lordship, availing himself of various pretexts, introduced into that district a Recollect religious; from this resulted a sort of schism, in which papers were written on both sides, insulting remarks were made, and neither party would yield. Like altercations occurred in other districts, because the Recollects tried to thrust themselves into the missions of the Dominicans. The "Lovers of the Cross" were a sort of beatas, who lived in a community, and, although they did not take the vow of chastity, observed the [rules of the] religious life; some of them belonged to the Tertiary Order of St. Dominic, and others to the discalced religious women of St. Augustine. It was made evident that these beaterios ought to be subject to the parish priests; but, bringing forward various pretexts, the Dominicans and Recollects disputed over the direction of these beatas.

In order to stop the scandals which resulted from these disputes, the bishop of Coriza assembled a [diocesan] synod in the village of Luctuy; it was the second synod held in Tungquin, and held its first session on June 24, 1753. Among the other points that were settled, action was taken on the "Lovers of the Cross," and on the distribution of districts. As the bishop was a Recollect, and the rest of those who attended the council were his confederates, everything was decided against the Dominicans; Father Hernandez, therefore, who was the only member of his order who attended the synod, protested against all its decrees, appealed to the Apostolic See, and went out of the meeting before it was ended. After the synod closed, the Dominicans, seeing that a Recollect was going to Rome to secure approbation for the acts of the council, sent another envoy, a Dominican, to prevent this. When the whole matter was examined in the holy Congregation, two districts were set aside for the Recollect fathers, and the rest were continued in charge of the Dominicans, the beaterios of the "Lovers of the Cross" were left subject to their respective parish priests. In regard to the [acts of the] second council of Tungquin, it was ordained that they should not be carried into effect until the holy Congregation should, after a thorough examination, agree to confirm them.

Returning to Manila, one of the good things which Señor Arandia did in his term of office was the expulsion of the Chinese. He sent away all the heathen to their own country, and, in order that hereafter they might not remain in Philipinas, he founded the market [alcayseria] of San Fernando,44 in which all the Sangleys who come here to trade must dwell until the time for the departure of their champans arrives; and then all must embark in their vessels except the Christians, who have permission to live in the islands, provided they devote themselves to the cultivation of the soil. The Spaniards who were interested in the residence of the Sangleys in Manila persuaded him that, if he expelled them, there would not be people enough to carry on the internal trade; and, in order to counteract this frivolous pretext, he established a [commercial] company of Spaniards and mestizos. This lasted only one year,45 because there was little need of it in some islands where there are more than enough to carry on this sort of traffic. The Asiatics are naturally slothful, and consequently enjoy greatly the kind of life — since it gives them food without labor — which they secure by buying and selling the commodities which are consumed in the country; and, even if some are unsuccessful, every one has a very moderate [amount of] trade; but there is hardly any one among them who does not carry it on very steadily. This abundance of petty traders makes their wares much dearer, since they pass through many hands before they reach the last buyer; and each trader, since he operates with little capital, must make large gains in order to support himself. From this it must be inferred that the Sangleys, far from being necessary to this commerce, greatly injure it; and it should have been considered desirable to lessen, in place of increasing, the number of these traders or dealers.

Notwithstanding the wisdom of this measure, Señor Arandia lost much in popular esteem by it; and this, added to others of his actions, brought upon him the hatred of the community. In virtue of the ample powers which he brought from the court, he drew up instructions for the alcaldes-mayor and the government of the provinces, in which he openly declared himself against the regulars. At the beginning, he had treated these religious bodies with respect; but, resenting some acts of disrespect manifested toward him by certain individuals, in these instructions he deprived the orders of the kitchen-boys who had been furnished to them by the king since the conquest, and the servants granted them by the crown for sacristans. Not content with causing them these losses,46 he made various remonstrances against them to his Majesty, in which he spoke of them with little civility; and in the instructions he spared no means of injuring them, seeking opportunity to speak ill of them even in those sections of that document which have no connection with the religious. The blame for all this was laid on his favorite, Don Santiago Orendain,47 who was the declared enemy of the ecclesiastics; but this could not excuse Señor Arandia for issuing directions which the king had the goodness to censure as soon as he saw them, for depriving the ecclesiastics of the groves of nipa palms which they held in La Hermita and Bagunbayan, for stirring up several groundless controversies with them, for imposing taxes on the goods which the religious in the provinces were sending to their convents,48 and for expressing his [unfavorable] opinion of them in public. He had a dispute with the royal Audiencia because he was not willing to render military honors to them when they went in a formal body, on occasions when he did not preside over their sessions. He imprisoned the treasurer and auditor of accounts of the royal exchequer, and caused them great suffering, because they had sent information to the court of some things that was contrary to the explanations given by him in his reports. Unwearied in the government, he conceived many projects which he considered necessary for the proper government of the islands. He talked of removing the arsenal from Cavite to the port of Lampon; and he ordered a ship to be built in the kingdom of Siam, which had such ill-fortune that in bringing it over to Manila it was driven to port in China three times, and once to Batavia, causing enormous expenses to the royal treasury.49 The governor made reports to the king, and proposed to him various plans for the promotion of [operations in] the mines of iron and gold. He abolished the corregidorship of Mariveles, annexing Marigondon and the other little villages of that shore to the district of Cavite, and forming from the villages on the opposite shore and from others which belonged to Pampanga the alcaldía which we call Batan.50 He made regulations for the soldiery, the royal exchequer, and the Acapulco ship51 — on all occasions giving many proofs of his zeal for the royal service, by which he was aroused to enthusiasm; but this disposition, ill directed by Orendain, was the cause for his being abhorred by every one. It was so wearing upon him that he reached the point of feeling a distaste for every kind of business, and experienced so great a failure of his vital powers that in the night of May 31, 1759, it was known that he was dying; and, after receiving all the sacraments, he expired at two o'clock in the morning of the following day.52 He left by his will two hundred and fifty thousand pesoty and one cannot guess how he gained them in the less than five years during which his term of office lasted; but at the hour of death he distributed them in a pious and Christian manner.

Through the death of Señor Arandia, the bishop of Zebu, Señor Espeleta, assumed the government. Soon afterward, the new archbishop of Manila arrived here, Don Manuel Roxo,53 a native of Tala [sc. Tula] in the kingdom of Nueva España; his Majesty had taken him from the post of canon and provisor at Mexico, for this see, giving him permission to be consecrated in Nueva España. He took possession of his church on July 22, 1759, and immediately claimed that he should be put in possession of the military government, which it seems belonged to him by the royal orders. The four auditors were divided in opinion, Señors Calderón and Davila deciding that the archbishop should assume the governorship, and Señors Villacorta and Galban that no change ought to be made. While they were in session in their hall, discussing this question, his illustrious Lordship Espeleta entered; he spoke with decision, and, in order to intimidate them more, made ready the artillery and placed the troops under arms; at these preparations the auditors and the archbishop gave way, and the bishop of Zebu remained in peaceable possession [of the government]. The first thing that he did was to revoke the ordinances of Señor Arandia, and to make some preparations against the Moros, who since the year fifty-four had been ravaging our provinces; but the event which made most noise in his time was the lawsuit against Doctor Orendain. Every one placed on him the blame for the actions of Señor Arandia; and the fiscal of the king, Señor Viana, believed that he had been placed under arrest in his own house by the favorite's suggestion. Orendain, either because his conscience stung him, or because reports had been spread that some design was formed against his person, took refuge in the Augustinian convent at Tondo. The fiscal made it a pretext for claiming Orendain from this asylum, that he should be arrested because he was treasurer for the Crusade, and, by his voluntary withdrawal [to asylum], indicated that he might prove to be a debtor to the royal treasury. He then left his refuge, and was imprisoned in the fort of Santiago, the authorities commissioning Señor Villacorta to bring legal proceedings against Orendain. It was found that he had hidden various jewels in the convents, and, while these investigations were being pursued, he made his escape from the fortress in the dress of a woman, going away in a coach, without the guard recognizing him, and took refuge in the convent of the Recollects. The auditor thus commissioned had recourse to the provisor, in order that the latter might give orders for Orendain's removal thence; but, as the provisor did not accede to this after three demands, the auditor sent a notary with soldiers, and removed Orendain by force from the sanctuary. The provisor declared Señor Villacorta publicly excommunicated, and his name was placed on the list. That gentleman had recourse to the royal Audiencia, which ordered the provisor to absolve the auditor; this was done through the cura of the cathedral, but ad reincidentiam, and for the period of thirty days—that is, if the accused did not return to the church within the thirty days, he would incur excommunication the second time. Señor Villacorta challenged the provisor, and this lawsuit became so tangled that various judges were challenged by one side and the other, and even Señors Calderon and Davila were challenged by the king's fiscal, who had taken part in the dispute; and there was no one who could give judgment in the suit, because some refused to take the responsibility, and others were challenged by one or the other party.

In such condition was the Orendain affair, when a decree arrived from his Majesty in which he appointed the archbishop as governor ad interim on account of the death of Señor Arandia. He assumed the authority in the year 1761, and put an end to this clamorous lawsuit by commanding that Orendain should leave the fort, and all his property be returned to him, with [his giving] security for all that he owed to the Holy Crusade; he also imposed on all persons perpetual silence during the time until his Majesty (whom he informed of his proceedings) should make some other decision. His most illustrious Lordship continued to rule the islands in much peace, fulfilling rather the office of father than that of governor, conciliating those who were turbulent, and extending his charity to the king of Joló, who was living in the fort with much lack of comfort. The governor quartered him in a house in Manila, decently furnished, with a coach and with menials enough for his service. He wished, besides this, to restore him to his kingdom, and after listening to the opinions of the leading persons in Manila, it was decided that the king Don Fernando and his son Israel should be sent back to Joló, and that they should take with them a guard of Spaniards, in order that the chiefs in that island should not compel him to abjure the Catholic religion which he had embraced. When they were ready to carry out this undertaking the English arrived [at Manila], the war with whom it is necessary to relate in separate chapters.54

1 The fiscal Arroyo declared that he had been imprisoned in order that he might not prosecute claims against the following persons in their approaching residencias: Governor Valdés Tamón, for the enormous sums which the royal treasury had lost during his government, which amounted to a million and a half pesos; the Marqués de las Salinas and the Marqués de Monte-Castro, confederates of the same Señor Valdés, for having appropriated from the royal treasury and from the public two and one-half million pesos; and Don Domingo de Otero Vermudez, [who had taken] more than two hundred thousand. (Concepción, Hist. de Philipinas, xi, p. 95.)

2 See enumeration of these funds in the historical sketch of the Misericordia, in VOL. XLVII.

3 It is thus stated by Concepción (Hist. de Philipinas, xi, p. 280): "With the pretext that the fathers of the Society [of Jesus] had usurped from them cultivated lands, and the untilled lands on the hills, on which they kept enormous herds of horned cattle— for which reason, and because the Jesuits said that these were their own property, they would not allow the natives to supply themselves with wood, rattans, and bamboos, unless they paid fixed prices—the Indians committed shocking acts of hostility on the ranches of Lian and Nasugbu, killing and plundering the tenants of those lands, with many other ravages. Nor did they respect the houses of the [Jesuit] fathers, but attacked and plundered them, and partly burned them, as well as many other buildings independent of these." All was plundering, rapine, destruction, and debauchery; the natives also rebelled against

the exactions from them of tribute and personal services. "The contagion spread to the village of Taal, and more than sparks were discovered in other places, although efforts were made to conceal the fire." The alcalde-mayor and the Jesuits tried at first to pacify the Indians, urging them to wait for the official visit of Auditor Calderon; but they could do nothing, the natives being rendered only more daring by this attempt. Troops were then sent from Manila against them; in the battle mentioned in our text several were wounded, among them the commanding officer, Sargento-mayor Juan Gonzalez de el Pulgar; but he succeeded in routing the enemy. The chief of the insurgents, one Matienza, took refuge in a church, but was captured and disarmed therein. Reënforcements were sent from Manila, and the rebellion was soon quelled. The leaders of the rebellion were punished in various ways, according to their prominence or influence; some were shot, others sent into exile or to the galleys; and amnesty was granted to the insurgents who would lay down their arms and renew their acknowledgment of vassalage.

To this may be added the following statements by Calderon himself: "By commission of this royal Audiencia, I went to a village outside the walls of this capital, to take measures for the completion of a small bridge, which was being hindered by some dispute, and to pay to Master Alarífe 250 pesos which had been offered to him for its construction. I proceeded to make inquiries regarding the lands and revenues belonging to the village; and I found that all the surrounding estates (on which the people were working) belonged to a certain [F., for *Fulano*] ecclesiastic, the Indians and mestizos paying him rent not only for these, but for the land occupied by their cabins, at the rate of three pesos a year for the married man, and one and one-half pesos for the widow or the unmarried man. And as it seemed to me that the person who, according to what was evident to my own eyes, was collecting about 30 pesos of land-rent, independently of the estates and houses belonging to him, was the one who rightfully ought to bear the cost of the little bridge, I announced that this cost should be collected from the persons who were owing rents for the lands. Receipts therefor were to be given to them, and orders were issued to the royal judges before whom such cases come first, that they must, if the laymen who make these payments should be accused before them, give the latter credit for these receipts; nor in all this brief summary, and in the measures that I took, would I notice the ecclesiastic who called himself the owner of all." "In regard to the representations of the convenience for the Indian who has built his hut in the grain-field, I believe that it is quite the contrary, and that it would be more expedient for him and for the commonwealth that he should not be allowed to build it there, or that he be obliged to change his dwelling, for those huts generally serve as refuge for persons bent on mischief; besides, as the Indian thus has no watchful neighbor to inform the religious minister of his doings, and no alcalde, he lives in too much freedom. But, granted that all this comes to an end, what right has the owner of the land to more than the rent from him who occupies it? And if with his *pilapis*, or pathway, and his house he occupies no more than 50 brazas—for which he has to pay the same as if he had rented a *cabalita*, which is a thousand brazas—and if he must pay the same rent, then lease to him the cabalita, including therein the house and pilapis; and with this the Indian will have land for planting his young trees, and for making some planting of grain."

These items are cited from a pamphlet issued (Manila, 1739) by the auditor Pedro Calderón Henríquez, entitled: *Discvrso ivridico, en qve se defiende la real iurisdiccion, y se hace demonstracion de la injusticia, que contiene el contrato de arrendamiento de solares en estas islas*; in it he "laments the great amount that the Filipinos were paying to the ecclesiastical power." This seems to have brought out a reply defending the ecclesiastics, *Apología por la immvnidad ecclesiastica, y por la licitvd de terrazgos, o alqvileres de tierras segvn la forma, estilo de algvnas estancias de estas islas Philipinas* (Manila, 1739); it is significant that this was published from the Jesuit printing-house, and the auditor's pamphlet from the college of Santo Tomás. Regarding both these, see Vindel's *Catálogo bibl. filipina*, nos. 1807, 1808; therein is cited the following paragraph from the *Apología*:

"48. In the cultivated estates or farms which the Society of Jesus possesses in these islands, the tenants pay nothing for the house-lot which they occupy, with the little garden which their houses are wont to have in addition; but they pay only for the other land which they cultivate. There is, moreover, an order from the superiors that no person shall be allowed on those farms unless he has the charge of some grain-field—and rightly so, since this is the purpose for which admission to the estates is granted to any one; although this does not prevent entire justice being shown to the old men, widows, and other people who are legitimately disabled, by allowing them to remain, as they do, in their houses without paying anything for these and without cultivating a field. Therefore, there is evident falsehood in what is said by a certain [N., used when name is not to be mentioned] author, at the beginning of no. 3, art. 2, in speaking of these estates of the Society—that is, that the tenants pay for the land which they cultivate and for the ground under the houses which they occupy. In Santa Cruz the same observance was in use at the beginning, and it still is followed among the tenants who work on the lands of Mayhaligue adjoining the said village of Santa Cruz, and have their houses in the grain-fields. But as in course of time the Sangley mestizos increased in numbers, and devoted themselves to other occupations — painters, gilders, and silver-smiths, etc., which trades they now exercise with dexterity — and many households were formed, up to the number of about three hundred and eighty, which they now reach, it became necessary to yield to their importunities; and for this college of San Ignacio at Manila to condemn the splendid orchards which it possessed there, and permit the said mestizos to establish therein their dwellings. And, as it is not right that the said college should suffer the heavy damage of losing the said orchards, which had cost it many thousands of pesos, ..."

4 Concepción says (Hist. de Philipinas, xi, pp. 278–280) that some investigation of this report was made before Torre's death, and seven of the wealthiest Chinese were arrested, "as being those most liable to suspicion in the proposed disturbance." These men were kept in prison for six months, the investigations being continued by Arrechedera and indicating that the "plot" was but a malicious fabrication, intended to harass Torre and thus cause his death. Finally, the governor, in view of their long imprisonment and the failure to prove any charges against them, released the Chinese prisoners, "under precautions and securities." One of the prisoners proved, by a note from the warden of the court prison, that the latter "had received the Chinaman as a prisoner, without being told from whom or by whose order." The further precaution was taken of sending back to China, in the champans that went that year, "no small number of Chinese, of those who were known to be strollers and without employment." Concepción states that Torre's government was rendered odious largely by a certain man in Manila, "who, on account of his rank and wealth, ambitiously lorded it over the community, causing its government to be subject to his pleasure, and did all that he could to cast infamy on the governor."

5 In these ships came the royal situado for the current year (1747), and 30,000 pesos on account of the arrearages due; moreover, the returns from the cargo of the previous year were unusually large, owing to successful sales at Acapulco. The vessels halted at the port of Sisiran, where the silver was disembarked, being sent overland to Manila; this was done through fear lest they might be attacked by enemies at the Embocadero. The galleon "Rosario" was sent with a cargo for Acapulco, but was driven back by contrary winds, because it was poorly constructed and difficult to manage. This placed the royal treasury again in great straits, because the situados were in arrears for six remittances;

Arrechedera appealed to the citizens and the clergy, who responded liberally—especially the archbishop and his chapter; "the Society of Jesus alone furnished 11,000 pesos—the royal promise being pledged for payment; and the obras pías also contributed to the common cause with their reserve funds." (Concepción, Hist. de Philipinas, xii, pp. 36–38.)

6 His family name was Martinez de Arizala; at this time he was fifty-two years of age. He was a member of the Audiencia of Quito in Peru (now in Ecuador) for seventeen years, and had been entrusted with various important commissions by the king.

7 Probably on account of his being a Dominican, the Chinese in and near Manila being mostly in charge of that order in matters of religion.

8 A full account of this revolt and its cause and progress may be found in Concepción's Hist. de Philipinas, xiv, pp. 79–107; and of its punishment by Lechuga, in xi, pp. 40–43. In writing the latter volume, he had not any adequate information regarding the causes of the rebellion; but later he obtained a detailed account of this from the Recollect fathers in Bohol who took charge of the natives after the expulsion of the Jesuits in 1768. According to them, the immediate occasion of the revolt was the arbitrary conduct of the Jesuit, Father Morales, who was, in 1744, in charge of the district of Inabangan. He sent out a native constable to arrest a renegade Indian, but the latter slew the constable, whose brother, Francisco Dagóhoy, obtained the corpse, and carried it into his village. Morales refused to bury it in consecrated ground, and it lay for three days unburied and rotting. Angered at this arbitrary and harsh treatment, especially as Morales had been the cause of the constable's death, Dagóhoy swore vengeance on the Jesuit, and persuaded the natives of his district to join him therein; 3,000 of them followed him, abandoning their homes and fortifying an inaccessible retreat in the mountains. On their way they plundered a large and valuable estate in that vicinity, named San Xavier, belonging to the Jesuits, which was well stocked with cows, carabaos, horses, and other animals. Soon afterward, Dagóhoy bribed an Indian to kill the Jesuit minister of Hagna, Father Lamberti; and afterward Morales was also assassinated by natives. The insurgents were numerously recruited through various acts of injustice and tyranny by the Spaniards, and the rebellion was assuming dangerous proportions. Bishop Espeleta of Cebú endeavored to persuade the insurgents to return to their allegiance, and offered them secular priests instead of the Jesuits; but they took this for timidity on the part of the government, and became only more emboldened. Twenty years later, Recollect missionaries were sent to Bohol in place of the expelled Jesuits,

and in the district of Baclayon was stationed Fray Pedro de Santa Barbara; he laid plans for reclaiming and reconciling the insurgents, and was partially successful; Dagóhoy and several other datos "returned to God and to the church" with their followers, several hundred being baptized and making then confessions. Nevertheless, they did not go much further, and although Bishop Espeleta endeavored in person to secure their Christian administration, "he could not secure from Dagóhoy any more than that he would build a church, in order to comply with his Christian obligations; but, as he was attracted by the lawless life which he had led during so many years, and by the gratification of being obeyed, the undertaking was delayed until the present time. Nothing was done save to erect the foundation posts, which had to serve for the present church." This last volume of Concepción's was published in 1792, and his later information was obtained probably in 1789, in which year he wrote this account. (Espeleta's last remonstrance with Dagóhoy was made, as stated by our writer, "in the year sixty-two;" but the context would indicate that it occurred after the labors of the Recollects began, and therefore the date is more probably "seventy-two," the word sesenta being printed for setenta, by one of the typographical errors so frequent in Conception's pages.) Fray Pedro de Santa Barbara was so delighted at his first success that he persuaded the civil authorities to withdraw the troops from most of the Bohol stations, and to publish a general amnesty (this was not later than 1770); but the result was, that the insurgent chiefs would not allow any of their followers to leave their strongholds under pain of death, and continued their habits of raids on their neighbors, plundering, and murder. Concepción expresses indignant surprise that this rebellion had been allowed to go long unpunished, with so great loss and injury to the peaceable part of the population.

9 These ambassadors were: for Mindanao, Father Francisco Isasi, rector of the Jesuit college at Zamboanga, and the sargento-mayor there, Don Thomas de Arrevillaga. For Joló, Isasi was also designated; but on his return from Tamontaca his health was so broken that in his place was appointed Father Sebastian Ignacio de Arcada, then in charge of the district of Siocon; he went thither accompanied by Arrevillaga, having been sent by Juan Gonzalez de el Pulgar, then governor of Zamboanga. (Concepción, Hist. de Philipinas, xii, pp. 75–106.)

10 The missionaries appointed to the Mindanao mission were the Jesuits Juan Moreno and Sebastian Arcada; but the latter was ill at the time, and died soon afterward; in his place was substituted Ignacio Malaga. See account of their mission in Concepción, xii, pp. 110–112, 138–141.

Those who went to Joló were Juan Ang[e]les and Patricio de el Barrio; they left Zamboanga on June 3, 1748, in company with Alimudin. For account of their mission, see Concepción, xii, pp. 114–138; he cites a diary and letters written by Father Angeles, and the report of Commandant Pulgar. He blames the Jesuits (pp. 146, 147) for misrepresenting the Moro sultans to the governor, and Pulgar (as being under their influence) for an unnecessarily hostile attitude toward the Moros.

11 Concepción states (xii, p. 134) that Alimudin was so infatuated for one of his concubines that he neglected his duties of government; and that his brother Bantilan bribed a man to assassinate the sultan, giving him six slaves and a thousand pesos.

12 Ferrando speaks (Hist. PP. dominicos, iv, p. 535) of "this sedition, actual or feigned (but on this point history has not made its final utterance)."

13 Forrest says (Voyage, p. 334) of Alimudin's visit to Samboangan: "He bought goods from Don Zacharias the governor, giving the Don his own price, made presents to the officers of the garrison, and lost his money to them, as if accidentally, by gaming with dice. Still resolved to ingratiate himself with the governor, the Sultan wanted to make him a present of forty male slaves, whom he had drest in rich liveries on the occasion. Many of them were natives of Papua or New Guinea. Zacharias refused the presents, suspecting the Sultan of some design. The Sultan then asked leave to go to Manila. He went thither, and said to the archbishop, 'I will turn Christian, let the Spaniards take Sooloo, send the stubborn Datoos to Samboangan; make me king there, I then will oblige every one to embrace your religion.' The Spaniards listened to him, and he returned to Samboangan with an armada."

14 See letter of the Jesuit Masvesi regarding this visit of the Joloan ruler, in VOL. XLVII, pp. 243–250; also account of it (1750), ascribed to Arrechedera, in Retana's Archivo, i, no. v.

15 Ferrando says (iv, pp. 538, 539) that Arrechedera sent the sultan to Binalatongan (in Pangasinan) for baptism; but that Alimudin was taken ill at Paniqui, on his journey, and it was therefore decided to baptize him there.

16 This catastrophe, one of the most ruinous of its kind ever known, occurred on October 28, 1746; Lima was wrecked by the earthquake, and Callao destroyed by a tidal wave—in Lima, over 1,100 persons perished, and in Callao 4,600. A detailed account of this event was published at Lima by order of the viceroy, Marqués de Villa Garcia, an English translation of which appeared in London (the second edition in 1748); and other accounts were published in Lima and Mexico.

17 See account of this controversy, the wretched condition in which the royal ships and galleys were found to be, and the loss of the "Pilar," in Concepción's Historia, xii, pp. 183–211; cf. Montero y Vidal, Hist. de piratería, i, p. 291, note. The vessel known by the names of "Rosarito" and "Philipino," which "had cost the royal treasury 60,666 pesos, had remained more than four years abandoned to the sun and rain, without any care;" and it was now valued at 18,000 pesos, a sum which, after more thorough examination of the rotting timbers, was reduced to 7,500. The Spanish government had ordered that six ships be at once constructed to proceed against the Moro pirates; and it was therefore necessary to hasten this work, without waiting for "red tape," hence Nebra's informal appointment. The "Pilar" was not a fragata, but a large ship; it sailed in June or July, 1750; its repairing and cleaning was so hastily done that the vessel began to leak before it left the Luzón coast. The commander, Ignacio Martinez de Faura, was notified of this, and that it was unsafe for the vessel to proceed into the open sea; he answered, "To Purgatory, or to Acapulco!" In the following October, pieces of wreckage were picked up on the eastern coasts of Luzón, which were identified as belonging to the "Pilar."

18 "The secretary of the government, who, protected in that quarter by the person who ought to have condemned his acts, pushed forward his designs and finally effected his purpose" (Ferrando, iv, p. 548).

19 "This [Dominican] province had already (in 1745) reported to his Majesty that the beaterio of Santa Cathalina was maintained in the form of observance provided by the royal decrees of February 17, 1716 and September 10, 1732; that it contained the fifteen religious which it ought to have according to the arrangements of its founder; that they observed the three vows of religious, according to the enactment of St. Pius V, issued on 28 [sic] in 1566; and that, although there had never been the slightest question raised on this point, some uncertainties were beginning to present themselves regarding the nature of their vows, and even whether dispensation from these could be granted by the archbishop of Manila." Accordingly, the Dominicans requested the royal decision on these matters; the king therefore decreed (June 20, 1747) that a committee formed of the governor, the archbishop, and the Dominican provincial, should carefully examine into the best method of carrying out the previous decrees. They did so, and, when their deliberations were laid before the royal fiscal, he demanded that the vows taken by these beatas be declared opposed to his Majesty's will. Sister Cecilia, as soon as she was placed in Santa Potenciana, divested herself of the religious habit, claiming that her profession was null—a claim which was irregular, "because the five years had

already passed which the laws and justice allow for proceedings of this sort." When the papal delegate disallowed the appeal of the Dominicans from the archbishop's attempted control of this case, they appealed to the Audiencia for protection from the fuerza exerted by the latter; but that court declined to interfere, saying that there was no fuerza committed. The archbishop then pronounced a definitive sentence in favor of Cecilia, and set her at liberty; she then married Figueroa, and they went to Nueva España. The Spanish government took no further notice of her case, save to refuse to the Dominicans permission to lay it before the Holy See. (Ferrando, iv, pp. 548–551)

20 This was Don Protasio Cavezas.

21 A minute account of this episode is found in Concepción's Historia, xii, pp. 212–230. The lady's name was Cecilia Ita y Salazar. She had been educated in the beaterio from childhood, and had been a professed religious for sixteen years.

22 "The royal decree issued in 1762 in consequence of the notorious litigation of Mother Cecilia did not decide that the beaterio should be extinguished, but only that new religious should not be admitted until those then living, who numbered nearly thirty, should be reduced to fifteen religious of the choir, in conformity with the provisions of its foundation," "and that the number of the fifteen beatas should be kept up, according to vacancies that might occur." (Ferrando, v, p. 151).

23 "The seizure of these champans was afterward the cause of a clamorous lawsuit incited by various officers against the master-of-camp Abad, accusing him of having kept for himself the best part [of the goods seized]. It was also proved that he employed the vessels of the royal navy in his mercantile speculations; this evil was very general in that period, and to it must be attributed, in large part, the scanty results of most of the expeditions against the Mahometan Malays of southern Filipinas." (Montero y Vidal, Hist. de piratería, i, p. 294.)

Another Chinese champan was seized by the Spaniards, apparently not long afterward, near Malandi; it was laden with goods for trade in Mindanao, which included a number of guns and other weapons, with ammunition. These were confiscated by the Spaniards, an act which was greatly resented by Jampsa, the sultan of Tamontaca, who therefore abandoned the Spanish alliance and sided with the hostile Moros. (Concepción, xiii, pp. 1–5.)

24 This proceeding took place at midnight on August 3, and the number arrested was 217 persons: these included Alimudin's four sons, his brother and sister, four of his daughters, five brothers-in-law, a son-in-law; a Mahometan jaddí ("the second

rank in that sect, equivalent to a bishop") and five panditas; also two prominent chiefs, one hundred and sixty of the sultan's vassals, and thirty-two concubines and female servants. (Montero y Vidal, Hist. de piratería, i, p. 298.) Cf. Concepción, xii, pp. 288, 289.

25 Alimudin and his household arrived as prisoners at Manila in September, 1751. Soon afterward the Manila government declared war, with fire and sword, against the Joloans and all those Moro peoples who aided them; permitting the enslavement of all who should be captured, whether men, women or children; and giving all their property and possessions to their captors, free from all royal dues or imposts. See copy of this proclamation in Montero y Vidal's Hist. de piratería, appendix, pp. 29–31. Concepción (xii, p. 344) regards this declaration of war as unjust; he adds that the Joloan captive princes, whose arrest was incited by ambition and greed, were so unfortunate as to lose their protector, Bishop Arrechedera, by death (November 12, 1751). In the same month died also Bishop Arevalo, of Nueva Caceres.

26 Here, as most often elsewhere, "captives" are synonymous with "slaves." Montero y Vidal (Hist. de piratería, i, p. 299) protests against this permission to enslave the Moros, as being contrary to the provisions of the laws of the Indias, which forbid slavery in Philipinas.

27 Concepción says (xii, pp. 345–352) that the master-of-camp in command of the fleet (who was Antonio Ramón de Abad y Monterde) was undecided whether to attack Joló, but was persuaded to do so by the Jesuits, who told him that the very sight of the Spanish squadron would ensure the surrender of the Joloans. The attack was made at the beginning of June, 1752, and was unsuccessful; Abad was angry at the Jesuits, who had led him into this difficulty, and quarreled with them. They retorted by accusing him to the governor, of conduct (in modern phrase) "unworthy of an officer and a gentleman" — that is, of neglect of official duty, mismanagement of the campaign, unnecessary sacrifice of his men's lives, and licentious behavior at Zamboanga. This was believed, until Abad was reported much more favorably by other officers of his fleet. See full account of his residencia (ut supra, xiii, pp. 36–85), in which he was acquitted from the charges made against him, but sentenced to pay the costs of the residencia.

28 These hostilities broke out in 1752, and for several years scourged the unfortunate Visayans. Concepción records many of these attacks in considerable detail (Hist. de Philipinas, xiii, pp. 5–36); the missions of the Recollects, as also those of the Jesuits in Mindanao (except those under the shelter of the fort

at Zamboanga) were the frontier outposts most exposed to the pirates, and it is these missions that Concepción chiefly mentions. The fort at Iligan, Mindanao, was besieged by two thousand Moros for two months; but a Spanish fleet was sent from Cebú, which obliged the enemy to raise the siege, after a great loss of men. This defense was conducted by the Jesuit in charge there, Father José Ducós, whose father had been an officer in the Spanish army; and this same priest rendered valiant service in other Moro raids in that region. Tagoloan and Yponan, in the province of Cagayan, Mindanao were besieged by the Moros; but the mountain Indians were called down to their aid by the Jesuit missionaries, and compelled the enemy to retreat. In Caraga, Surigao was attacked, and the Christian inhabitants, with their two Recollect missionaries, were compelled to take flight and seek refuge in the mountains; they were hunted there for weeks by the enemy—one of the priests being finally captured and taken to Lanao—all this time, enduring terrible hardships and suffering, which caused the other (Fray Roque de Santa Monica) to become hopelessly insane; he was afterward brought to Manila, but died there in a demented condition. "The district of Surigao, rich through its famous gold-mines, and now in most wretched condition," was devastated and ruined. The enemy did the same in the island of Siargao, where the Recollect missionary, Fray Joseph de la Virgen de el Niño Perdido, was slain while endeavoring to lead his followers against the pirates. Nearly all the population—of Surigao, more than 2,000 souls; of Siargao, more than 1,600— were either slain or carried away captive. The district of Butuan was laid waste and some two hundred captives seized; the little military post at Linao, up the river, alone escaped, mainly through the difficulty of ascending the stream. The Moros attacked the island of Camiguin, which was so bravely defended by its natives that the pirates were repulsed—especially by "one of the villages, which consisted of people of Moro origin from the Lake of Malanao, from which they had withdrawn on account of domestic dissensions, and settled in this island. They are of excellent disposition, very good Christians, courageous, and have an irreconcilable hatred for those enemies." Here they were led by their Recollect priest, Fray Marcelinc de el Espiritu Santo, "a robust native of La Mancha," who with them fought so valiantly that the enemy could not make a landing. Romblon had so good a fort that it could repel the foe; Ticao was so poorly defended that the people, with their missionary, Fray Manuel de Santa Cathalina, could only take to flight—the priest being afterward captured, and finally ransomed for eight hundred pesos. In several places the missionaries were either slain or captured by the pirates; and these raids were extended, the boldness of the enemy increasing, even to the coasts of Luzón, in Batangas and Zambales. The government took what precautions it could, but these amounted to little save in the vicinity of Manila, Cebú, and Zamboanga; military and naval forces, and supplies of all sorts, were deficient, and there was much official apathy and corruption.

29 "This unfortunate attempt cost the treasury 36,976 pesos, and a galley that was seized by the Moros" (Montero y Vidal, Hist. de piratería, i, p. 301).

30 "In Manila the indignation against the disloyal Ali-Mudin knew no bounds. All clamored for the punishment of so ignoble a race, sorrowfully recalling the fact that the amount expended in courting him and in the expenses of his sojourn there was more than 20,000 pesos, without counting the 6,000 pesos and the military supplies sent to establish the Jesuits in Joló" (ut supra, p. 299). Later, the authorities at Manila hardly knew what to do with Alimudin; he would probably have been put to death, but it was feared that the Moros would retaliate by slaughtering their Christian captives, who numbered some 10,000. Fatima procured the return (in the summer of 1753) of fifty-one Christian captives, and negotiations were made for peace between Manila and Joló; and in June, 1754, Bantilan surrendered sixty-eight more captives, and a Spanish galley and champan. Faveau, who had carried on a brilliant campaign against the pirates with his little squadron, made a favorable report to the governor of the good intentions of both Bantilan and Alimudin; and stated that the return of the latter to Joló was desired by his subjects, and that Bantilan was willing to resign in his favor. Arandía sent most of the Joloan prisoners back to that island, retaining the sultan and his eldest son as hostages until the full accomplishment of the treaty; they remained there until the capture of the city by the English (1762), who afterward restored them to Joló (see VOL. XLIX). Ferrando (iv, pp. 541–543) considers that Alimudin was unjustly suspected and ill-treated, and defends him from accusations of disloyalty to the Spaniards and to the Christian religion.

31 "The Sultanship in Sooloo is hereditary, but the government mixed. About fifteen Datoos, who may be called the nobility, make the greater part of the legislature. Their title is hereditary to the eldest son, and they sit in council with the Sultan. The Sultan has two votes in this assembly, and each Datoo has one. The heir-apparent (who, when I was there, was Datoo Alamoodine) if he sides with the Sultan, has two votes; but, if against him, only one. There are two representatives of the people, called Manteries, like the military tribunes of the Romans. The common people of Sooloo, called Tellimanhood, enjoy much real freedom, owing to the above representation;

but the Tellimanhood, or vassals of the adjacent islands named Tappool, Seassee, Tawee-tawee, and others, being the estates of particular Datoos, are often used in a tyrannical manner by their chiefs. I have been told that their haughty lords visiting their estates, will sometimes with impunity demand and carry off young women, whom they happen to fancy, to swell the number of their Sandles (Concubines) at Sooloo." (Forrest, Voyage, p. 326.)

32 For detailed accounts of the events here briefly mentioned, the Moro wars, the imprisonment of Alimudin, the ravages committed in the islands by those pirates, etc., to the end of Ovando's government, see Concepción's Hist. de Philipinas, xii, pp. 230–419, and xiii, pp. 1–250. See also the account of the "Moro raids repulsed by Visayan natives," ante; it is inserted mainly to represent more vividly, in the words of a probable eyewitness, a typical raid by Moro pirates on the peaceable Christian natives.

33 To this name should be added, "Santisteban, Echeveria, y Alvero" (Concepción, xiii, p. 250); he was a knight of the Order of Calatrava.

34 See Concepción, Hist. de Philipinas, xiii, pp. 250–287, for details of these reforms.

35 See Concepción's account of this eruption (xiii, pp. 345–350); it lasted from September to December, 1754 and was accompanied by severe earthquakes, one of which lasted half an hour.

36 Ignacio María de Alava, "Commander-in-chief of the naval forces in Asiatic waters," was a personal friend of Zúñiga, to whom the latter dedicated his Historia. In a preliminary notice to his Estadismo (p. 3 of Retana's ed.) he says that Alava desired to become acquainted with the Philippines from various points of view, and invited the priest to accompany him therein. Alava arrived at Manila on December 25, 1796, and remained in the islands until January 7, 1803; he reorganized the naval forces and the arsenal at Cavite, with much energy and ability, but had various controversies with Governor Aguilar. Afterward he held important posts in the Spanish naval administration, and died on May 26, 1815. See Retana's note concerning him (ut supra, ii, p. *562), and Montero y Vidal's Hist. de Philipinas, ii, pp. 345–359.

37 The exploits of this militant Jesuit are described by Concepción, in Hist. de Philipinas, xiii, pp. 148–168, 178–188, 296–319.

38 The name given her in baptism was Rita Calderón; the marriage occurred on April 27, 1755. See Concepción, xiii, pp. 333, 334.

39 "The people of Magindano, and their neighbours, known commonly by the name of Oran Illanon, as living near the great Lano, are very piratically inclined. Neither can the Sultan of Magindano restrain his subjects from fitting out vessels, which go among the Philippines, to Mangaio, that is, cruise against the Spaniards: much less can be restrained the Illanos, being under a government more aristocratic; for, on the banks of the Lano, are no fewer than seventeen, stiled Rajahs, and sixteen who take the title of Sultan, besides those on the coast. When the Spanish envoy sailed from Magindano for Samboangan, Rajah Moodo sent a vessel, as has been said, to convoy him across the Illano bay. This is a proof the Spaniards are not on good terms with the Illanos. These, within ten years before 1775, have done much mischief to the Spaniards, among the islands called Babuyan, at the north extremity of the Philippines; and, at this time, they possess an island in the very heart of the Philippines, called Burias, where has been a colony of Illanos, for many years, men, women, and children. The Spaniards have often attempted to dislodge them; but in vain: the island, which is not very large, being environed with rocks and shoals to a considerable distance." (Forrest, Voyage to New Guinea, pp. 301, 302.)

40 Fray Mateo González founded this mission to the Batanes. He made his profession in 1667, and came to Manila four years later, being then twenty-seven years old. He was sent to the Cagayán missions, and was stationed in the Babuyanes Islands during 1673–84 (save in 1677–80, at Lallo-c). In 1686 he made a visit to the Batanes, where he was well received; they contained over 3,000 souls. Leaving his companion there to study the language, he went to Manila to secure support for his new mission, to which he returned with Fray Juan Rois; but hardly two months passed before the unhealthful climate and many privations brought mortal illness on them. González died on July 25, 1688, and Rois on August 10, following. With this the Batanes mission came to an end until (in 1718) it was revived by Fray Juan Bel. (Reseña biográfica, ii, pp. 155–157.)

41 "Action was taken in a session of the royal treasury officials on the execution of the orders in a royal despatch which notified this government to establish on the mainland of Cagayan the people who were dwelling in the islands of the Babuyanes; for this purpose the sum of five thousand, three hundred and ninety-eight pesos was sent from the royal treasury of Mexico, definitely allotted to this transportation. The migration was agreed upon, the money was spent, but the only result was the

transfer of some families, the greater part of them remaining in their own islands—where, as they were accustomed to that mode of life, they desired no further privileges than their own liberty, even though it be with necessary inconveniences, which they felt little or not at all, being free from the yoke since their youth." (Concepción, Hist. de Philipinas, xi, p.304.)

Cf. Salazar's sketch of the history of these missions, in chapter xxiii of *Hist. Sant. Rosario* (in our VOL. XLIII). See also, for both early and later events therein, Ferrando's *Hist. PP. dominicos*, iii, pp. 550–588, and iv, pp. 254–258, 330, 582–585.

Concepción (ut supra) does not mention the date of the royal decree; but Ferrando states (iv, p. 423) that it was dated March 14, 1728, and that it granted for this purpose the sum of 3,398 pesos; the "3" may be a typographical error for "5," the amount as given (but spelled out) by Concepción. Ferrando says that some three hundred families removed to the mainland, but that many more remained in their islands.

42 This is more fully described in the previous document, "Later Augustinian and Dominican missions."

43 See Ferrando's Hist. PP. dominicos, iv, pp. 576–582.

44 Arandia made a census of the Christian Sangleys in the islands, and found that they numbered 3,413. He established the market here mentioned, that of San Fernando, at first intended to be simply a pavilion in which trade might be carried on; the heathen merchants to return immediately to their own country, without going inland from Manila or having any dealings with the natives. But, as it was soon apparent that the exigencies of weather and trade required larger and more permanent quarters, Arandía had a plan made for the necessary dwellings and storehouses, by a Recollect lay brother who was an excellent architect (whom the governor had appointed superintendent of royal works); and a contract for building it was made, at a cost of 48,000 pesos. Half of this amount was contributed by a citizen of Manila, Fernando de Mier y Noriega, the other half being supplied from the royal treasury; as a reward for this service, he was made warden of the new market, an office carrying a salary of fifty pesos a month, and passing to his children and descendants. (Concepción, xiii, pp. 357–360.) The king, however, restricted this privilege to Mier's life.

45 See Concepción's account of this enterprise (xiv, pp. 167–171). The amount of capital raised was 76,500 pesos, in shares of 500 each; with this, the company began to buy goods (ropas) to supply the public necessities, and sold these in their own shops, in each of which were two Spanish agents, no Sangley having anything to do with these shops. It was planned that the company, having bought goods at wholesale—they found that

they could purchase thus at sixteen per cent less than they paid for the same goods at retail—should sell at only thirty per cent above the first cost; "of this [gain] eight per cent must be paid to his Majesty to make up to the royal treasury the deficiency arising from the loss of the licenses that the infidels had paid; ten per cent went to the shareholders; and the remaining twelve per cent was kept for the payment of salaries, and for a public fund for the promotion of the industries and products of the country." Their capital was found insufficient to make their purchases; indeed, this lack had always been felt when the Sangleys conducted the trade, but their industry had supplied it; the directors therefore applied to the Misericordia and other administrators for the loan of the reserve funds held in the obras pías. The latter were at first disposed to aid the company, but later declined to do so, following the advice of certain theologians whom they consulted. The auditor Pedro Calderon Henriquez gave an opinion contrary to this, saying that the obras pías had gained great profits through the voluntary concession and tolerance of the citizens, who ought not to be the only ones to make sacrifices for the public good; and that "in these islands they had winked at the business transactions of the confraternities, which are not carried on in other regions, on account of the convenience which the merchants found in having money ready for investment in their commerce." The governor therefore demanded from the Misericordia 100,000 pesos of their reserve funds, and from the Third Order (of St. Francis) 30,000; and with these funds the company was for the time floated. (Among the advantages expected from this enterprise were: lower prices than the Chinese asked for goods, the same price the year round, the retention of all profits within the country, and the certain support of the twenty-one families belonging to the company's employ.) Another great hindrance was found in the general practice of using clipped money in this trade, which caused great losses. This and other difficulties caused the dissolution of the company within the year, and it was unable to do more than save the capital invested therein.

46 Ferrando says (iv, pp. 587–591) that Arandía cut off from the hospital of San Gabriel 800 pesos, out of the 2,000 which it received from the communal fund of the Sangleys, for whose benefit the hospital was founded; and this amount the Dominican province was obliged, through motives of humanity, to make good from its own treasury. Moreover, he insisted that the Augustinian provincial, Fray Juan Facundo Meseguer, should reveal to him the private reasons which he had for removing two of his friars from their charges in Indian villages. This was in reality an attack on all the religious bodies, who all resolved to make common cause on the governor, and forthwith sent to

the king a remonstrance against the governor's proceedings; this checked Arandía, who desisted from his demands against Meseguer.

47 Vindel's Catálogo, tomo i (Madrid, 1896), p. 94, cites from Rezabal y Ugarte's Escritores de los seis colegios universitarios (Madrid, 1805) mention of works left by Viana, existing in the archives of the Council of Indias, among them "Ordinances for the government of the Indian provinces of Filipinas." This, with the hostility which his letters and other writings exhibit toward the religious orders, indicates the possibility that Viana had some responsibility for the instructions here mentioned by Zúñiga.

48 According to Concepción (xiii, pp. 360–366), the tax here referred to was a general one, called "the royal impost," an ad valorem duty levied on all the products of the provinces, brought in the coasting trade to Manila; it was established, in view of the depleted condition of the royal treasury, for the maintenance of the royal fleets against the pirates and the defense of the internal commerce of the islands, and was exacted from all persons concerned, without exempting any one, whatever his rank or estate. The Dominicans were unwilling to pay this tax on certain commodities which they were sending to their convents in Cagayan, alleging that these were not commercial articles, and that they were exempt as a religious body. This was of no avail, and their vessel was seized; but, either through their representations at court or because Arandía had not first asked the royal permission for this measure, it was censured by the government and the duty removed.

49 See Concepción's full account of this venture (xiv, pp. 208–275). It will be remembered that Bustamante had attempted in 1718 to open up commerce with Siam (VOL. XLIV, p. 152); but this was a failure, through the apathy of the Spaniards. In the year 1747 a Siamese ship came to Manila with merchandise, and another four years later; these were well received there, and allowed to sell their goods free from duties. On the second ship came a Jesuit, Father Juan Regis Aroche, as envoy from the king of Siam to establish friendly relations with the Manila government; he proposed to Ovando to send an expedition to Siam to build there a galleon, then needed at Manila for the Acapulco trade. As the royal treasury had not the funds for this, Ovando formed a stock company, with a hundred shares, each of 300 pesos; 30,000 pesos were thus raised (said by the Jesuit to be enough to build the ship) — "with the idea that afterward the king [of España] would vouchsafe to buy it, and the gains would be divided pro rata among the shareholders, whose profits would be considerable even if the ship were sold at the usual and reasonable price." Accordingly Captain Joseph Pasarin was

sent to Siam (March 18, 1752), and made arrangements for the construction of the ship, which was facilitated and aided by the king of that country; labor was there abundant and cheap, yet the cost of the ship was much more than had been planned, and not only was a second remittance made from Manila, but the king furnished nearly 13,000 pesos besides. Pasarin set out on his voyage to Manila with the new ship, but, when in sight of Bolinao, a fierce storm drove the Spaniards back, and finally compelled them to land in China. They went to Macao, refitted their damaged ship (for which a wealthy Portuguese lent them, without interest, 20,516 pesos), and set sail for Manila on April 28, 1755; storms again drove them from Bolinao, and they were compelled to put back to Macao, and to remain there five months until the north winds should subside; Simon Vicente de la Rosa again generously aided them with 5,000 pesos. Returning their voyage on December 12 of that year, unfavorable winds again attacked them, and they were obliged to make port in Batavia. (January 12, 1756). Here Pasarin fell sick, and on his recovery found that the shipbuilder whom the Dutch had detailed to repair the galleon had fled with certain goods which he plundered from it, and twenty-eight of his seamen had deserted; at last he secured a new crew, and reached Cavite on July 6, 1756. This galleon was named "Nuestra Señora de Guadalupe," or "La Mexicana;" its keel was 120 English feet long, and its capacity was 1,032 toneladas; it was built entirely of teak; the entire cost of vessel, equipment, and construction was 53,370 pesos. The king of Spain disapproved the enterprise; and when the accounts of the company were settled, it was found that they were still indebted to the extent of 9,520 pesos. The galleon was sold at public auction for 10,000 pesos.

50 Concepción furnishes an interesting account (xiv, pp. 76–79) of the abolition by Arandía of the "rotten borough" of Cebú. During the term of Governor Arrechedera, he received a request from Juan Baraona Velazquez, governor and chief magistrate of Cebú province, that in view of the lack not only of regidors there but of citizens who could fill that office, the governor should confer it on certain persons named by him, among them two who were the only permanent (Spanish) settlers there. Nevertheless, affairs soon returned to their former condition: of the five persons thus appointed, one was long detained in Manila, and one died; another was deprived of office for harsh treatment of the headman of the Sangleys, and still another for failure to perform his duties. "Thus, only the regidor Espina was left, and in him much was deficient, if he were not actually incapable; for he could not read or write, and his judgment was not very sound." Velazquez therefore proposed that these offices be extinguished, and some suitable

person be appointed from Manila to assist him in ruling the province. Nothing came of this, and his successor, Joseph Romo, applied to Arandía for relief, saying that for two years no election of alcalde-in-ordinary had been held, and the office was exercised by the regidor Pedro Muñoz—the same who had ill-treated the Sangley—"of whom alone that municipality was composed;" that the latter had obtained his post only ad interim, and now refused to surrender it to Romo. "In view of this report, Señor Arandía decided that these remnants of the city should be abolished, leaving it with only the name of city, and that it should be ruled by its chief magistrate, as alcalde-mayor of the province; and in this wretched condition was left the first city of this sphere, endowed with privileges by our Catholic kings, and worthy of other and greater consideration. Its lack of citizens transformed it into so dry a skeleton; and, although this measure was provisional, necessity has made it perpetual." Buzeta and Bravo say (Diccionario, i, p. 555) that since then Cebú had been governed by a gobernadorcillo, like any native village; and at the end of that same volume they give a table of the population of Cebú province in 1818, which shows that the ancient city of Santisimo Nombre de Jésus contained no pure Spaniards, its population of 2,070 souls being all native or Chinese except 233 Spanish mestizos. Its present population, according to the late U. S. census, is 31,079—of whom 793 are natives of China, 131 of America, and 168 of Europe.

51 He had witnessed personally at Acapulco the careless, disorderly, and even fraudulent manner in which this trade was carried on by the Mexican merchants, who contrived to secure the advantage in every way over those of Manila. He therefore imposed severe penalties on all who on either side should practice frauds. He also appointed four of the most distinguished of the citizens of Manila to register, apportion, and appraise the goods sent thence; but the only result was that these men took the best for themselves, and consulted their own profit; he therefore revoked their commissions and sharply rebuked them. Arandía also made many reforms in the management of the Acapulco ship, its supplies, and its men, both on the sea and in port. (Concepción, xiv, pp. 171–183.)

52 Le Gentil and Marquina are cited by Montero y Vidal (Hist. de Filipinas, ii, p. 14) to show that Arandia died by poison or other violent means.

53 His full name was Manuel Antonio Rojo del Río y Vieyra.

54 At this point properly should come the documents which relate the invasion of the islands by the English, their capture of Manila, the consequent disturbances in the provinces, etc.; but the great length of this episode, and the desirability of bringing

all this material together in one volume, induce us to place it all in VOL. XLIX, completing this present volume with the noted memorial by the royal fiscal Viana, written nearly a year after the evacuation of Manila by the English.

MEMORIAL OF 1765

By Francisco Leandro de Viana. MS. dated February 10, 1765.

Source: This document is translated from a MS. — apparently a duplicate copy of the first original, and bearing Viana's autograph signature — in the possession of Edward E. Ayer, Chicago.

Translation: This is made by Emma Helen Blair.

VIANA'S MEMORIAL OF 1765

Part I

In which is shown the deplorable condition of the Philipinas Islands; the necessity of preserving them, with respectable forces; and the method for attaining this, without the costs which hitherto [have been incurred], and with increase to the royal exchequer.

Chapter First: Of the present unhappy condition of these islands1

1. There is no greater misfortune in the world than poverty; all have a contempt for it, and all regard it with displeasure. No one honors the poor man, however heroic and eminent he may be; his subordinates serve him unwillingly, and readily show him insolence. He has no success, for lack of money; and, in fine, every undertaking costs him immense labors, fatigues, vigilance, and sorrow.

2. It is literally this which is occurring in these islands. The Moros deride us, and display their superiority compared to our weakness, which certainly is ignominious to the Catholic arms, and to the reputation of the [Spanish] nation. When we had forces for punishing them, they were curbed and humiliated; since they have seen us poor and weak they have displayed their perfidy and boldness, and are treating us with the greatest insolence ever seen — for they invade even the villages along this bay, without there being, on our side, any means to prevent this.

3. The vassals of his Majesty, both Spaniards and natives, live in the sorrow which is aroused in them by their melancholy reflections on our poor and miserable condition. The Indians, who are civil only when they

fear some punishment, regard their sovereign with little respect, and the Spanish nation with disgust at seeing it humiliated by the English, the Dutch, the French, and even the Moros; and they judge that the Spaniards are somewhat more than the Indians, but much less than the other nations. And, although they are confounded at the glorious successes which our armies have gained against the English since the capture of this military post, and at the heroic valor with which the unfaithful provinces have been punished, when they become aware of our actual poverty that will be enough to destroy their reverence and respect for the acts of the superior government, and to make them bold to commit any insolence, for our lack of means to restrain them from it.

4. For this same reason, nothing can be undertaken that will avail against the Moros who harass us,2 or against the Indians who refuse obedience to the commands laid on them. The consequence of this is, that the scanty funds in the royal treasury are being consumed; that it is deprived of the receipts which it could have if we were in a respectable condition; and that a zealous governor of these islands labors and watches, in weariness and grief, to procure the remedy for so many evils, under the impossibility of finding it.

5. If we look at the condition of this fort and of that at Cavite, we shall lament, as is natural, the necessity of repairing their fortifications and building some new ones, of clearing out the ditches, of tearing down buildings, and of other works which will be deemed indispensable. If we turn our view to the artillery, we shall find it so defective, and part of it so useless, that for the defense of these forts it will be necessary to spend many thousands of pesos. If the gun-carriages which are needed and are actually lacking are built; if the forts are supplied with the gunpowder, balls, grapeshot, bombs, grenades, and other implements of war, and with iron, nails, mantelets, cordage, and oil, and, in short, with everything which ought to abound in the [royal] storehouses: the cost of all these things, which are necessary, will be enormous. If attention is given to the need of ships for transporting [hither] the situado, and of other smaller vessels for sending aid to the military posts, providing them with supplies, driving away the Moros, and transporting property from the provinces, one will be astounded at the contemplation of these expenses. And, after all, he will draw the conclusion that nothing of what I have mentioned can be undertaken, for lack of money; that the Moros will keep us in a state of continual fear; and the Indians will act as caprice leads them; that at the first outbreak of war the forts will be found entirely defenseless; that the military posts will be exposed to destruction; and, in one word, that the lack of troops and money places these islands in imminent risk of their total

destruction, by various paths, and our sovereign and the Spanish nation in grievous danger of losing their honor, reputation, and influence — which must be averted by such means as are possible; and one of these is, the abandonment of these domains.

6. If, then, they produce nothing; if to maintain them must cost so much that it weakens the royal exchequer, to the injury of other and more important domains; if for lack of money the honor of the Catholic arms cannot be maintained in these distant regions; if we are exposed to being the plaything of all the nations; if we cannot resist or confront the feeblest enemy who may attack us; and finally, if we must endure the ignominy of being discreditably deprived of these faithful vassals, with the loss of all that they have: it is better to anticipate these losses in good time, to abandon or sell these regions, and allow to all [their inhabitants] free opportunity to make their property secure and take refuge in other dominions, where the power of our beloved kings and lords may shield and defend them.

7. This is the method of saving expenses, and employing those funds for other and more useful purposes, and averting the ignominies to which we are exposed — with danger not only to our property but to our lives. For we are surrounded by ferocious and inhuman enemies, such as are the English — who, warned by the events of the late war, will give no quarter if they return to these islands, on account of not exposing themselves to remain as prisoners within the walls of Manila and Cavite — the Moros, who will come to the aid of the said English, or alone by themselves if they see us very weak (and in every way those people are terrible, for they know not what humanity is); the Sangleys or Chinese, who are equally barbarous and bloodthirsty; and even the Indians, who also are cruel and ferocious.

8. The recent example of Pangasinan is the most melancholy warning. What obstinacy and blindness! what insolence and aversion toward the Spaniards! What treasons and apostasies! What murders, so inhuman and cruel! It is certain that the Indians desire to throw off the mild yoke of the Spaniards; that they are Christians, and vassals of our king, simply through fear, and fail to be either Christians or vassals when they consider us weak; and that they neither respect nor obey any one, when they find an opportunity for resistance.

9. The revolted Indians in the island of Bohol solemnize weddings among themselves, confer baptism, and perform other functions of the Catholics, for which purpose they have some persons who perform the duties of the father ministers in the villages; and this mockery, this scorn, this contumely they display for what is most sacred in our religion. They have fled from the villages, and live in their freedom in the hills; yet for this conduct they have experienced only kind treatment and promises of

pardon, to which they do not, and never will, pay any attention. If we had troops and money, those insurgents would be reduced; they would be good Christians and vassals, and the royal treasury would possess the receipts from their tributes; for only the fear of punishment is adequate to subject the Indians, and draw them toward what is right.

10. More recent is the case of Pangasinan, whose natives had just been making the same mockery of our Catholic religion, and showing the same contempt for it; but chastisement has reduced them to being Christians and vassals to our king. It is argued from this that, so long as we have not the forces for coercing the Indians, they will be our greatest and most terrible enemies—from whom we cannot free ourselves, save by the measure of abandoning the islands, in case we do not maintain them with respectable forces.

Chapter Second: Of the difficulties which will result from abandoning these islands

1. Not many years had passed after their conquest when it was recognized in España that, in order to support them, it was necessary to expend much money; and the question arose whether it was more expedient to maintain these new domains, or to abandon them. Opinions were expressed on both sides: some urged that but little advantage had resulted to the crown from spending immense sums of money in this country, so distant from its sovereign—who, besides the fact that it did not promise him much profit, could not render it assistance with the promptness which was necessary. Others, on the contrary, urged that under no circumstances ought these islands to be abandoned, which were conferring such glory on our arms, victorious in the four quarters of the world, in which resounded the power of our sovereign, and his royal and Catholic zeal for the salvation of so many souls.

2. Our king and sovereign Don Phelipe the Second, of glorious memory, embraced this latter opinion, with that apostolic and heroic resolution, so celebrated in our histories, that "for the sake of one single soul that might be saved, he would consider well employed the moneys that were being spent in these islands."

3. I believe that to this religious motive others were added, of policy and state, for maintaining these islands, which, although at the beginning they would consume much money—as occurs in every new colonizing enterprise, which [sort of work] is not done for nothing—at the same time promised great advantages, on account of the valuable products which they yielded, and the great number of people who were conquered. Efforts in this enterprise were made for several years, with the greatest ardor;

the chimerical projects of Terrenate and the Molucas were begun, which cost us infinite expense; and, on the other hand, we were harassed by the Moros, with the Dutch, who were aiding them as enemies to this conquest, which they feared would be their ruin—an indication that we had a better opportunity than they to aggrandize ourselves with the commerce of all India, which would have yielded to us the very profits which they feared to lose. And we, occupied in defending ourselves from so many enemies, have not thought of making any progress, but only of leaving everything as the famous Legaspi established it—and yet continually with new burdens, on account of the creation of new offices, the increase of missions, and other expenses, which exceeded the income of this royal treasury, and were made up from that of Mexico.

4. Freed at last from the aforesaid enemies, [a time of] serenity and calm began in these islands, and much progress might have been made, to the benefit of the royal exchequer; with its forlorn condition, and the interested motives of those who were managing it, the zealous and disinterested governor Don Fausto Cruzat promptly made himself acquainted. He collected much money which had been regarded as lost; he erected or rebuilt very costly works, as the galleon "San Joseph," the palace, the halls of the royal Audiencia and the accountancy, with prisons, storehouses, etc.; he left much money in the royal treasury; he prevented the remittance of large sums which were due from the Mexican treasury; and he practiced economies which were very considerable, and suited to his own example of interest, zeal, application, and ability. But the reduction which he made in the military force, in pay, and in the royal situado, was not the best idea for the security of these islands, and for supplying their urgent necessities— especially as no increase of the royal revenue was established in place of the said reduction. For as a consequence—and the receipts of the royal treasury having been diminished, when they might have been increased—and with the necessity of holding the Moros in check, with costly expeditions and the construction and equipment of some military posts, our expenses were increased; and since these were greater than the incomes, the islands have not retrieved their condition since that time. They have had but few troops, and this government has not been able to make itself respected, or to restrain the invasions of the Moros. Nor is it able to undertake enterprises that would be useful in the provinces, in order that these might produce for the royal revenues the great increase which they bid fair to yield, and for which plans would be made, [if the support of the government could be given], by those who were of opinion that these islands should be preserved. As is admitted by [those of] all nations, these islands are the most fertile, abundant, and rich, and the country the most delightful, in all India; and no other region

is so well suited for [the center of] a flourishing commerce, on account of their situation. [For they lie midway] between the empire of China, the kingdoms of Siam and Cochinchina, the islands of Celebes and Molucas, the kingdom of Borney, Vengala, the coasts of Coromandel and Malavar, Goa, Persia, and other populous regions which have made the [mercantile] companies of Olanda and Inglaterra rich. With greater reason would they be able to increase the wealth of España, if in these islands were cultivated their many valuable products, which are greatly esteemed in the aforesaid colonies, and if these products found there the market which foreign goods now enjoy. The whole matter consists in restoring our commerce with the same courage and perseverance which the foreigners display, for which design the abandonment of these islands would be very pernicious—even laying aside religious motives, which are powerful to the Catholic zeal of the Spaniards.

5. I find another and greater objection to the abandonment of these islands; that is, that the English would securely establish themselves therein, for they have shown themselves eager and greedy for the advantages which the islands present. In that case, they would easily carry on, by way of the Southern Sea, an illicit commerce with Nueva España—where they could land wherever they might please, and without difficulty make themselves masters of the Californias, in order to continue, with this advantage, the discoveries by which they have sought to find a passage to the Eastern Indias by the [route] northwest from Hudson's Bay (called thus from the name of an English captain). With this object there was formed, at the beginning of the eighteenth century, a company of English merchants, who, as a result of their latest enterprises (in the years 1746 and 1747),3 have reasonable expectations of finding a way of communication between the Northern and the Southern Seas, according to the critical account of a modern geographer.

6. West of Canada and of the Misisipi River is the great gulf of the Western Sea,4 which falls [into the ocean] above [i.e., north of] Cape Mendocino; it was discovered by the Spaniard Martin de Aguilar, and it is judiciously conjectured that it extends a considerable distance toward the lands of the northern region in which is situated the strait of Anian, according to the discoveries of the Russians in 1728, 1731, and 1741—which have a certain agreement with those of the aforesaid Aguilar, and especially with those which our admiral Don Bartholome Fuente and his captain Pedro Bernarda made in the year 1640,5 north of California and northwest from Canada.

7. The former navigated along the coast of California four hundred and ninety-six leguas to the north-northwest, as far as the lake which is called Lake de los Reyes [i.e., "of the Kings"], and reached Canoset; he crossed a

lake, and by a river—to which he gave the name Parmentier, which was that of his Spanish interpreter—he arrived at another lake, which he named Fuente; it is one hundred and sixty leguas long and sixty wide. From this point he passed to another lake, called Ronquillo (from the name of a captain in that squadron), and in one of the villages there he learned that at a little distance toward the east there was a ship, in which it was supposed that there were Spaniards; they found an English ship, which had reached that place by the current from Bafin's Bay, or else that of Hudson's Bay.

8. Captain Bernarda, who had directed his course to the north, arrived at Minhaset, a village of America; he entered a lake four hundred and thirty-six leguas long (which he named Velasco), the extremity of which extends northeastward, as far as 77 degrees of latitude, and by a river which flows from the said lake to the southwest he came out at the sea. Again going to the north, he continued his navigation to the northeast in the sea of Tartaria, as far as 79 degrees of latitude, always following the coasts. He sent ashore a Spaniard, and he assured him that he had seen the extremity of the gulf of Davis's Strait, or of Bafin's Bay; and that in that place there was a freshwater lake at the latitude of 80 degrees, and mountains of ice toward the north and northwest. From this the said captain concluded that there was no passage or communication between the said strait and the Southern Sea; but the English regard these relations as the effect of the Spanish policy, which hides the actual discoveries of Admiral Fuente. As if there were not a similar refutation of error in the voyage which the merchants of Zelandia undertook in the year 1592, as Samuel Ricard6 relates, with the idea of passing over to China by way of the coasts of Tartaria! On the contrary, the English suspect that there is a passage to the Southern Sea by way of Hudson's Bay; and they are continually searching for it, with the greatest ardor and perseverance—for which enterprise they will have, without any doubt, motives which encourage their expectations. It is enough for my purpose to show how substantial is the advantage that would result to the said English from being masters of these islands, in order that they may establish themselves in the coasts of the Californias, and thus render easy the illicit commerce and the discoveries that I have mentioned.

9. Even without these suspicions, it cannot be doubted that in case of war breaking out the English could attack our domains in the two Americas from these islands, by the coast of the South [Sea]; and from Europe, by the opposite coast—diverting our forces in one direction, in order to strike a blow in security, where it may be most to their advantage; and to this risk we expose ourselves by abandoning these islands. But, notwithstanding this, I conclude that if we must ignominiously lose them, by not maintaining them with respectable forces, it would be better for us to abandon them

rather than to encounter such a calamity. This, in my opinion, would be accomplished in the first hostilities [that might break out], since the English, who are arrogantly establishing their factory in Joló to secure the profits of their commerce in that kingdom, will much more willingly establish themselves in Manila, whenever an opportunity is afforded them; and they will profit by whatever now benefits the Spaniards—and much more, on account of their greater application and industry, which regards the entire circuit of the world as narrow for the extension of their commerce.

10. The dominions ceded to the English by España and Francia in North America, as far as the Misisipi River, furnish to that nation the means for continuing the discoveries which I point out; and it cannot be doubted that, at the same time, they are seeking for a connection between the two seas—to which the inquisitive disposition of the English will devote itself, with the energy which hitherto [they have displayed]. They can open a route, by land if not by water, to the Californias, where any settlement [by them] would be very injurious to us, but very advantageous to them if they possess these islands. But without them the English could not maintain such a settlement, except at great cost in sending to it supplies in ships, which would have to navigate either by way of Cape Horn,7 in order to go along the coast of the South—without fear of encountering resistance from the Spaniards, since a dozen Englishmen, and half as many Indians to guide them, will make the crossing, and fortify themselves in any part of the southern [i.e., Pacific] coast of America—or by the Cape of Good Hope [Buena Esperanza], the Gulf of India, and the Straits of Malacca, in order to cross over from there, by way of these islands, and afterward make the same voyage as do the ships of this [Acapulco] line. These voyages, so protracted, will hold back the English from any settlement on the southern coast of America. However, if these islands belonged to them, they would immediately execute that project, in order to secure the advantages of this great commerce and of the illicit traffic which they would carry on in Nueva España—just as now they are conducting it from Jamayca and Honduras among all the Windward Islands [Islas de Barlovento] and in part of the Americas, with notable injury to the commerce of España and to the royal duties, of which they are depriving his Majesty with so many illicit importations [of foreign goods].

11. Many other difficulties which would ensue from the abandonment of these islands can be seen in the Extracto historial8 of the commerce of Philipinas, to which I refer—contenting myself, lastly, with calling attention to what we have lost by the Dutch having made themselves masters of the Molucas, the commerce of which has compensated them for the enormous expenses which they incurred. This subject also is treated by the said Extracto historial, and by the chronicles or histories of these islands. It

is sufficient to say that the Dutch have enriched themselves with the cloves and spices of the Molucas, from which the Spaniards obtained nothing but great expenses, with no mercantile advantage; that with the said products they have drained the silver from our dominions; and that with this money they have waged most cruel war against us.

12. Let a computation be made of the expense which the Molucas caused us, and of the loss which we have experienced from abandoning them; and even he who is least versed [in such matters] will concede that the latter is vastly greater than the former. For ten years' expenditures for preserving the Molucas are not equal to the increase of strength which we have given every year to our enemies since they gained possession of those islands. I assert that we would not have abandoned that valuable piece of territory if our Spaniards had been as industrious and assiduous in trading as are the Dutch; or if they had realized what they lost, which has been the immense treasures which the Dutch have gained. But ours is the singular misfortune that we regard the land as useless that does not abound in silver; nor will we consent to be convinced that commerce is the most safe of mines, if the products which our provinces yield are promoted, cultivated, and worked up.

13. The importance of the Molucas was not thoroughly understood until we lost them; nor will the loss resulting from the abandonment of the Philipinas be realized until they are in the power of some other nation, less indolent and negligent than ours. Then their exceedingly rich products— cinnamon, cloves, pepper, nutmegs, cotton, gold, iron, and the others which are yielded in great abundance (as will be said in its place) — will be cultivated and gathered up; those foreigners will sell us these very fruits, which now we cannot appreciate, and with them will take away our money; and in any war we shall be ruined by the gains which our abandonment [of the islands] will produce to those [who possess them].

14. I believe that in view of these reflections, and of what I am going to explain, every good Spaniard will be convinced of the necessity of preserving these islands—even though it shall be at greater expense, and without the powerful incentive of religion—on account of the great benefit which can result to the monarchy if we open our eyes to avail ourselves of the advantages which these dominions offer to us, as I attempt to demonstrate in this writing.

Chapter Third: Upon maintaining the islands with respectable forces

1. Assuming the difficulties which would follow from abandoning them, which is the first measure proposed, the second seems indispensable — to place these forts not only in a condition of ordinary defense, but in one of entire security, in order to avert the ignominy and discredit of our arms, and to render worthy of respect the name of our king and sovereign, and that of the Spanish nation, which certainly have lost much of their honor in this part of the world, at seeing the derision which the Moros have repeatedly cast at us. And it has been a special providence of God that since the shameful loss of Manila our arms should regain the reputation which they had lost in the siege of this fort, by some glorious successes — so complete that they were extolled by the enemies themselves, and caused admiration throughout India — in order to show that the loyalty of the Spaniards, even when their forces were most feeble, could conquer the strongest enemy and avenge their injuries. But this glorious and heroic example of fidelity and valor — by which all the people distinguished themselves, under the orders cf their commander, Don Simon de Anda y Salazar — ought not to lull us into living in excessive confidence that, in another invasion (which may God not permit), we shall be able to accomplish the same results; for the hand of God is not always ready to work miracles, and He desires that men shall aid themselves, in order that He may aid them.

2. I say, then, that it is very easy to make these fortified places so worthy of respect that there will be no forces in this part of India able to capture them. With the same ease any person can begin to form, in his imagination, a basis of brave soldiers, of fortifications, etc.; but he will strike on a reef from not knowing how the increased expense which must necessarily burden this undertaking can be supported. For this end, I will propose some measures, after showing the way by which to make ourselves respected.

3. The towns of Manila and Cavite ought to be placed [in a condition of defense] with the plan of fortifications in the modern style which shall be furnished by the engineers who may be consulted, or may come from España, for this purpose. This expense will be very great, as is naturally obvious; and perhaps with the same expenditure the entrance of the bay could be fortified to prevent the entrance of ships and leave this place in a condition conformable thereto — devoting all attention to the said entrance and to the port of Cavite (in which the courts, the [royal] offices, the storehouses, etc, ought to be), because its situation, aided by art, will make the said port impregnable, and its maintenance less costly and more secure.

4. The town of Manila is of no use without the port of Cavite; and the latter, without the former, is more useful and less costly. Any enemy who attempts to capture this town [of Manila] can secure the same advantages by seizing other lands on the shores of the bay, because all is alike, but

useless, without the said port; and the expedient of abandoning this town (which, on account of its uselessness, does not merit the expenditure of so much money), and employing the same expense in fortifying, if that can be done, the entrance of Mariveles, is more advantageous and safe, and less costly. It is more advantageous, because then no vessel can enter the bay, to invade the villages along its shore, as the Moros now do; more safe, because while any [hostile] squadron would be wasting time in opening a passage by which to find entrance into the bay and lay siege to Cavite, opportunity would thus be given for various military measures which would render difficult the capture of the said port; and less costly, because not so many soldiers are necessary to guard the fortifications of the said entrance and port as to man the great extent of the walls of Manila — which, according to intelligent persons, needs a garrison of at least three thousand men.9

5. There is a sort of flat boats which are called "floating bastions" [baluartes en el agua]; they are of shallow keel, but of a strength which can support artillery of large caliber. This is a most admirable invention for defending the entrances of ports; those who understand the subject will give more minute information regarding these vessels, which, added to the fortification of the aforesaid entrance [of Mariveles], will make it impossible for hostile ships to enter the bay.

6. There is no doubt that Manila, as I have said, is unnecessary if Cavite is well fortified; but it is also certain that at Manila it is easier to bring in supplies, and for all the troops and the citizens to remove, with their property, to the provinces, where the enemy cannot attack them. These reflections, and the difficulties which there may be in fortifying the entrance to the bay, will be better foreseen by those who understand the subject.

7. Besides the two ships, which are necessary for the trade with Nueva España, there ought to be at Cavite two others in reserve, which could serve in any outbreak of war for the guard and defense of our fortifications, and even could be sent out for capturing the ships of our enemies which might come from Europa and from the coasts [of India] to trade at Canton, for the latter pass in sight of the coasts of Ilocos and Cagayan, and visit without fail Pulaor, Pulicondor, and Pulizapato. These ships [at Cavite] ought to have competent naval officers; and even in time of peace they will be very useful for keeping the coasts clear [of enemies], for transporting troops to the military posts, for any expedition against the Moros, and for reconnoitering and surveying the lands, and the shoals and dangerous places of our islands and seas, and discovering new routes. The navy, shipyard, and arsenal of Cavite should be placed under such regulations as shall be considered most suitable; and as warden of the said port there should be appointed a competent naval officer, or some one of the builders of ships, with the

title of superintendent of the arsenal and shipyard, in order that affairs may progress in proportion to his ability.

8. The expense of the two ships which must sail to Acapulco is paid for by the same royal duties which have been hitherto paid, for there have always been at least two galleons for this purpose. As for the additional two ships, and some fragatas besides, it can be estimated that they will cost one hundred thousand pesos a year, besides their construction; this can be carried on in various parts of these islands, with evident saving of expense on account of the exceeding abundance of timber and the low wages of the workmen.

9. The principal defense and security of these islands consists in the troops. In every province there ought to be fifty soldiers, with their officers, at the disposal of the alcaldes-mayor. In this way the reduction of the villages would be made easier, without which all the rest is absolutely idle and useless. As fast as the villages are reduced, they offer greater advantages for both spiritual and temporal things; and thus could be established what would be very beneficial to the Indians and to the royal exchequer, as will be explained later.

10. With a thousand soldiers distributed in the provinces—and these in time of war could retreat to the forts—and with three thousand who may be permanently stationed in the forts, the port of Cavite and the forts which may be erected at the entrance of the bay will be impregnable. Or, [if it be a question] of not undertaking this work but of maintaining the fortified post of Manila, the said number of troops will likewise be sufficient; for the Dutch, the English, and the French, who are the powers that we can fear in India, have not the facilities for coming to conquer our towns with so many marines as there would be soldiers in our garrisons aforesaid; and, on the other hand, they may fear lest we invade them with part of the said military force and of the militia (which, disciplined on the plan that I propose in my memorandum of suggestions, will exceed six thousand men, besides the veterans). With that force, and with the enormous number of men who could be obtained from these islands for [making] earthworks [para faginas] and for other construction, the name of our sovereign and of the Spanish nation would command so much respect in this part of the world that no one would dare to invade us.

11. The permanent garrison of Manila and Cavite, according to the regulation by Señor Arandia, contains two thousand men, divided into twenty companies; and the plan which I propose for the security of the said towns and of the provinces calls for another two thousand men. From these can be formed another twenty companies, of a hundred men each; and, since usually these companies are at no time complete, it will be necessary,

in order to keep them full, to increase the said plan by another thousand men, in order that the [regular] footing of four thousand men may always be maintained. They can easily be recruited in Nueva España, and [sent over] by every ship to replace those who may die; for we have learned by experience that the Americans, if they are well disciplined, are remarkably well fitted for soldiers. They are barbarians in courage, and are daring and resolute; they fling themselves into the greatest danger as joyously as into a dance; and whether on the march or in guard duty, in heat or in rain, and in the most distressing fatigues, they are always gay, contented, and good-humored. With the same aspect they endure poor food, a scanty supper, a hard bed; and, finally, they are very obedient, and their virile powers are quite spent [son de potencias mui despejadas] usually—so much so that on this account they usually have all the vices which are natural to man. But strict discipline and punishment are a great restraint on them; and, with the example of four or five hundred veteran soldiers who might come from España, a very respectable military force could be trained here—with the additional consideration that they are better able than are the Europeans to endure heat and rain, and other hardships, which ruin the latter and make no impression on the former. But it is indispensable that some officers of rank should come from España, to lay good foundations for this edifice, for in no other way can it be permanent.

12. In order that this force may serve willingly, and be reliable, it is necessary to increase their pay. It is impossible to have good officers unless they have sufficient pay to support themselves decently, and it is certain that they do not have it; the same thing is true of the soldiers, relatively; and on this account it is found that both officers and men serve by compulsion, for, by leaving the service, they make a better living, and are more highly esteemed. A captain with [a salary of] twenty-five pesos, a lieutenant with eighteen, and an alférez with fourteen, cannot feed, clothe, and house themselves; and in order to appear on the streets neat and clean, they are forced to practice a thousand stratagems and deceits, which cast discredit on the body of officers and injure their reputation among the citizens. The honorable officer who does not conform to this [sort of] life, or who has means to support himself in some other way, or who adds to his income by trading, escapes by leaving the service; and the soldier deserts, and takes refuge in one of the provinces, where he lives better and has more comforts. Therefore, in order that they may serve the king with affection, willingness, and honor, both officers and men should receive a corresponding rate of pay.

13. This, it seems to me, ought to be fixed at the rate of fifty pesos for the captain's pay, forty for the lieutenant, thirty for the alférez, ten for

the sergeant, eight for the corporal, and five for the private soldier; and in this proportion for the sargentos-mayor, the adjutants, and others. With these salaries all the military could support themselves decently, and the service would be desirable; young men of good standing would devote themselves to it; there would be emulation among the officers, and, if these were competent, among the soldiers also—who, with such pay, would not be so eager to desert the service.

14. Computing the annual expense of the aforesaid forty companies, according to the proposed schedule of pay, it would amount to very nearly the sum of three hundred and twenty thousand pesos; and adding thirty thousand pesos more, for the pay of the corps of artillerists whom we ought to have, the annual expense would be about three hundred and fifty thousand pesos. [With that force,] there would be men for the detachments which we may need to send on special service, for the expeditions that may be necessary, for proceeding wherever necessity may call for aid, and for the ships and the galleys; and, above all, for rendering ourselves respected and feared, in times of either peace or war.

15. This increase of troops and pay, compared with the pay and troops stated in Señor Arandia's regulations, amounts to the half more; and I reckon it, with that of the artillery, at two hundred thousand pesos more of expense; this, with the hundred thousand applied for the navy alone, will make three hundred thousand pesos of increase to be charged to this royal treasury. Computing the cost not by the said regulations, but by the plan which I have just proposed, the entire cost of army, navy, and corps of artillery amounts to four hundred and fifty thousand pesos annually.

Chapter Fourth: On the facility with which these islands can produce for the royal exchequer more than what it needs for the said expenses

1. Having constituted the aforesaid military force—or half of it, in order that the expense may be less at first—the reduction of all the Indian villages ought to be resolutely undertaken, as a matter that is absolutely essential, without which all the rest will be useless. This reduction made (which can be accomplished in less than a year), enumeration will be made of the tribute-payers in all the provinces; after the reduction their numbers will be greatly increased, because the heads of barangay will not be able to hide the tributes as easily as they now do, or to commit thefts and dishonorable acts, as they have hitherto done. The ordinances will be made duly effective, especially in regard to plantations, and other measures will be adopted that are beneficial for the better government, both economic and civil, of the villages; government buildings will be erected in the chief towns, at least,

that may serve to shelter the alcalde-mayor and the troops that he will have; also a storehouse, in which to keep the property of the royal exchequer. Good schoolmasters will be employed for the instruction of the Indians, and for teaching them our language; and the matters in which the father ministers should have the right to intervene, and those in which they ought to forbear, will be strictly regulated, without any dispensation. The cultivation of the land will be conducted with the utmost care; and, finally, the tribute will be increased, to the rate of two pesos a head each year. Although this is a very moderate impost, and is profitable not only to the king but to the Indians, in order to draw them out from their continual and pernicious slothfulness, this branch of revenue will produce annually one million, six hundred thousand pesos. This addition to the royal treasury, even when some deduction is made, as is ordinary, will not only support the expenses of my plan for army, artillery, and navy, but a considerable amount of silver will be left for other allotments from the royal exchequer, and for indemnifying the expenses with which the islands have been burdened, from the time of their conquest until now.

2. The other increases and savings which the royal exchequer can make in its various branches I have set forth to his Majesty and to the superior government, and I will furnish a still more detailed account whenever it shall be deemed necessary. It is sufficient [here] to know that these can amount to some four hundred thousand pesos, and that, when added to the income from the tributes, the two items will amount to two millions of pesos annually; and even if half a million be deducted for contingencies and losses, and another half-million be spent in making payments, a million still remains as savings. Even considering the matter as gloomily and distrustfully as possible, there cannot fail to be an annual saving of half a million of pesos, as any one will understand who is moderately acquainted with the affairs of these islands.

3. With such receipts in the royal treasury, and with the aforesaid soldiery and their pay, and with navy, artillerists, and military supplies, what enterprises cannot be undertaken in these islands? Will this not be the most considerable establishment in all India? Will there be forces that can overcome us? Will the English, who have their forts and factories, with the necessary garrisons, venture again to invade this place? On the contrary, will they not fear, and with just cause, that we, superior then in forces, will attack them in their own colonies? I think that no one will doubt that the advantage is ours, assuming that my plan for savings and increases in the royal revenues is practicable; and I believe that, however numerous the difficulties which may accumulate in carrying it out, all will admit the suitability of these islands for attaining it, if only it be undertaken in earnest

and followed up persistently by all the governors; for if the military forces be placed on the footing that I propose, all the rest will be overcome without special difficulty; and I dare stake my head on it.

4. In order that the islands may enjoy the peace, tranquillity, and comfort which they should have, with evident benefit to the royal revenues, it is absolutely necessary to inflict exemplary punishment on the Moros of Jolo and Mindanao, whose insolence, perfidy, cruelties, piracies, seizing of captives, and deceitfulness have ruined these wretched provinces, and will entirely annihilate them unless the remedy be applied — and there is no other, than to attack them in their own territories, and give them no quarter; to destroy them, or else intimidate them so that they will never forget [their punishment]; and to put a stop to their raids, by some small forts, which can keep them in subjection — imposing on them a heavy tribute, which will indemnify the expenses of the expedition and the costs of the said forts and soldiers. The enterprise is easy and safe, when we have the men and the money; and the advantage and even necessity is the greatest one of these islands. Upon this I could expatiate at length, since this is a matter upon which I have worked with considerable application; but this point is sufficient, as being one of those most essential to the prosperity of these islands, and to make it evident that at the same time we can succeed in depriving the English of their factory in Jolo.10 This is another of the more important matters, since in either peace or war they will entirely ruin these islands: in peace, by frauds and commercial intrigues; and in war, with small forces.

5. For the execution of all the aforesaid, and in order that the [military] establishment proposed may suffer no delay or procrastination, it would be expedient for his Majesty to give commission for this to the governors, and to the ministers of the Audiencia, with the insistence which is merited by this project, so assured and so beneficial; and the amplest powers should be given them to proceed in such manner as they shall judge, by the majority of votes [in councils of war], to be most expedient. For in consulting his Majesty in regard to some uncertainties, and waiting for his royal decisions, the delay of at least three years will be experienced; and in so long a time the postponement of action cannot fail to be injurious to the enterprise, and to cool interest in its continuation, when it ought to be pursued with the greatest ardor, zeal, and efficiency, deferring for this all other affairs, as being less important.

6. The first thing which should be attempted is, that his Majesty issue commands — provided he approve the project for making these domains respected, and the plan for economies and increases in the royal revenues — to the viceroy of Nueva España to send over here money and soldiers, in

order to serve as a foundation for the work that is to be undertaken. For this is necessary to be done, even if there were no such project; for in its present condition the place is without defense, and the government without forces to make itself obeyed; and there is no medium between the two extremes above stated — to abandon this country, or to maintain it with honor; and the latter cannot be secured without spending money, and without having sufficient troops to garrison the forts.

7. If to these succors from Nueva España were added two ships and five hundred soldiers from Europa, a corresponding force of officers, and abundance of military supplies — which could come to these islands by way of the Cape of Good Hope — great advantages would ensue. First, all the vassals in these islands would rejoice at seeing such succor as never before had been seen in them; second, the Indians would have some idea of the power of our sovereign, since, as a people of material ideas and little penetration, they do not consider or understand more than what enters through their eyes; third, they would feel more respect, fear, and dread, which is that which holds them in check, and obliges them to be Christians and vassals of our king. Fourth, such aid would serve as a terror to the Moros, and would allow the provinces, overwhelmed by their invasions, to take breath; fifth, all the soldiery would be disciplined and organized after the example of the said five hundred veteran soldiers, and with the sergeants and corporals of the latter a good corps of officers could be formed, filling vacant posts with them in place of the untrained and inexperienced (to whom can be given other appointments in the posts of alcalde-mayor, corregidor, etc.). Sixth, in these neighboring provinces the reduction [of the villages] and the increase of tribute could be immediately undertaken, without risk of resistance on their part; and when the undertaking was concluded in this region, where it is easier to carry out such a measure, it would be continued in the other provinces, one after another. Thus in a short time the benefits set down in this project would be obtained, and with them the troops and their pay could be increased, fortifications and ships built, supplies provided (which could be done here), and the Moros who harass us destroyed.

Chapter Fifth: Of the arguments which justify the increase of tributes

1. As this matter is discussed with the greatest scruples by all the authors, it has seemed to me desirable to explain, as briefly as possible, the reasons which I consider just for the increase of tributes which I mention in the preceding chapter. I see therein from the start the obstacles and difficulties which this delicate question will occasion; but I will bring

together the considerations·which no author denies in this discussion; I will adapt their doctrines to the Indians of these islands, in order that the justification of my design may be evident; and I will conclude with touching upon some objections which have been raised by the most learned persons whom I have consulted on this point.

2. From the confusion and disorders of ancient times originated the selection of kings, to whom and to their successors the respective kingdoms entrusted the power of establishing laws; of forming towns, and of maintaining them in peace, justice, and social order; of appointing persons for government, civil, economic, and military; of establishing tribunals; and, in fine, of providing their vassals with all the means conducive to their greatest comfort and security. The people bound themselves to contribute means for meeting these expenses, with the tributes and regular charges which might be necessary. By this mutual obligation between the kings and the vassals, the latter must be protected, defended from enemies, and maintained in peace and justice; and in return and acknowledgment they must also pay the tributes, since these are employed for the common benefit, and secure the stability and solidity of the state. If St. Paul counseled that tributes be paid to the heathen princes, with how much more reason ought they to be paid to our Catholic monarchs!

3. The payment of tributes is binding in the tribunal of conscience, under [penalty of] mortal sin, and with the obligation to make restitution when they are fraudulently withheld; and this opinion no author questions. But, as it is not possible to determine the quantity, opinions are divided, and many persons expand this matter, urging that the excessive imposition of tribute exonerates from the obligation to pay it, and establishing [the fact of] the said excess on various arguments, although I know not whether these are solid as is necessary. For, in order to speak with assurance on this matter, neither theology nor jurisprudence is sufficient; but it is necessary to know also the science of government and that of administration—which are little understood by some who clamor against excess in the tributes, without knowing whether or not there is any.

4. In matters of government, a statesman who is adorned with superior talents will distinguish the expenditures which are necessary from those which are needlessly incurred; he will know whether the tributes are sufficient to meet the obligations of the crown; and he will make a calculation of the incomes and expenses of the royal exchequer. This neither the jurist nor the theologian can do, without knowledge of these matters, which are remote from their professions, and consequently they cannot be sure whether the tributes are sufficient, or are extravagantly spent, in order that they may establish the [charge of] excess in them, or the [right of] relief from

paying them, or the [justice of] scruples at imposing them. But the theologian and the jurist who may have the said information will doubtless declare with most correctness, whether the tributes are excessive or moderate, and whether there is obligation to diminish them or necessity for increasing them, in order that sovereigns may not experience the aforesaid scruples, or the vassals have cause for not paying the tributes.

5. It cannot be denied that in all the nations of Europe the tributes have been increased in this century, as the Mercuries publish it; and this is right, because continually new things are discovered which render the old ones useless — for instance, a fortification which formerly was considered impregnable is [now] regarded as very frail and weak. On the other hand, the exertions which a power makes oblige it to incur greater expenses, and all of the powers strive to place themselves in a state of equilibrium which can render their respective domains secure. The abundance of silver has raised the prices of commodities, and, as everything costs much more than formerly, and the necessity for expenditures is infinitely greater, the increase of tributes cannot be avoided, nor can the vassals be excused from the clear obligation to pay them, in proportion to the [demands of the] times, which cannot be the same.

6. The pious feeling with which the Indians have been regarded has rendered still more delicate the question of the tributes which have been imposed upon them; nevertheless, all our authors agree in justifying not only those which at first were laid upon them, but those which for just reasons were afterward increased. Moreover, it was decided by a council of very learned men whom the emperor Carlos Fifth consulted that the Indians ought to pay the same tributes which the other vassals were paying in España, appraising their value, and moderating the tax according to the resources of the tributaries and to what each province could carry and endure;11 and from this proceed to the laws which have been established, and the royal decrees that have been issued, for this purpose. These ordinances are even more benign than the aforesaid decision; for really the poverty of the Indians has been exaggerated more than is just, and it has been believed that by these moderate measures the conquest of the Indias, both spiritual and temporal, would be more easily effected — which I do not attribute to that, but to the great reverence which the reputation and glorious achievements of the Spaniards occasioned in the Indians.

7. Taking for granted then, the moderation (as all admit) of the tributes paid by the Indians, especially in these islands — where they paid only at the rate of four reals for each tributary, and of one real a head which was afterward imposed in addition, one entire tribute finally paying ten reals, in accordance with ley 65, tit. 5, lib. 6, of the Recopilación de Indias, without

there being, from the year 1602 until now, any further burden upon them—and assuming, as an unquestioned fact, that there has been a continual increase of new offices, new military posts, and many expenses in these very islands; as also that the urgent needs of the crown are now incomparably far greater than in the past century, it seems that by an undeniable conclusion the increase of tributes ought to be lawful, in proportion to the increase in the said expenses. For without the tributes the king cannot fulfil his obligations as such, in regard to his vassals; nor can the latter omit to contribute the means for their own preservation and security, which is what the sovereign must endeavor to obtain for them.

8. What reason will there be for the vassals in the peninsula of España being the only ones to be laden with an increase in the tributes, and for the vassals in the Indias not bearing the same increase? One class is under the same obligation as the other to pay their share to their king, for the necessary expenses of the monarchy. Let, then, a survey be made of the taxes and imposts which have been increased in España since the conquest of the Indias, and it will be seen what increase of tributes has been imposed upon the Spaniards in order to defray the expenses of the crown, while in the Indias hardly any increase has been made—although it accords with equitable justice that all should bear these burdens which conduce to the common welfare, and assure the stability and permanence of all the dominions.

9. Even when the expenses of these islands were less, the tributes were not sufficient; and every year the generosity of our sovereign has sent and is sending the situado12 from Nueva España—which, [even] with the product of the tributes and of other royal taxes, is not enough to satisfy all the obligations of this royal treasury. This is an argument which demonstrates that these vassals do not contribute to their king the amount which, in the opinion of all, they are under obligation to pay; for they ought to pay that which his Majesty spends for their comfort, for their spiritual and temporal government, for the administration of justice, and in defense of their persons and property. Besides all this, they ought to contribute to the royal revenues for the expenses of the wars, and the maintenance of troops and forts, of the navy, of state officials, and of the royal household—which, as indispensable and general expenses, ought to be exacted from all the vassals. But not only are these expenses never exacted from the vassals here, but these islands have been supported at the cost of the labors and fatigues of the other vassals, without any reason being found why one class should enjoy more privileges than the other while they receive equal benefits.

10. There are probably in all the world no vassals who are less burdened than are the Indians of these islands. They eat and drink without paying

alcabala or any impost; the fabrics with which they clothe themselves, if made in the islands, pay nothing, and if they are of foreign make they bear no heavier burden than the light one of the customs duties; in the polos and personal services to which the king assigns them, he furnishes them with rations and pay according to the tariffs and ordinances of the provinces; and, finally, each Indian pays, at the end of the year, only five reals, from the age of eighteen years to that of sixty. I agree that at the beginning it was proper to proceed with this moderation, because the said tribute was then considered sufficient for the expenses, and those of the monarchy were also less in those times, on account of the scarcity of silver, which caused all commodities to be cheaper than they are now; and, finally, because they had not been conquered by wars occasioned by their own perverse conduct, in order to impose on them heavy tributes at the discretion of the conqueror, as is just in such cases. For they submitted of their own accord, and our conquest was made not because they had previously furnished us with causes for war, but for the sake of their greater good, both spiritual and temporal; for this reason their tribute ought to be more moderate, but not so much so that, in order to relieve these vassals, it should be charged back to the others (as it has been, unjustly), in order to support these islands. For it does not accord with justice that exemption should be granted to these Indians from their obligations, as vassals, to pay their share toward the expenses of these dominions and of the entire monarchy, in [due] proportion; and that this favor [to them] should prove injurious to the rest of the vassals, who certainly are more worthy of consideration [than these], since they are more useful.

11. "In the time of their heathendom, they ought to be considered as slaves rather than as vassals of their tyrannical petty kings, to whom they paid service as vassals. These tyrants employed them in their grain-fields, and in gathering pearls, shells, gold, dyewood, amber, and civet; in timber-cutting, and in the construction of vessels; in a word, the people had nothing more than the labor appointed to them by their tyrant masters" (thus I explained the matter to his Majesty in a report of June 5, 1760, and [here] will copy exactly the rest of its contents regarding the increase of tributes). "Your Majesty conquered these dominions and these peoples, making rational beings from brutes, Christians from heathens, and rich people from poor ones. Your Majesty gave them the freedom of the sea, the rivers, the lands, and the forests; established a governor, an Audiencia, and other courts, in order that they might be defended from their enemies and maintained in justice; formed bishoprics, with bishops and curas; and, in fine, you completed these benefits with the many privileges which are contained in the laws of the Indias, without further burden to them than the

payment by each Indian of five reals. At the same time, they were able to pay much more, as it is just they should, considering that every vassal ought to contribute to his king and natural lord whatever is necessary to maintain the vassals in peace, justice, and social order; but in these islands not only does your Majesty not obtain what is needed to pay these expenses, but your Majesty supplies, and has supplied, an immense amount of money. If the rest of your vassals contributed in this proportion, your Majesty could not maintain your dominions, for you spend vastly more than what they yield to you; nor could the Indians of these islands, moreover, be instructed and governed if your Majesty spent upon them no more than you obtain from the fund of the tributes. Therefore, in order that these obligations may be reciprocal—that of your Majesty to maintain the Indians in social order, and theirs to contribute for the same—it is necessary that the tribute be proportioned to the expenses, and larger than what they are at present paying."

12. Let these reflections be prudently considered, for, even without the constraint of the foregoing ones, they show the lawfulness of increasing the tribute; and at greater length I have stated the disposition of the Indians, as I also explained to his Majesty in the said report: "They are a people who are given up to sloth; they work one day for the food for the entire week, and the rest of the time they are without occupation, and most often [spend that time] in gambling or drinking. That is a very unusual Indian who takes pains to have a comfortable house, and to accumulate some little property for the comfort of his children; for he [usually] only works for his food and for wretched clothing, for paying his tribute, and for gambling. This is more usually the case; as also is it certain that there are no vassals who have better opportunities for being rich, or can do so more easily. Those who were exempted from going to cut timber paid the overseer five pesos, three reals each, in order not to be obliged to do this work for the period of one month; and in this is evident the facility with which they make money when they choose, and when necessity urges them."

13. Here comes in well what the governor has set forth in a memorandum of suggestions regarding the increase of the tributes, and I will extract from it what answers my purpose: "Among the numerous vices which are occasioned by the incredible laziness of the Indians, one is that of gambling. When they gamble on a cockfight, a multitude of people assemble, and all of them carry ready money for this purpose. The Indian women adorn themselves with many chains of gold, with pendants, and with rosaries ornamented with gold; with rings and bracelets of tumbac, and with many buttons of the said metals on their chemises. The Indians are accustomed to

use much silver, and some gold and tumbac, on the said buttons and those on their jackets; in rings and clasps; on their knife-belts13 and weapons ornamented with silver. For a burial they pay out twenty, forty, or sixty pesos; they spend enormous amounts in the banquets at their weddings, in the functions of gobernadorcillos, and in other things, which prove that the Indian, notwithstanding his great slothfulness, has money for everything except for the tribute."

14. There is no province which does not yield many and excellent products, and, if the Indians were willing to apply themselves to a very moderate [amount of] labor, they could pay a larger tribute, and [yet] live with more comforts; for there are probably no vassals in all the world who have such facilities and opportunities for becoming rich as have the Indians of Filipinas. But this condition is not attained when there is slothfulness; and what means have the Spaniards used to banish this vice? None; for we are as languid and negligent as the Indians, and have left them in their freedom without seeking either their advancement or our own. The Spaniards do not go out of Manila, where all are gentlemen; they regard it as unworthy to devote themselves to any other pursuit than commerce; they employ themselves in swindling and begging alms, rather than seek a living in the provinces; and, more than all, they live in utter idleness. They loiter about, divert themselves with gambling and other vices, and become insolent in their licentious mode of speech, even that which they do not understand. For this reason Manila is the commonwealth most abominable for malicious tales, slanders, and factions,14 for sloth and licentiousness; for even the citizen of most wealth and he who is most occupied will have at least ten months which he does not know how to employ.

15. Such is the example that we set to the Indians, and they imitate us so perfectly that they all desire to live as the Spaniard does, to wear the same costly ornaments, and to be rich—but without labor, and without ceasing to be idle or to divert themselves with all the other vices. If the many Spanish vagabonds who wander about Manila and its environs were distributed in the provinces, they would trade therein; they would marry Indian women of rank, would become rich with some application and labor, and would thus furnish a good example to the Indians. In this way the foreigners (and especially the French) have established their colonies, free from the error of our pernicious vanity, inaction, and sloth; and we, although better warned than they, are unwilling to change our ideas, but prefer to maintain the Indians in the same state of idleness.

16. The means for their not being idle is, that the Spaniards should work, and encourage and aid the Indians to cultivate their lands and utilize their products. An ordinance should be published that no Indian may be a

gobernadorcillo or official of his village unless he cultivate and gather in a certain portion of rice, wheat, sugar, cacao, cotton, wax, or other product, regulated by what each province produces; that if they do not cultivate their lands they must lose them, the lands being adjudicated to other persons, in order that these may cultivate them; and that exemption from tributes, polos, and personal services be granted to those who shall most distinguish themselves in tillage and harvesting. The idea is, to stimulate them in this manner to the tillage and cultivation of the lands which his Majesty grants to all the villages and the Indians who dwell in them; and these measures are very gentle compared to others which were decreed by the municipal law of the Indias. For in one of the ordinances of Mexico it is decreed that "the Indians must not be allowed to be idle, or to wander about as idlers and vagabonds; but they must work on their farms." The authorities could compel them by force to obey this, as Señor Solorzano proves by various arguments in book 2, chapter 7 of his Política Indiana, demonstrating that no Indian would work if allowed his liberty, "through his natural inclination to an idle and easy life," as is definitely stated in ley 1, tit. 13, lib. 6 ("Of the Indians"), and many others of the same Recopilación; and that the Indians resist work "because they are exceedingly slothful and fond of idleness, and are inclined to abandon themselves to intemperance, licentiousness, and other vices which idolatry occasions among them; and as they are so little covetous, and are content with so little for food and clothing, many passing their lives in the manner of beasts, some force and compulsion is necessary to make them give up this mode of life; for the devil prompts and persuades them not to serve or aid the Spaniards.

17. "On this account it has always been regarded as best to keep them occupied and at work, and in their heathen condition the same was done by their Ingas [i.e., Incas] and Montesumas—to such an extent that, when they lacked profitable and necessary occupation, their rulers set them to work at others that were only for pleasure, and of no use or benefit; they were even made to collect little bags of lice, and to cut and carry to the mountains stones of enormous size."

18. All this description seems written for the Indians of these islands, and he who may have any experience with them will decide that, in order to remove them from their sloth and their vices the increase of their tributes is indispensable, as is the necessity of compelling them by the said measure to perform work that is useful to the king, and likewise to themselves, in both spiritual and temporal interests—so much so that one can and ought to

form the gravest scruples at allowing the Indians to remain in their present condition, since it is the origin of numberless evils (from which I shall pray God to deliver his Majesty and his ministers), through consenting to this so pernicious sloth, and not applying some remedy to it. At the same time with the increase of the tribute, the abundance of products and the wealth of the islands will be greater; for if the Indians now do a certain amount of work in order to pay five reals, they will be under necessity of working three times as much in order to pay two pesos.

19. In Nueva España, Señor Solorzano regards as lawful and very just the tribute of eight tostons (which are four pesos, each of eight silver reals), for each Indian, one-half more15 than what I rated in the increase which is here proposed. He who has any knowledge of the said kingdom and of these islands will admit that the said rate is very moderate; for the Indians of America do not enjoy so great an abundance of products or so wide a market as do the natives of these islands. Also, there they have not, in proportion [to the extent of the country], as many troops and as many military posts as here; and these natives have fewer burdens of polos and personal services, and much less hardship, than those of Nueva España. Notwithstanding these advantages, which furnish just reason for imposing on these islands the same tribute which is regarded as just in Nueva España, I am fixing the rate at one-half less—for with the two pesos for each Indian I think that there will be more than enough to place the troops, the fortifications, and the navy, on a more respectable footing; to defend these vassals from the invasions of Moros and other enemies; and, by saving to his Majesty the royal situado and making amends for the enormous expenses which have burdened these islands, to furnish to the royal revenues some increase, and have means with which to meet the needs and obligations of the crown.

20. The difference which there may be between the Indians who were conquered by arms and those who voluntarily subjected themselves to our sway (as were those of these islands) is also found in the said regulation of rates, by which the latter will pay but one-half as much as the former; for this circumstance that I have mentioned does not relieve them from the obligations and burdens of vassals—although on account of it they have the right to be treated with more clemency, as they have been treated hitherto, and will be in the future—paying the two pesos as tribute, in order that his Majesty and the other vassals need not defray the expenses to which the people of these islands ought to contribute, since these conduce to their spiritual and temporal welfare, and to the preservation and security of these dominions.

21. Besides this, it ought to be borne in mind that, from the first years of this conquest until the one in which we now are, nearly all the provinces have at various times rebelled and risen in arms; and not one of our authors doubts that for this kind of offense the Indians ought to be punished by an increase of their tributes, that this may serve them as a warning and example; for they [thus] lost the right to be treated with the mildness which their first voluntary submission deserved. If the Spaniards had proceeded after this fashion in these islands, it would have been an easy matter to increase the tributes, in order to save the situados. Moreover, with the examples in this war [*i.e.*, with the English] we have most rightful cause for punishing, by some such means, the traitorous and revolted provinces, by [imposing] not only the two pesos of tribute, but much more, in order to make some distinction between the Indians who have continued faithful to our king and those who have rebelled and acted disloyally.

22. With these brief reflections the minds of those who have entertained some doubts or scruples in regard to the increase of tributes which I proposed in the preceding chapter would be convinced; but there would be other difficulties to overcome in this exceedingly delicate matter. People will tell me (as I have sometimes heard it said) that any person who proposes the increase of tributes commits mortal sin, and incurs the excommunication of the bull of the Cena. But I will reply with the upright and pious intention which has influenced me to write on this subject—on which, in my opinion, depends the preservation of these islands and their Christian churches; for they will certainly be lost in a few years unless they produce [means] for the expenses which they occasion, or unless his Majesty increase the royal situado; this is a difficult matter, and he is under no obligation to do so. And it is sufficient for me, in order not to incur the said excommunication, that the bull of the Cena is not received in España in regard to matters of temporal government (in which our sovereigns are absolute), but only in what concerns ecclesiastical discipline, and the purity of the faith and the Catholic religion, in which the Spaniards have always affirmed the blindest obedience to the supreme pontiff and vicar of Christ on earth.

23. Nevertheless, I regard with the most profound veneration and respect all that is contained in the aforesaid bull, and its provisions regarding government taxes and tributes make me hesitate; for, assuming (as a good Catholic) some influence of the Holy Ghost for the said pontifical declaration,16 my mind would be full of remorse if at the same time when I defend the increase of tributes I did not oppose the malversation of their proceeds, the superfluous expenses, the lack of economy in those who

administer them, and the numberless thefts from the royal revenues, which are the strongest objections that can be raised against my proposal.

24. It is certain that the vassals are under obligation to pay tribute to their kings, but it is likewise certain that they have the right, in equity, that what they pay as tribute be well employed, and that punishment be administered to those who steal, extravagantly spend, or misapply those funds; for in the honest administration of the royal revenues consists the greatest comfort of the vassals and the prosperity of the [respective] monarchies. The remark made by a celebrated French writer is [worthy] of note: that if the ministers of the king of España in the Indias were not so dishonest the royal incomes would amount to more than those of all the powers of Europa. The vassal complies with the obligation which rests on him, but the kings do not fulfil theirs; for they let go without punishment all the theft, all the robbery, all the iniquity committed by their ministers. I am well aware that there cannot be government among men without these defects and vices, which without exception are utterly incurable, and all the nations of the world have committed them from the time of Adam; but he who knows our general misgovernment of the Indias and the numberless robberies which are committed [therein] will be astounded to see that the criminals are not punished. [At the same time] he is certain that the royal revenues are in great part consumed by those who manage them, while if some exemplary punishments were inflicted the thefts would be greatly checked; that, by not curbing these, heavier burdens are laid upon the vassals; and that these protest against the tributes which are imposed upon them, [levied] not strictly for the maintenance of the dominions, but in order to enrich the officials, who (especially in the Indias) make enormous fortunes with what they obtain by defrauding the royal exchequer—or, to speak more correctly, by plundering those who pay tribute.

25. If in the collection, administration, and allotment of the royal revenues there were application, zeal, disinterestedness, and economy, it is evident that the vassals would not be compelled to contribute with so many imposts and taxes; for with what is plundered and misapplied in one year the expenses could be met for the half of the following year, and perhaps, instead of increasing the taxes, it would be possible to make some reductions of these to the vassals who should be considered most burdened.

26. I have not the slightest doubt that the tributes which have been hitherto paid in these islands are not sufficient for maintaining them in a condition so respectable as that which I have already proposed; and if for this chiefest reason I have defended the increase of tributes, I likewise retract this opinion in case our court do not apply the most effective remedies, in order to check the robberies and malversations which during

my time I have seen, and that they may not be responsible before the stern tribunal of God for such hardships to the Indians, and for the robberies, which will be committed in greater number in proportion to the increase in the funds which will be handled. For, strict as is the obligation of the vassals to contribute to the expenses, or pay tribute, equally so is that of the sovereigns to make proper distribution of what is contributed, and to endeavor that it be not misapplied; and so long as kings do not fulfil this obligation, by appointing zealous and disinterested officials, and punishing with the greatest severity those who are not such, there will be few persons who will venture to express opinions in favor of increasing the tributes. But [when such measures are taken] I will be the first to withdraw from this statement of my opinion; for I have always believed that the aforesaid condition [of honest administration] was inseparable from such increase.

27. I will note other objections which have been made to me against increasing the tributes; but, before mentioning them, I protest my veneration and blind obedience to the royal decrees of my king and sovereign, whose upright conscience will consider what is most in accordance with its internal peace, the rectitude of his royal intentions and the comfort of his vassals, by mercilessly punishing those who defraud the royal treasury, and issuing such other commands as are expedient.

28. There are many who restrict the powers of the sovereign which I mentioned in section 2 of this chapter, and who say that the [various] countries, when they instituted kings, did not dispossess themselves of all the authority which the people of the nation possessed; but that the latter reserved something, especially in the matter of taxes, which were proposed and demanded by the kings, while the vassals granted or denied them—[the objectors] drawing conclusions from this ancient method, and (especially in our España) from the convocation of parliament [cortes]; that the power of the king to grind his vassals is not absolute, and that these do not depend in such matters on the will of their kings alone. I frankly state these objections, which, even though they be paltry (on account of the positive opinion of the sovereign, supreme, and absolute power of our kings, who recognize no superior on earth), it is expedient for those who ought to anticipate them not to overlook; for, in order to render a question clear, and to foresee all the difficulties in its decision and practical result, a knowledge of the replies and objections which may be made is always helpful. I content myself with pointing these out, and repeating my [assertion of] invariable obedience to the royal commands of my king and sovereign, as I stated in the preceding section.

29. [Some] persons will also raise objections against what I have stated in the fifth section, that in all nations imposts and taxes are increased,

according to their necessities and exigencies, and that, when this time [of urgency] is ended, the vassals are set free from such burdens; but that in España there is no impost which may not be perpetual, as has generally been the case with all—and the "Man of San Quintin" demonstrates it in his memorial, attributing the ruin of the monarchy to [the imposts,] the millones and sisas especially.17

30. These and other objections I will answer briefly, by saying that the presumption of the law by which it is believed of all public officials that they conduct themselves conformably to justice, so long as quite the opposite is not evident, is stronger and more effective in favor of kings and their wise prime ministers—who, with more enlightenment, a profounder knowledge of the [affairs of] state, well-known zeal for the welfare of the monarchy, and the proper maintenance of their lofty honor and character, have decided and will decide these matters, in which we who are inferior and of more limited abilities ought to render subordinate our own opinions, and honor with the utmost respect their wise decisions, persuading ourselves, as is just, that in their councils they have borne in mind all the considerations which can produce the most advantageous judgment, before it is made known to the public. For however satisfied one may be with their reasoning, he would admit that he was convinced if it were possible for him to hear the substantial arguments which influence the royal proceedings of our sovereign—on account of which I, more than any other person, submit these productions of my dull intellect to the superior comprehension of his Majesty and his zealous ministers, protesting that I do not presume to furnish enlightenment on these subjects because I might think that they do not possess it, but in order to manifest my intense desire that what is understood to be beneficial to the state, to the glory of the nation, and to the welfare of all the vassals, may be carried into execution.

31. It will be necessary to assume that the increase of tributes in these islands will be resented in the greater part of them, and that, in order to obtain it, the precaution of stationing fifty or sixty soldiers in each province will be necessary; in view of this, the Indians will not cause the least trouble, while if they see us without military forces the aforesaid increase will be entirely impracticable.

32. Equally it must be assumed that so long as the Moros invade the provinces the Indians will resist paying tribute; for they will represent that for the defense of their villages they are employed during most of the year in making bulwarks, stockades, and little strongholds, and with weapons in their hands, on account of having no aid from the king which will secure them from the said invasions; and in truth they ought to be heeded in this point. To this end I repeat that in these islands some respectable forces are

necessary, and with them must be punished the haughtiness and insolence of the Moros; for at the sight of this example the Indians will be encouraged, they will attend to their labors, they will regard with respect the affairs of his Majesty, and they will assuredly pay the tribute which may be imposed upon them, without danger of their revolting. To this end, a circular edict or decree should be drawn up, in which, suiting the mode of expression to the disposition of the Indians, should be fully explained to them the motives which constrain us to the said increase, and the obligation under which they lie to pay their share of the expenses for their spiritual and temporal maintenance under the mild sway of our Catholic king and sovereign, and for freeing them from the tyranny and servitude to which they would see themselves reduced if these islands should, for lack of military forces, pass over to another sovereign.

33. This edict or order, carefully prepared, and translated into the idiom of each province, can produce many good results if we proceed with an understanding of the character of the Indians, and [in accordance] with the ideas that are necessary, which ought to be communicated, by instructions, to all the alcaldes-mayor and corregidors of the provinces, according to the circumstances of each one—imposing the most severe penalties on those who do not exactly fulfil the orders which the government may entrust to their management and conduct, and offering corresponding rewards to those who shall distinguish themselves in the execution and success of the new order of things, which ought to be established in each province.18

34. In order to [secure] the observance of the said ordinance, it will be expedient that when the tribute is increased the salaries likewise should be made larger. An alcalde-mayor has twenty-five pesos of salary a month, which makes three hundred pesos a year; but before he leaves Manila for the province to which he is assigned he spends a larger sum [than that] in the fees for his documents and in the notary's office, and for the securities [that he must give]. In three years his term as alcalde comes to an end, and the expenses of his residencia cost him four hundred to five hundred pesos; and it needs but little less for the settlement, presentation, and despatch of the accounts of the royal revenue. Thus all the salary which he receives on account of being alcalde, which amounts to nine hundred pesos in the three years, is not sufficient for the aforesaid expenses; for the rest of their maintenance have been invented the thefts from the royal revenue which they handle, and from the Indians within their jurisdiction. For this reason, and likewise because these offices have usually been sold, as a rule they are filled by men who are not very trustworthy. But if suitable pay were assigned to them, there would be many persons of known probity who would seek them, transgressions could be more severely punished, plundering would

be decreased, the appointees would furnish better bondsmen for the security of the royal exchequer, and the Indians would not experience oppression.

35. The poverty of the alcaldes-mayor, their being loaded with debts when they go from Manila, and the ambition to become rich in a short time, draw them into trading with the product of the tributes in each province; they buy vessels, lade them with goods, and convey these to Manila, or send them to other provinces. If the vessel sink, if the Moros seize it, or if it run aground on some shoal and the goods are damaged, or if any other disaster occur, the alcalde loses nothing, for he possesses nothing; and the damage is suffered by the king alone.

36. All this would be remedied by paying them more; for there would be more reliable alcaldes, and they could be compelled to deposit in the royal treasury every year, by means of their agents, the royal revenue of their respective provinces, in order to avoid the aforesaid contingencies, which here are common.

37. With better alcaldes, all the provinces would be well governed. For what is more melancholy than to surrender authority over them to persons who are incompetent, nobodies, in distressed circumstances, vicious, and thieves? How is a man of this sort to govern fifteen, twenty, or forty thousand Indians? If he cares for nothing except for conducting his own business, how is he to attend to the affairs which concern the king and the Indians? If the alcalde is inefficient, or coarse, or ill-bred, or of little capacity, how is he to govern well? how is he to administer justice, and how civilize his subjects? How is he to furnish reports on subjects which his limited intellect does not comprehend or fathom? How is he to look after the cultivation of the soil, the collection of its products, making plantations, and other things for which the ordinances provide?

38. This disappointment, this disorder, this misgovernment, and the thefts from the royal revenue can only be avoided or remedied, for the most part, by increasing the tribute and giving larger salaries to the alcaldes-mayor, the corregidors, and the other officers of justice in the provinces. There is occasion for the same increase of pay in the posts of public and royal officials, and the subordinates in the accountancy of the royal exchequer, in order to stimulate them to better work and greater zeal and application in the affairs of the royal finances.

39. In the royal storehouses there would be an end to the incredible infractions of law and the thefts by the storekeepers, by giving this position to honorable Spaniards, with suitable pay; and abolishing the mischievous abuses in the waste and consumption of supplies—with unchangeable

regulations for the incomes and expenditures; for the respective account-books of the storehouses and the appointment of an auditor for verifying them; for the credits and debits of the accounts, with vouchers for them; for the obligation and responsibility of the storekeeper; for the weekly inspection which ought to be made by the royal officials, in order to acquaint themselves with the condition of all these matters, and ascertain whether or not they are properly attended to; and for many other things, which contribute to greater economy in the royal revenues.19

40. In order that there shall not be such confusion, it would be expedient to separate the storehouses, or divide what belongs to the artillery and military supplies from all the rest; and to abolish the dependence of the storehouses at Cavite on those of Manila, making the regulation that in the said port be entered and unladen whatever is necessary for the equipment of ships, galleys, and other vessels of the king, without its being necessary that the vessels from the provinces which come with property belonging to the royal account should unlade their cargoes in these storehouses [at Manila], from which various goods are sent back to the said port. This causes greater expense, on account of the detention of the seamen, and because of the vessels and men that afterward are employed in conveying to the said port what [supplies] it needs, in which also they are exposed to the uncertainties of the sea. This is avoided and spared by the direct discharge of cargo in the said port, where, in fact, the main storehouse ought to stand, because there three-fourths of the goods belonging to the royal account are consumed.

41. The superior government gives orders for the hasty equipment of some vessels to cruise against the Moros, and for other purposes. The cordage, the sails, and all the rest, are sent from the Manila storehouse; the said vessels set sail, and come to supply themselves with provisions at these storehouses. Who does not see the loss of time and the increase of expenses which are uselessly incurred, and which could be saved if the storehouses at Cavite contained what they need?

42. Although what I have touched on in these last sections may seem a digression from the object of this chapter, they will be excused by those who remember what I had already stated in section 26, and by those who think that the increase of tributes will facilitate the increase of salaries. This measure will give the superior judges more discretionary power for punishing the thefts and illegal acts which are diminishing the royal patrimony, to the injury of the vassals — who have no right to complain that those who render them faithful and disinterested service should be well paid; but their right in justice calls for punishment to those who, receiving

suitable pay, satiate their covetousness with the blood and sweat of those who are wretched.

43. With the increase of tribute, numberless other matters could be regulated, for the settlement of which it is needful to begin spending money. All my plan and project is based on this chapter, for in no other way — although these islands can be supported with the economies which I set forth to his Majesty in my advices of the year sixty, without the necessity of the royal situado — will it be possible to place the country in the respectable condition of strength which can oppose the nations who are established in this part of India, or to produce so great advantages to the royal exchequer. I therefore desire that these reflections of mine be carefully considered, in order that, with other opinions that carry more authority than mine, the royal and upright conscience of my beloved king and sovereign may make such decision as he shall hold most expedient; and I shall content myself with having brought forward what is dictated to me by fidelity and affection, the zeal of a good Spaniard, desire for the glory and increase of the monarchy, and the general welfare of these islands and of the entire [Spanish] nation.

44. And if, notwithstanding the cogent reasons which justify the increase of the tributes, it be preferred to employ with these vassals an extraordinary degree of mercy, without a resulting deficiency in the means for supporting the islands with respectable forces this could be made practicable by establishing the tithes20 for the maintenance of the ministers of religious instruction, that of the cabildo of this holy metropolitan church, with its archbishop, and the suffragan bishops with their churches; for the wine for masses, and the oil for the lamps; and even for the missionaries — all with the saving, for the royal exchequer, of these great expenses.

45. Nearly all the provinces have their military posts, with the garrisons corresponding to the greater or less danger of enemies; and this expense is another of the heaviest incurred by the royal exchequer, which would be able to save it (in default of the increase of tributes) by laying upon the Indians and mestizos the burden of such contribution as shall be deemed necessary for maintaining the said military posts. [This would include] the pay of the troops in garrison, the cost of transporting them and of the shipment of provisions, clothing for the men, and the purchase of necessary arms; for all this would contribute to the benefit of the provinces and of their inhabitants.

46. And if, for the same reason which I have stated for the military posts, there be exacted from the natives of the provinces the cost of the thousand soldiers distributed among them who are mentioned in sections 9 and 10 of chapter third, the total saving to the royal exchequer will exceed 260,000 pesos, or will come near to 300,000. With this, and the product from the

tributes (if these are paid as hitherto), and from the other sources of income, there will be in the royal treasury funds sufficient for the maintenance of the islands according to my plan, provided that the rules be observed which I set forth in my memorandum of suggestions and in my advices to his Majesty. Thus will be secured these objects: to make our power respected throughout India, to avoid the expense of the royal situado which comes from Nueva España, and to gain the many advantages which have been mentioned. I shall speak of these in the second part of this work, in which I am going to treat of navigation and commerce, the gains from which will be more than enough for maintaining these dominions, even if the tributes are not increased.

Part II

Of navigation and commerce: the method for establishing them in these islands, and their great benefits.

Chapter First: In which it is demonstrated, with examples, that no power can make itself respected in the world without navigation and commerce

1. I do not presume to utter new things, but to arouse the minds of Spaniards to follow the examples of the other nations, to which end I have drawn from the works on history, both ancient and modern, what confirms this idea. [This chapter is interesting, but the limits of our space make it preferable to omit most of it, as having but slight connection with our main subject; the following sections are worth retaining.]

17. In the fifteenth century was begun the manufacture of woolen stuffs [paños] in Inglaterra; for before that they sold (as we are now doing) their woolens to other nations, especially to the Flemings and the people of Brabant—from whom some seditious persons went over to the said kingdom, about the year 1420, and taught manufactures to the English. Monsieur de Thou,21 however, attributes this establishment [of a new industry] to Queen Isabel [i.e., Elizabeth], and to the disturbances, on account of religion, in which the great Duke de Alva and the Inquisition of España were insulted—without having borne in mind, when he allowed his pen to move with the envious and bitter temper that swayed him, that, many years before the revolution of some of the seventeen [Netherlands] provinces which threw off the mild yoke of the Spaniards, the artisans of Lovaina [i.e., Louvain] had already introduced the manufacture of woolen stuffs in Londres.

18. The French, who in the opinion of Cardinal Richelieu were totally unfitted for commerce, have made with it and navigation the most felicitous progress, especially since the reign of Louis Fourteenth.

19. Nor must I omit the height of glory and power to which the empire of the Muscovites has been raised since the reign of the great Czar Peter. That nation was ferocious, barbarous, and slothful, and had no intercourse with other and foreign nations. That glorious monarch formed the design of civilizing the vassals of his Russian empire, and of turning their inclinations toward political affairs, the sciences, the fine arts, and the great advantages which result from so praiseworthy occupations; but [even] his uncommon intellect found no other means [for this] than that of navigation and commerce. But he went incognito to Inglaterra and Holanda, under pretext of renewing certain treaties, but in reality with the idea of gaining instruction in those two sciences, which were his only aim. In this he actually succeeded, by dint of immense labor and mechanical occupations, which, if apparently they were unworthy of a prince, were afterward (as they still are) those which most enhanced his glory. Not to linger over what is well known, I conclude with what is to my purpose: that the great Czar Peter established commerce in his empire, overcoming insuperable difficulties; and from the year 1697 (which is the real date of that enterprise) to the present time so marvelous has been the progress of that empire that its forces by sea and land, its wealth and products, its manufactures, its vassals transformed from barbarians into civilized beings, learned men, and politicians, yield to [those of] no other power—all being due to commerce, which in the short time of sixty-seven years has wrought these apparently incredible prodigies.

20. The Swedes and Danes22 also have made much progress through this means; and the Portuguese, glorious in their conquests and discoveries, have constantly declined ever since they neglected navigation and commerce, regarding these as occupations unworthy of their nobility.23

21. Almost the same has happened to our España; what fear, what respect, what terror, did not our armadas inspire in the four quarters of the world? There was no power that could resist them; but, not to linger on the glories of our nation, I leave that to the histories which relate them— especially those of the reigns of the pious king Don Fernando, the Catholic monarchs, the emperor Don Carlos Fifth, Don Phelipe Second, and Don Phelipe Fourth, who certainly protected navigation and commerce. I will assert [here] only what answers my purpose: that our navy declined, our great manufactures in Sevilla, Segovia, and other places retrograded, and our commerce deteriorated, with the continual wars; and, as we did not repair this damage, we were at the same time promoting the commerce of the other nations. These have made themselves rich through our negligence and

inactivity — selling to us all the more commodities the more we abandoned manufactures, and with their gains increasing their shipping the more that we gave up shipbuilding — until in these latest reigns our shipping and commerce were reëstablished. But it is necessary to extend our commerce further, in proportion to our vast domains; otherwise, we keep them greatly exposed [to danger]. For it has been now thoroughly proved that navigation and commerce have rendered formidable and terrible the forces and power of the nations who have practiced them, as also that from the decay or neglect of these activities has proceeded the ruin of kingdoms.

Chapter Second: Of the liberty of the Spaniards to navigate by way of the Cape of Good Hope

1. Some may think that this navigation is prohibited to the Spaniards by the treaties of peace, and that on this account we have not established a commerce like that of the Dutch, English, French, Swedes, Danes, and other nations. But it is certain that there is no such prohibition, and that our natural inactivity, laziness, and lack of application to commerce, has been the cause of our not undertaking the aforesaid navigation, which is equally free to us as to all the other powers. For the prohibition that the Englishman, the Dutchman, and the rest can lay upon us is, that our ships may not enter their ports, just as they have been forbidden to enter our ports; but they cannot hinder us from navigating in all the seas of the world, in accordance with natural right and the law of nations. That law does not allow the dominion of the sea to any power, according to Grotius, Heinsius, and others — contrary to the Mare clausum [i.e., "closed sea"], of the Englishman Selden,24 who in regard to the dispute of the year 1653 defended the [English] dominion of the White Sea, and the right of forbidding this navigation to the Dutch; but they maintained their freedom with powerful fleets, and with the same arguments which justify the freedom which the Spaniards possess for navigating by way of the Cape of Good Hope.

2. As the Dutch have always regarded these islands with suspicion, fearing some injury to their own commerce, they likewise have striven in every way to make amends for the damages which they fear. One of these is the extension of our commerce, because it diminishes their own; and, in order to hinder it, they have sometimes chosen to avail themselves of article 5 in the treaty of Westphalia in 1648, and of article 10 in that of Utrecht in 1714 — in which is confirmed the said article 5, wherein it is provided that "the Spaniards shall retain their navigation to the Eastern Indias, in the same manner as they enjoy it at present, without being authorized to extend it further; as likewise the inhabitants of this Low Country [i.e., Netherlands] shall abstain from frequenting the places which the Castilians possess in the

Eastern Indias." From these expressions, and from the demarcation [made] by the supreme pontiff Alexander Sixth, the Dutch—who claim, by right of conquest, to enjoy the privileges and prerogatives of the Portuguese—try to argue that our ships have no right to navigate by way of the Cape of Good Hope, nor along the regions of Asia—the Coromandel Coast, Vengala, the Red Sea, etc.—intending that these Philipinas Islands shall be the limits of our navigation to the west.

3–8. [In section 3, it is shown that the demarcation of Alexander VI was made only to check possible disputes between the great Catholic nations of Spain and Portugal, and its provisions referred only to their discoveries of lands and isles, and not at all to the navigation of the sea, which no power can claim, "since it is not fitted for other dominion than that of God." Section 4 shows that the Portuguese and Spaniards have frequented each other's ports, without any difficulties arising between them over the navigation of those seas, which has not been and could not be forbidden to the Spaniards; and that even if the Portuguese had had any such exclusive right it could not pass over to the Dutch when they conquered the former nation in India, especially as privileges granted by the Holy See to its Catholic followers could not be claimed by Protestants. In section 5 it is asserted that the previously-cited article 5 of the treaty of Westphalia does not forbid navigation past the Cape of Good Hope, but only the entrance of Spaniards or Dutch into ports belonging to the other power; that navigation on the high seas is, "by natural right, free to all the world," and the object of the treaty was to protect both powers in their respective possessions and commerce. As further proof of this, Viana cites (in his section 6) the Hague treaty of 1650, and comments on it in section 7. In the following section he shows how the Dutch are claiming what was never granted by Alexander VI, who separated only the conquests of Spain and Portugal, and not their navigations in the high seas, a distinction which has been observed in the practice of both countries, "who have freely navigated and traded through all the seas of the East and the West." He claims that Japan and China "are, without doubt, included in the demarcation of Castilla."]

9. Equally within the demarcation of España are included the kingdoms of Siam, Camboja, Cochinchina, and, in the other direction, Borney, the Molucas, and the other islands of the Malays—as was declared in the year 1524, by the geographers appointed for this purpose by the crowns of Castilla and Portugal, to whose decision the respective sovereigns agreed. As for the prohibition of navigation, if the demarcation of Alexander VI were to have been observed, it was clear that the Dutch must admit the right of the Spaniards to prevent their navigation through the seas of the kingdoms and provinces here enumerated, as also through those of Japan

and China, to which the Dutch ships go every year; or else that they have not any right to forbid to the Spaniards the navigation by way of the Cape of Good Hope. For by the admission of those very Dutchmen, in a letter which the governor of Batavia wrote to the governor here [at Manila], in regard to a balandra seized by the Spaniards in the island of Mindanao (which belongs to the crown of España, and is within the limits of the aforesaid demarcation), they say that the Spaniards could not enjoy dominion over the rivers and ports of Mindanao, and that only the authority of the petty king there ought to be acknowledged; and they add that it is lawful for any power to navigate there, and make observations on the situation of those lands and towns, and to trade therein with the vassals of the princes who possess them. This carries conviction [of the principle] that as little ought the Spaniards to recognize in Eastern India any other authority than that of the princes of the ports and towns where their ships make port; and that it is lawful to navigate through those seas, to reconnoiter those lands, and to trade with their vassals, as has been done hitherto. For our ships have gone to their ports, where they have been well received, as happened recently with the ship named "Guadalupe," in the past year of 760; and those who have come to this city, under various flags—Moro, Armenian, Malabar, Chinese, Siamese, and others—have met the same friendly reception.

10–11. [Viana asserts that, although "long use and immemorial possession may be a certain title to dominion over the sea," in such instances as that of the Venetians over the Adriatic, and the Greeks over the Ionian, this cannot be true of the claim made by the Dutch (as having conquered the Portuguese settlements) to the dominion of the great seas that lave India and Africa. These waters are too vast to be possessed by any one power, and have always been freely used by all nations. Moreover, the influence of Alexander VI and his successors had always been in favor of the Catholic monarchs of Spain, and of the preservation of the law of nations—"which presumption is taken for granted whenever for just cause temporal dominions are changed by the paramount power of the supreme pontiff."25 He also cites Solorzano to support his contention. The final section repeats the statement that the Dutch cannot forbid the Spaniards to navigate through the seas of India, and past the Cape of Good Hope; and adds, "Would to heaven that we had the eyes to perceive the advantages of this navigation, which are the following." Thus he prepares for chapter iii.]

Chapter Third: Of the advantages of the commerce carried on by way of the Cape of Good Hope

1. The distance of these islands [from España] deprives our court often of news; occasions delays in the correction of so many infractions

of law; retards all governmental measures; gives opportunity for the commission of many iniquities; discourages those who are zealous for the royal service; causes incredible expenses to the royal exchequer, and to the inhabitants of these islands; and detains the citizens here, as if in a place of banishment,26 since they are not at liberty to return to España, nor have they means to pay the expenses of the long and grievous journey over land and sea, by way of Acapulco. All this would be in great part remedied by carrying on navigation and commerce by the Cape of Good Hope.

2. The clothing for the troops is brought from Mexico; it costs much, and serves only to kill the soldiers. If it came directly from España, it would be of better quality, cheaper, and more suitable for garments; and our [Spanish] manufactures would have this market.

3. The wine for masses comes by way of Vera Cruz; it crosses the entire kingdom of Mexico, and is shipped at Acapulco; and it arrives here with so many leakages, damages, and costs for transportation that it costs very dear—and sometimes it is mixed with water, to replace what the muleteers drink on the route [across Mexico]. If it came by way of the Cape, there would not be this uncertainty about celebrating mass and the wine would cost much less.

4. The iron which has been purchased here from the Dutch, English, and others at very high prices would cost much less if it came directly from España, and foreigners would not carry away our silver. I say the same of the lead, copper, gunpowder, balls, bombs, grenades, and cannons, which have always been bought from foreigners, on account of the negligence of the Spaniards—who, although they have [material for] all the said [supplies] within the islands, go outside to find it, for lack of application in working the mines.

5. The many thousands of pesos which the king has expended in the transportation of missions by way of Nueva España, the detention of the religious in the said kingdom in order to await the galleon (for which delay the king pays), and the amount that is contributed for clothing to the religious orders of St. Dominic and St. Francis, would have been largely saved, and can be thus saved in the future, if the said route be established. Among the ships of that navigation will come to these islands many belonging to the commerce of Cadiz, and on the other hand other ships will go to Cadiz from here, among which there will be many who will undertake [to convey], some one article and others another of the numberless commodities which can yield some profit. With this trade it will be known what the Philipinas are; our court will have more light [about them]; the infractions of law and the iniquitous acts, of which it will have accurate information, will be

punished; and the measures of redress will not be delayed for four or five years, as is now the usual case.

6–7. [Viana (in section 6) reminds the government of the great advantage which the proposed route would give in sending news of an outbreak of war with any power, enforcing this by the ignorance of the Philippine colony, in the late war with England, of any hostilities with that country, of which Manila learned by the coming of the English squadron to attack that city. He urges (section 7) the lack of available shipping along the South American coast, and "the incredible amount of money which the equipment at Acapulco of the fragata 'Santa Rosa' (which by accident arrived at the said port from Perù) cost; and the injuries which would have followed to these islands if the divine Providence had not made ready the said fragata for our succor. Thus will be seen the advantage of the aforesaid navigation and commerce, for, without its costing the king any money, he will have in Cadiz vessels for carrying out the orders and despatching the succors and provisions which his royal compassion shall regard as expedient."]

8. Conducting our commerce from these islands to España by way of the Cape of Good Hope, the commerce of the foreigners must necessarily be diminished, and they will not obtain so much silver from us. In most years there come to the port of Canton, in the empire of China, twenty-four, twenty-eight, or thirty ships—English, French, Dutch, Swedish, and Danish; they carry our pesos fuertes (which is the money most valued in China and throughout India), and some European commodities, as fine woolen stuffs, and Brussels camlets [carros de oro] (which the Chinese use for their outer garments27 in the winter-time), some pearls, and clocks, and much wine; cochineal [grana] from our own America, and the opium of India, are also two main lines of this commerce.

9. Such is the lading of the said ships, which return to Europa with chà or tea, and with some porcelain, some articles of furniture in lacquered or varnished wood, rosewood escritoires, and candlesticks and other articles of white copper;28 and, finally, they carry a great amount of silk, both raw and in fabrics, which is their principal lading. The raw silk is used for the European manufactures, and with the fabrics they transact most of their trading. Each of the aforesaid nations has its agent in Canton, who during the year disposes of such goods as his ships could not sell; he furnishes to the Chinese the designs [for fabrics] which are every year invented, and they weave the stuffs of the same width as those of Europa. Afterward they sell these, as coming from Francia, Inglaterra, and other European countries, without any one being able to detect the fraud except those who have been in these islands—where it is notorious to all that this is true; and he who may doubt it will find this statement confirmed in the "Universal Dictionary" of

Sabary.29 A large portion of the said fabrics or stuffs come to Nueva España in our trading-fleets, and, although they are of the same quality as those which the galleons carry from here to Acapulco—with only the difference that the latter are wider and somewhat more lustrous than the former—there is a very great difference in the prices; for the mere name of "French" or "English" confers value and estimation on the said fabrics throughout the kingdom of Mexico, and the mere name of their being "Chinese" renders those which go by way of Acapulco of little value.

10. This fraud only the traders of Manila thoroughly understand, because they see it every year; the traders of Cadiz would be equally aware of it if they carried on commerce in the empire of China, as the foreigners do. They would also discover in the same way numberless small wares of Canton make which are sold in España as made in Londres and Paris, as is the case with the snuff-boxes of all kinds, whether gold or silver, or of tortoise-shell or other material; with lace-bobbins [palillos] of mother-of-pearl, ornamented with gold, and those of finely lacquered or varnished work, painted; and with various other curious articles of mother-of-pearl, ivory, etc.

11. All of these desirable articles, and many more, could be obtained by our ships, if they came via the Cape of Good Hope to these islands, which are on the route to Canton. At Cadiz they could take on cargoes of woolen stuffs, which here are used for riding caps and coats,30 liveries, and in China for outer garments, as I have said; Brussels camlets, which both here and in that country are greatly used; wines (and thus the Swedes, who carry it from Cadiz to Canton, and the Dutch and the English—all of whom carry away our money, and make us pay sometimes a peso fuerte for a single bottle of red wine, and for that of Xeres—would be deprived of this [source of] profit); hats, which the foreigners sell to us at high prices; silk hose and thread under-stockings; mirrors; crystal chandeliers; branched candlesticks, and lanterns; vases, cups, and other kinds of glassware; European paper; thread for sewing; britannia linens, fabrics from Cambray, etc. (which are brought at much cost from Batavia); silver and gold galloons and laces, which also the Dutch sell (and would to Heaven that the great extravagance of Manila in this respect might be prohibited!); and numerous other articles, which persons who have a practical acquaintance with commerce can name better than I, and which, if used, would be recognized as highly beneficial.

12. Of course the said lines are of recognized utility and large profits, both for the Spaniards who may ship them by the said route of the Cape, and for those who will buy the goods in these islands, at more moderate prices. Above all, the profit would remain among Spaniards; our Spanish manufactures would have this additional market; we would succeed

in stopping the foreigners from draining away all our silver. For it is an intolerable grief to good Spaniards that, when more than two hundred millions of pesos have come to these islands since they were conquered, there are not now found in them eight hundred thousand pesos in ready money. [This is] because our own inactivity and lack of application causes us to buy from foreigners the very articles with which these dominions abound, or which they bring from our own España—as is the case with the iron, the copper, the lead, the saltpetre; with the cinnamon, cloves, and pepper; with the wines; with the woolen stuffs; with the mirrors; with the hats, hose, galloons, and other articles, of which some are manufactured in our España, and others are produced in these islands.

13. The Spanish ships which make their navigation by way of the Cape could supply, as I have said, these islands with what they need, and carry from them to Canton many excellent products which the foreign ships cannot include in their cargoes. Such are birds'-nests, nacre or mother-of-pearl, carey or black tortoise-shell, indigo and dyes from Pampanga, balate, tapa, deer's sinews, hides, sybucao, ebony, lumber, and other things, which have a great consumption in China; on this account every year cargoes of these commodities are carried thither by the champans which come here to trade, and by the barks which depart from here for Emui and Macao. With these products, and with the commodities from España, the said vessels would ship at Canton the same goods that the foreigners are taking on; the royal duties at Cadiz would be the same; our manufactures would be greatly promoted; the profits would be as great [to the Spaniards] as the losses to the said foreigners; the products of these islands would be cultivated according to the market for them; and, finally, in time many other advantages and benefits would be made evident.

14. The said ships returning from Canton by way of this city, in order to pursue their voyage to Cadiz, could carry some products of the islands— such as very fine petates or mats, hats of the same kind, and cotton; tortoise-shell, palomaria; tamarinds, dragon's blood; manungal,31 and jars of the same wood, which is very medicinal; various especial roots; gold; sibucao, which resembles brazil-wood, for dyeing; pepper, which yields very abundantly wherever it is cultivated; sugar, which does not cost here two cuartos a libra; dried candied fruits; and, finally, they would have the benefit of the cinnamon, with which our mountains abound from Samboanga to Caraga in the island of Mindanao; it would be the most valuable line of commerce. These mountains are in the same degree of north latitude as those of Ceylan, where the Dutch obtain all the cinnamon; and it is judged, on account of their location, that the quality of the cinnamon also is the very same. For in Ceylan likewise cinnamon grows that is thick and gummy,

like that of Samboangan, and if the latter were cultivated like the former, it would be equally good.32 The cinnamon of Mindanao will be as good as that of Ceylan if the king prohibits the latter in his dominions, and facilitates the consumption of the former; and if the Spaniards had begun to sell their cinnamon before the Dutch did so, ours would now be of better quality than theirs.

15. As soon as I arrived in these islands and had made myself somewhat acquainted with this subject, the inactivity and indolence of our people caused me much sorrow; for although we possessed this exceedingly rich treasure, there had been no one who devoted himself to its development. This I explained, among other things, to his Majesty in my report of June 5, 1760, showing what these islands could produce, the valuable products with which they abound, and the possibility of maintaining them without the situado which annually comes from Mexico. In the following year came Don Nicolas Norton Nicols,33 who, it seems, proposed at the court the project for [developing] the cinnamon, and brought a royal order from his Majesty that he should be aided therein. I did so, with the utmost energy and readiness, and this famous and skilful Englishman began to make plantations in Caraga; people assure me that he would have carried this work to completion if God had not taken away his life, through the grief which he experienced at the attack on us by the English, from whom he expected no favor. It was necessary that a foreigner should accomplish what no Spaniard had done in some two hundred years;34 he died on account of our misfortunes, and now there will be no one who will devote himself to the same enterprise; for these citizens have no thought of any further occupation than their everlasting laziness, nor have they the spirit to risk four reals, or any zeal for the nation.

16. Even without its cultivation, there is a wide market for all the cinnamon which comes from Samboangan. The greater part of it is used in these islands, for chocolate, and brings a very good price; for ragouts and for liquors, it is stronger than that of Ceylan; and it is being shipped, as for several years past, to Nueva España. In Samboangan no cinnamon is procured besides what the natives gather in order to better their wretched condition, but this produces a sufficient quantity. This is enough to prove that if the Spaniards would apply themselves to the cultivation of the cinnamon of the said mountains; to making new plantations, the bark of which, as being more delicate, would yield better cinnamon than that of Ceylan; and to gather what Nature herself produces, without any [human] labor: this commodity alone would be capable of enriching the islands and the Spanish commerce, and of annihilating that of the Dutch. The Dutch company supports existence, notwithstanding its many losses and

obligations, on the cinnamon and [other] spices, fixing the prices of these at its pleasure, as being masters of this commerce—which indemnifies them for their losses on other things, and for the incredible costs of fortresses, troops, and [commercial] establishments in the aforesaid island of Ceylan (which would not be incurred in our cinnamon mountains).

17. The iron is another valuable product of these islands; there are mountains of this metal, the ores of which yield seventy-five per cent, only twenty-five per cent being lost in the fire. To judge from the abundance of ores in the said mountains, iron to supply the world can be obtained from them. Before the English came to attack us, the working of these mines was vigorously pushed; it was in charge of Don Juan Solano and Don Francisco Casañas. In less than eight months they established furnaces, coalpits, barracks, forges, and other facilities, and they mined a large quantity of iron; but everything was destroyed, as a result of the loss of Manila, because some malevolent persons went to plunder and destroy all the works. But it is absolutely certain that all the iron can be obtained [here] which the islands need for nails, plows, bolts, cannon-balls, bombs, grenades, cannons, and *carajayes*, and for other uses, which amount to more than one hundred thousand pesos every year, without the iron costing three pesos a pico. [It is also certain] that if this money remains within the islands—an amount of which hitherto the Dutch, English, and Chinese have drained us—they will become rich, and diminish the commerce of the foreigners.

18. The commerce in the iron that is necessary for these islands will alone produce, in fifteen or twenty years, more money than what they now have; and if the Indians were compelled to clothe themselves with the fabrics of the land, even with the little commerce that we have the islands would abound with silver. The trade with Nueva España in iron would be extremely advantageous to his Majesty; for the mines of Sonora and other provinces further inland cannot be worked, on account of the transportation from Mexico of the great amount of iron and quicksilver that is necessary; and this, and the expenses which are added for the conveyance of silver to Mexico, leave very little profit to the miners.

19. In carrying the iron from these islands and the quicksilver from Peru to Acapulco or to La Navidad, these effects can be transported in small vessels, and with little expense, to the coast of Guadalajara; they will cost less than if purchased in Mexico; at least thirty or forty pesos will be saved on the transportation of every arroba; and, if on the return trip by the same route the silver is embarked for Acapulco, there will be a great saving of freight in the transportation of this metal.

20. Let a computation be made of the money which must have gone out from the islands since their conquest, in order to purchase the very products

in which they abound, and the amount will be incalculable for the items of cinnamon, iron, saltpetre, and other products. Let also computation be made of what the outlays must have been for purchasing wines, mirrors, and the other things which, as I have stated above, could be brought directly from España; and it will be seen that by our own fault we have enriched our enemies, and that we could have annihilated their commerce and increased our own with only the sources of gain which are pointed out in the present exposition. Then let us, even though it be late, have the discernment to avert our total ruin, by striving, with glorious emulation, to secure the greatest prosperity for the Spanish nation.

Chapter Fourth: Of the necessity for forming a company in these islands

1. By a royal decree dated at Sevilla on March 23, 1733 (in which the project was carried out which was approved by his Majesty on April 26, 1732), there was established by our lord Don Phelipe Fifth, of undying memory, a company with the name of "Royal Company of Philipinas,"35 under fifty-eight articles and stipulations. These were full of the most unusual privileges and liberties that can be granted, and were even more advantageous to the Spaniards than those which Louis Fourteenth granted to the French for their Oriental Company; but I do not know exactly for what reason—some attribute it to the loss of Torres's trading-fleet—the paternal affection did not prove effectual with which our beloved king and sovereign took an interest in making the Spanish monarchy prosperous by the extension and promotion of commerce (the only means for securing wealth), imitating the examples of almost all the nations of Europa, who, in order to become rich, have established their companies in the Orient.

2–12. [In these sections Viana expands this last statement, enumerating the nations who have enriched themselves by the Oriental trade, and the companies formed in each for this purpose. First were the Genovese and Venetians, who traded with India by way of the Red Sea; they were afterward driven out of this trade by the Portuguese, in consequence of the discovery by the latter of the route via Cape of Good Hope. (Section 3.) "Portuguese trading-fleets of thirty ships came to the commerce of India every year, and for Brasil alone sailed fifteen to twenty ships laden with merchandise from India—besides others which carried on trade in China, Japon, Persia, Arabía, Mosambique, Melinda, Sofala, and other regions. But now that commerce is so reduced that only one or, at most, two ships sail from Lisboa yearly, which would not be the case if they had established a company with adequate capital, which is the only way of making commerce lasting." The Dutch at first bought spices from the Portuguese, and then resold them at a huge profit to the other European nations; but Phelipe II prohibited the spice trade to Portugal, and the Dutch therefore formed a company to operate in the Orient, and trade directly with its peoples. As finally constituted in 1602, this company had (section 6) a capital of 6,600,000 florins ("according to Savary"); and "in less than four years the members received the principal of their shares with the great profits which they obtained." At the time of Viana's writing, the Dutch company were maintaining "twelve thousand men, regular troops, in their twenty-five fortresses in India, and were able to equip 30,000 militia in their colonies, especially that of Batavia" (Savary). Viana cites another authority, Samuel Ricard, who places this militia force at 100,000, and states that the company employed in the Eastern trade more than 160 ships, each carrying thirty to sixty cannon, besides forty ships of the line (which number was increased in time of war). This enterprise ruined the commerce of the Portuguese (who had been the first to open the sea-route to India); "from that time until now it has steadily diminished, and is the poorest in all India; this has been the result of their not having formed a company with capital, and with respectable forces to oppose the conquests which the Dutch made. For they had a better opportunity than the latter, and it would have cost them less to maintain a flourishing commerce, as was that which they already possessed, than it cost the Dutch to establish a new commerce by dint of money, conquests, fortifications, and enormous expenses." The English company (section 8) sent out its first fleet (of four ships) in the year 1600; its capital was 369,891 pounds sterling. After various fluctuations of fortune, it was reëstablished in 1698, and attained great prosperity, so that its capital had increased to 1,703,422 pounds. In Viana's time, "the ships from Madrast for London (more than fifty in number) carry annual cargoes of five to six million pounds, according to the estimate of Sabary; and, taking into consideration the increase which this commerce has had since he published his famous work, the 'Universal Dictionary,' it must by this time be worth some ten millions. This does not include the operations of the private English traders who traffic among the colonies of India; this may be inferred from the duties which they pay in Madrast, which, at the rate of five per cent, produce for the company 80,000 pagodas. This sum amounts to 120,000 or 130,000 pesos, estimating the pagoda at twelve and sometimes thirteen silver reals." The English company were maintaining in constant operation 150 ships and fragatas, and more than fifty smaller vessels, employed in their commerce between India and London alone; to the great expenses of this navy must be added those of the company's forts and garrisons in India, which indicate how enormous were their profits. An Englishman told Viana that the king of England was owing to the company more than 36,000,000 pesos, the amount of loans which they had made to the crown in various emergencies. The Oriental commerce of the Dutch was further encroached upon (section 11) by the trading companies formed later in France, Sweden, and Denmark, and proposed in Prussia;36 these were protected and fostered by their respective governments. The commerce of the Dutch "would have been ruined if it were not for their being exclusive owners of the spice trade—of which only the Spaniards are able to deprive them, since we have in these islands cinnamon, pepper, cloves, and nutmeg." As all those nations maintained forts, garrisons, and war-ships, the necessity of opposing these armaments with like forces has imposed on the Dutch enormous additional expenses. Viana says (section 12): "I know not what reason there can be why that which is so beneficial to all the powers should not, with even greater cause, be an advantage to España, which holds her conquests in peaceable possession, and has valuable products in her dominions; moreover, she has forts and ports which at little cost can be rendered impregnable, and better opportunities than any other nation for a very flourishing commerce. Yet she labors only to enrich her enemies, abandoning to them the commerce which our people are unwilling to carry on, and surrendering to them our treasures and wealth, in exchange for the greater part of the commodities and products which our own lands produce."]

13. If the Spaniards would form a company in the islands, similar to the foreign companies, and according to the pious anxiety with which the magnanimous heart of our beloved king and sovereign Don Phelipe Fifth, of undying memory, was concerned in this matter, all the nations who trade in India would have the same experience as the Portuguese and Dutch. Our commerce would annihilate or [at least] diminish that of all the India companies, who cannot find a market for their goods if they do not trade these in our dominions—and this they could not do if the Spanish company had large capital, and ships for navigation and trade in España and the Americas. If we could fortify the towns and garrison them, as has already been explained, the other nations would find themselves under the necessity of spending much more than they now do, in order to defend themselves against our power, if war should break out. This increase of expenses on the one hand, and diminution of their commerce on the other, are two excellent principles, which promise many advantages to the Spanish company—which, as it is not, like the others, compelled to incur these expenses, will be able to sell its commodities at lower prices, and the gains will be more certain.

14. In order to facilitate the establishment of this most beneficial company, the royal protection of our sovereign is absolutely necessary, and with it must be banished the contemptuous notion that the Spaniards form of the commercial career; for that notion usually leads them to keep their

chests full of silver, for which they sell the products of their family estates. As a rule, the Spaniards spend with great economy what is necessary for their maintenance, especially those in the little hamlets throughout the kingdom; and, as they enjoy no commerce, they deprive themselves of the benefits arising from commercial activities, with detriment to their families and to the public welfare. On the other hand, they imagine that there is too great a risk in the remittance of their silver by sea, because they are so little (or not at all) acquainted with nautical science and mercantile affairs; and, as timidity prevails in their minds over ambition, they consider themselves fortunate to keep their riches under their own eyes, without thinking of investing them. But they would take hazards on their money, if they were touched by that eager desire for gain which is inseparable from all commerce, and which is stimulated by the lure of profits.

15. There are, of course, many persons whose ability enables them to understand thoroughly the benefits of commerce; but they live remote from the marine ports, they have not trustworthy acquaintances to whom they can confide the management of their capital, and they sorrowfully deprive themselves of the benefits which they would derive from its employment, the result of which is that they lead idle lives, or sometimes yield to an extravagance which is excessive and impairs their fortunes. Even more melancholy than all that I have related is the sight of the Spanish nobility, without any occupation, and, as a rule, reared in extreme ignorance and idleness. This is the source of many excesses, the beginning of ruin to the most robust constitutions, a hindrance to the generation of children, and a cause of the lessening of population which is continually growing more worthy of consideration.

16. Let there be formed, then, an Oriental company, and let the nobles of the kingdom contribute its funds; the profits [on these] will awaken in them a liking for commerce, and they will become acquainted with this most useful branch of knowledge. They will maintain their [business] relations, they will have some occupation, and will not use up their fortunes with vicious habits; their children will be brought up with a liking for commerce, and the fathers will have the satisfaction of employing some of their sons in appointments under the same company. This is the most certain means for securing the happiness of families and the prosperity of the entire monarchy; for, if commerce and the naval service (which follows the other closely) are promoted, there will be no vagabonds or idlers. Rather, idleness will come to an end, and with it many vices, on account of the enormous number of men whom a company with large capital needs to employ by land and sea — not only for its business positions, but for manufactures and navigation, in which persons from all spheres of life find an opening.

17. What a number of people must be employed by the English and Dutch companies in the more than one hundred and fifty ships which each company maintains for its commerce, and in the various colonies in which they have established that commerce! And what advantages result to these two powers from keeping so many people busy, maintaining them at the company's expense, and freeing them from the idleness in which they would [otherwise] live! If those countries had not so great a commerce, vagabonds and idlers would abound in them; but this class of people is not seen there. On the contrary, there is great application to all the arts and sciences; for all have employment, and all are useful—some in manufactures, others in the military or the naval service, and others in commerce, etc.

18. The attainment of these fortunate advantages depends on whether our beloved king and sovereign will assure to his vassals all his royal protection for the promotion of the said company, following the example of his glorious father, Don Phelipe Fifth, ever to be remembered; for the money of the royal treasury is the main foundation for this great and most useful enterprise. For it cannot be doubted that, animated by the same spirit, there will be many contributors to the capital of the said company— all the nobility of España, from the highest rank down; the guilds of Madrid, which now form a body of considerable importance; all the merchants of España, the two Americas, and these islands; some foreigners; and many religious communities, who have set aside the proceeds of their funds for pious contributions—convinced of the benefits of this commerce, and of the prosperity which will ensue to the Spanish nation; and regarding it as certain that (as will be mentioned hereafter) our Spanish merchants, if assured of their gains by way of these seas, and the method of supplying the Americas, in great part, with the materials for clothing which they need, without the burden of the royal imposts, will not long for the illegal purchase of foreign commodities.

19. There are also other advantages, worthy of being known, which render the above-mentioned project more feasible. One of these is the abundance of timber for the construction of ships; at least ten ships can be built every year in these islands; and, by taking care of their many forests, even if a hundred ships were built now there would be enough timber left to construct every year the ten that I have mentioned. The Viscount del Puerto greatly praises (in book 9, chapter 10, article 2 of his Reflecciones militares37) the project of a friend of his (whose name he conceals) for forming a company in these islands; and among the products which it yields he mentions the timber called tiga (it is not known here by this name), extolling its strength, and setting forth the advantages of carrying this wood to España as ballast for the ships.

20. This wood (of which, according to the said author, the strong ships of Philipinas are built) is in my opinion the teca [i.e., teak], which comes from the Coast; or that which is known here (and I am inclined to think that this is meant) by the name of molave. This abounds in all the islands, and is so compact that it petrifies in the water, which I myself have seen; of it are made the ribs of the ship's frame, the knees, and all the principal timbers that strengthen the ship. The keels are made of another wood, equally strong, which is called guijo; it never rots in the water, nor does the boring worm, which is bred on the ships in the port of Cavite, penetrate it. There are other woods as useful as the guijo, and among them is the dongon, which is better. As a rule, the lower masts are made from the mangachapui, which is another timber of especial value; for, although it is somewhat heavy, it never splinters, and is very elastic. The yards and topmasts are of palo maria; and for whatever is made of boards the lavan, the banaba, and the tangili38 are also used, from which kinds of wood very long and broad planks are obtained. There are pines here, and various other kinds of trees, which can be put to the same use; and plantations could be made of the teca tree (the wood of which lasts more than a hundred years in the water), for there is more than enough land for this purpose in the vicinity of Manila and Cavite. Likewise, sawmills could be built, in order to save the expense of [hiring] sawyers; also dry-docks, for careening the ships and preserving them under cover.

21. In Ilocos are manufactured the blankets which serve as sails for our ships; and canvas can be made (as it has been) of excellent quality and in enormous quantities, for there is no end to the cotton which is and can be gathered, with the greatest facility, and of the finest quality. Moreover, on the many tracts of land which the sloth of the Indians leaves untilled hemp could be cultivated—which, even if it should not yield well on the lands of one province, would without doubt succeed on those of another; for there is nothing among all the products of the earth which is not afforded by these islands, by searching for the climate—whether hot, cool, or temperate—which is suited to the needs of the crop. Flax would be produced with the same ease as hemp, without any other cultivation than that which rice receives on irrigated soil [en tubigan]; and the seed of both these plants has been sown, and is yielding very well, in the province of Cagayan.

22. There is much pitch, and cordage is so abundant that it can be supplied to all the ships of España, with what is made here; and, in order that it may be evident whether it is suited for this purpose, I will explain in detail how on this may depend the question of saving the expense of purchasing cordage in foreign kingdoms, by availing ourselves of that produced in our own dominions. [The fiber used for] cordage is both white and black; the

former is known by the name of abaca, which is obtained from the bark of a tree resembling the plantain, the trunk of which is heckled like [the stems of] hemp. The fiber is very harsh; tar scorches it, and for this reason no tar is used in these ships; it is stronger than hemp, as experience has shown. It is usually of service no longer than for one voyage; the threads shrink much, and on this account all the cordage here is heavier than that of Europa. On twisting it, it is apt to break, and in order to avoid this it is cured by placing it for some time in salt water, and drying it in the sunshine, then storing it until it is needed; for if this precaution be not taken, and it becomes spattered or moistened with fresh water, it will soon become rotten. With some additional expense the cordage could be made finer and smaller, without changing its quality; it would then be more easily handled, and the manœuvers of the ships would be more expeditious.

23. The [fiber for] black cordage (known as cabo negro)39 is obtained from a plant which they call gamù, very similar to the coco, and it is a veil which covers the entire tree, from the top down; it grows out between each pair of leaves [entre òja y òja] of the gamù, like long hair, or tufts of hair. It is exceedingly harsh, and for this reason it is used only for cables, of all sizes, and to some extent for tackle and rigging; and there is nothing with which to compare its strength. It lasts many years, but it is necessary to keep it either under water, or uncovered, where the dew and the rains bathe it; and in dry weather water is thrown over it, either salt or fresh, for its better preservation; for if it stands in the sun and wind, without these precautions, the threads break, and it loses its extraordinary strength. It is also preserved by keeping it in a shady place, where the wind strikes it but little. These two kinds of cordage are exceedingly abundant in these islands.

24. There is another sort of cordage, [made] from the husks of the coco, which is superior to the other two; for with the said fiber the ships can be calked, and [even] after many years the bonote (thus they call it) comes out as fresh, strong, and sound as on the day when it was thrust between the planks. Of this species also there is a great abundance.

25. The anchors can be cast here, by putting into operation the iron mines of which mention has been made; and I can say the same of the cannons, the balls, the grape-shot, the bombs, and the grenades. For, I repeat, there is iron in these islands for supplying all the world, and there are men enough to mine and manufacture it, if there be brought from España some skilled directors (who are not found here). If it be desired to work the copper, there are mines of this also, although I cannot speak with the same certainty of these as of the iron mines; for I have not come across any records to show whether the said metal has been worked at any time, and what the product

was. The same thing is true in regard to the lead mines, but I have seen ores from Paracale, which were smelted at Bacolor, by order of Don Simon de Anda; and I do not doubt that, if we had skilled master-workmen in this and other industries, many useful discoveries would be made through the agency of the aforesaid company, whose funds would allow the expenses that a private person is unable to incur.

26. To this concourse of advantages ought to be added the most important one that our Indians are exceedingly ingenious in the construction of ships. They do not understand arithmetic, or proportions and measures, or the computation of the weights of the various parts, or anything which requires knowledge; but if they have masters who will furnish to them models of the works, they imitate everything with the greatest accuracy, for they have exceedingly keen eyesight, and indescribable facility in making whatever they see. For this reason we have here excellent carpenters, calkers, and the other artisans necessary for the construction of ships, and in whatever number may be desired.

27. There is not an Indian in these islands who has not a remarkable inclination for the sea; nor is there at present in all the world a people more agile in manœuvers on shipboard, or who learn so quickly nautical terms and whatever a good mariner ought to know. Their disposition is most humble in the presence of a Spaniard, and they show him great respect; but they can teach many of the Spanish mariners who sail in these seas. In the ships of España there are sure to be some Indians from these islands, and investigation can be made to ascertain what they are. The little that I understand about them makes me think that these are a people most suited for the sea; and that, if the ships are manned with crews one-third Spaniards and the other two-thirds Indians, the best mariners of these islands can be obtained, and many of them be employed in our warships. There is hardly an Indian who has sailed the seas who does not understand the mariner's compass, and therefore on this [Acapulco] trade-route there are some very skilful and dexterous helmsmen. Their disposition is cowardly, but, when placed on a ship, from which they cannot escape, they fight with spirit and courage.

28. Let it be considered, then, whether these circumstances are worthy of regard, and highly advantageous for the company of which I am speaking—which likewise can save much money in the difference of wages; and any one will reason that not one of the foreign companies has had the opportunities which these islands possess for the establishment of a company, since all these things which are easy and of little expense for the Spaniards were almost insuperable difficulties for the Dutch, the English, and the French—who succeeded in overcoming them by dint of silver, of

conquests, and of fortifications; and by bringing from Europa supplies which we do not have to bring, because they abound in these islands.

29. In order not to be prolix in relating other advantages which the companies in general possess, as compared with the commerce of private persons, I refer to those which are set forth by the distinguished Don Miguel Zavala (in his celebrated memorial40 to Phelipe V of blessed memory), whose authority alone would be sufficient in order that no means should be neglected for establishing the aforesaid company in these islands; and I pass to other advantages which the said author explains. But first I will point out what relates to the fortunes in the Indias, which do not pass to the grandsons; this is accounted for by the vicious way in which the creoles, as a rule, are reared—the indolence and vices in which they are brought up, and the luxury and prodigality to which they are accustomed from childhood. If these fortunes, or the greater part of them, were [invested] in the company, they would not be so easily wasted; and, even if the sons should save nothing from the profits, they would keep the principal which their fathers might bequeath to them in the aforesaid company. Or, in case there were some persons so reckless as to sell their shares, others would buy these, and the commerce and its gains would always remain for the benefit of the Spaniards.

30. With the funds of a company, enterprises could be undertaken that would be both extensive and easy. The province of Pampanga alone is capable of producing more sugar than can be consumed in China (to which the Sangleys carry it when it is cheap), in the coasts of Coromandel, Malabar, and Vengala (where it is scarce, and is sold at a high price), and in all the ports of India; having a market, all that is required of this product will be supplied in abundance, especially if the said company encourages the Indians to cultivate their lands. It would be the same with the dyes; and with deer's hides, sinews, and *tapa* (or dried meat) which all come from the same province, and are sold to the Chinese who come here to trade. By establishing a mart in the capital [of Pampanga], on the company's account, it will gather in all the said products, in exchange for cloth, especially if credit be given to some persons until the time of the harvest; and the gains will be enormous, since profits will be made on the sale of the cloth, on the purchase of the products, and on the export of these to other colonies.

31. The same method ought to be observed in the other provinces for promoting the cultivation of the lands and the abundance of so highly valuable products as they yield; by this means there would be obtained in Pangasinan all the gold which the infidels bring down from the mountains there, which exceeds three hundred thousand pesos each year, and with that which is brought from other provinces reaches five hundred thousand

pesos. This commodity is very useful in all the commerce of India, and can also be carried to Europa, as is done by the English and Dutch, to whom regularly comes the gold from Philipinas; its current price is at the rate of sixteen pesos for the tae of 22-carat metal (each tae has the weight of ten reals), and in this ratio is purchased that of 21, 20, 19, and 18 carats.

32. In the provinces of Ilocos and Cagayan there might be excellent factories, to work up the great amount of fine cotton which they produce; and, by bringing skilled workmen from the Coast, the figured cottons which are brought thence could be made [here]. In all the Visayan Islands, in the province of Camarines, and in that of Albay, are made the choicest and finest webs, which they call nipis; and others, of commoner quality, which they call guinaras, and use for shirts. In Cagayan and Ilocos are woven very fine handkerchiefs, towels, coverlets, table-linen (which is of as good quality as that made in Flandes), terlingas, etc.; and if only these provinces are stimulated, and factories established with good master-workmen, the company can easily manufacture at least all the cloth which the Indians consume. As these number a million of souls, if we allow to each one an average consumption of no more than one peso, this would amount to a million of pesos; and the greater part of this amount, which now the Chinese, the Dutch, and the English carry away, would remain in the islands, and would increase the profits of the Spaniards and the losses of the said foreigners.

33. The cacao is very abundant and cheap, and if it could find a market in other colonies and kingdoms the crop of it would be still greater, because the Indians would devote themselves to its cultivation.41 Entire groves of the coffee-tree could be planted, since it yields fruit everywhere; it is milder than that of Mage [i.e., Mocha?] and its fruit is gathered in the year when it is [first] planted, on account of the richness of the soil. Rice and wheat, if the natives applied themselves [to cultivating these], as they would do if they had a market for them, would be sold at good prices throughout China (where these grains are scarce), in Cochinchina, in Siam, in Camboja, in Pegu, and sometimes in the Malabar and Coromandel coasts. Wax — of which these mountains are full, and which is sold by the infidel Indians who inhabit them — has a great consumption here, and much of it is shipped to Nueva España; and if it were bartered for cloth, as was said above, it could be procured in greater quantity. Tobacco, oil, and sulphur are very abundant. Horses are valued in the said coasts, and, although there are many of them in these islands, there would be more if the ranchmen had a better sale for them; for at times they are accustomed to kill the horses, in order to dry their flesh and sell it. Carabaos and deer, whose flesh is likewise dried, yield some pesos. In fine, the following are recognized articles of merchandise

in different places in China, Cochinchina, Camboja, and Siam: sugar, rice, cotton; indigo, dyes, sibucao (a sort of Brasil-wood), deer's sinews, pepper, black tortoise-shell (called carey), nacre shells (or mother-of-pearl),42 birds'-nests, ebony; tapa (or dried meat), balate and camaron (both which are shellfish), and bonga; cables of cabo negro—all of which commodities these islands produce. [To these must be added] cochineal from Nueva España, fine cloths and camlets from España; lead (which also is produced by these islands, although it is not mined), and other articles, as stated above, of which better information will be given by practical merchants.

34. For Vengala, the Coromandel and Malabar coasts, Persia, Zurrate, and other parts of India, are found useful indigo, sugar, sibucao, sulphur, siguey, birds'-nests, cotton, rice, gold, and horses; and, in one word, all that has been said in the preceding chapter (speaking of the private commerce which could be carried on via the Cape of Good Hope) ought to be understood, with greater reason, of the commerce which can be carried on by the company of which this chapter treats. For this reason I omit what I said there of the cinnamon and other products which the company could develop, with its funds and systematic arrangements, better than an individual could; for the latter may die, and the former continues perpetually to carry on the enterprises of manufactures, mining operations, the cultivation and promotion of crops, and the exportation of all these to foreign kingdoms and colonies. For all will be successful in these islands with the Indians, who, if well paid, will do what they are ordered to.43

35. I have already mentioned the indescribable readiness with which our Indians learn perfectly whatever they see, even without the necessity of a master to instruct them. There are some who write well, without knowing how to read, as they have had no teacher; for by their natural inclination they devote themselves to imitation of the letters, and easily succeed in doing so, without being able to read what they write. This is one proof of their readiness, above mentioned, but they have still more of it in embroidery. It is a marvelous thing to see, that there is hardly an Indian who cannot embroider, and that they learn this art without any teacher save their own attention and their extraordinary patience. The hands of the Indian women are the most delicate, for every kind of sewing and needlework; and the company, by availing itself of this skill of our Indian men and women, could employ an innumerable number of people in embroidery, needlework, and the making of hose—they make them of fine quality, in Zebu of cotton, and in La Laguna of silk—and obtain much profit through these industries, in finding a market for them.

36. Near Paracali in the province of Camarines there is abundance of rock crystal, very transparent and choice. In the province of Cagayan are

some stones that are very singular and rare; one of these is emerald-green veined with gold or golden-brown, and when well polished it looks like a mirror, or like the finest jasper. Another is a stone as white as marble, similar to that which abounds in the mountains of San Matheo near Manila (from which has been made the paved floor of the Society's church in this city); and who knows what Nature is keeping concealed, for our enlightenment, in the provinces and mountains of these islands? Assiduity, good taste, and the desire for knowledge would discover many things if there were Spaniards here who would devote themselves to the investigation and examination of the many rarities in the plan of Nature.

37. If there were any chemist and herbalist here, this likewise would be an immense aid for making further discoveries and experimenting with many trees, roots, herbs, and medicinal stones. For instance, the narra;44 in cups made from the wood of this tree water becomes, in a very short time, of a most beautiful blue color, and people say that it is useful for curing obstructions; the wood called manunga, which is extolled for its remarkable virtues; the seeds of the catbalonga, or St. Ignatius's kernels, which are already known and esteemed in Europa; the shell in which the cocoanut grows, in which water soon becomes exceedingly bitter; bezoar stones; and innumerable other articles from which homely remedies are made here, among the Spaniards as well as among the Indians. The latter make much use of the remedies produced in the islands, and know some, both herbs and woods, which cure the most hideous and bloody wound in twenty-four hours. The rhubarb45 may be smelled [sehuele] in many woodlands, and no one is acquainted with it; the herb of Calamba is especially good for preventing, by [the application of] its juice, the bad results of a blow or fall. More than all, in the mountains of Mindoro there is a tree called calinga, the bark of which has a delicious odor, which smells like cinnamon, cloves, and pepper all combined; I made a small quantity of chocolate, using the said bark powdered instead of cinnamon, and it was very pleasing to the taste. In the ship "Santissima Trinidad," which the English captured, I was sending to Madrid some lozenges and many pieces of the said bark, which is a delicious flavor for seasoning ragouts; and I have used it in my household. Señor Anda also sent to Madrid the aforesaid bark, and, I think, chocolate made with it powdered. So great is the abundance of these trees that there are mountains, many leguas in extent, which produce them.

38. If the foreigners had these trees, they would have already introduced in the world the use of this commodity, with enormous profits; and we, if we possessed industry, and zeal for the interests of the nation, would have been able with this tree, to lessen the consumption of the cinnamon and cloves of the Dutch. Let these points be considered, and the advantages will

be recognized which can assuredly be expected by the company which may be formed in these islands—regarding it as certain that nothing will make progress, except by this means; rather, this colony will in a little while go wretchedly to destruction, without the least hope for its reëstablishment.

39. By way of conclusion to this chapter, I will note as the last (and an important) advantage of the aforesaid company the conspicuously fair treatment and friendly reception which the Spaniards have experienced, and may expect, throughout India. Our silver [money] is in good repute in all regions, and those peoples, especially the Chinese and the princes of India, show the greatest eagerness and make great efforts to obtain it, as being the most valuable for them; and, although the Dutch, English, French and other powers trade in this part of the world with our pesos, the Spanish ships are always better received in those ports, because they carry more silver and more products of these islands, which are held in very evident esteem.

40. Since I have been in Manila, I have seen only the traders from Canton and Emui in China visit this port,46 except the ship "Guadalupe," which went to the [Malabar?] Coast; and through its captain and officers I have heard of the friendly reception which they met in all the ports of India. But in other days the commerce of this colony was more extensive. In China it was established in the year 1598, and has been maintained without interruption; the king of Camboja asked this government for aid, and it was sent to him in the year 1594, leaving commerce with that country established. In the same year the king of Siam sent an embassy to open commerce with these islands, and in 1599 the said commerce was actually begun, by vessels which went from these islands, and which came from Siam, with which country the Spaniards have maintained the most friendly relations. This was recently experienced in the case of the ship which was built there in the year 53, by order of our governor the Marques de Ovando, who sent thither letters for the said king of Siam; and the latter, in virtue of these, furnished a sufficient sum of money, and gave all the other assistance which they asked from him. In the year 718, the same king of Siam granted a piece of land, in order that the Spaniards might establish a trading-post there.

41. In the year 1596, commerce with these islands was established in Cochinchina, and the Spaniards declined to establish a trading-post [on the land] which this king afterward bestowed upon them. In Tunquin also the Spaniards undertook their commerce; and in Zurrate, Vengala, and other kingdoms of India, both Moorish and heathen, they have been equally well received. Although, on account of the reverses of this commonwealth and the lack of courage in its merchants, the Spaniards have given up this commerce for several years past, it cannot be doubted that the aforesaid

company has the opportunity to establish itself advantageously, furnishing a market for the products of these islands, bringing hither those of the said kingdoms, and establishing (if that shall be expedient) some trading-posts—with which their purchases will be at more reasonable prices, and their gains in España and Nueva España more assured.

42. Here at the same time another advantage presents itself. The commerce which now is carried on with Acapulco by private persons suffers many losses, occasioned by the unsuccessful fairs there. These losses originate in the necessity of selling the goods in order to send back [to Manila] the money that they produce; for even if the merchants lose in the sale something on the principal which they shipped, it is necessary to sell their goods in order to repay what they obtained from the obras pias for their investments. If the goods are left in Nueva España, in order to take advantage of an opportunity for better sale, they cannot meet the cost of the expenses, and here find themselves tormented by their creditors. The company cannot be placed in such straits, but will always sell their wares to advantage and profit; for when in Acapulco they do not obtain good returns on the merchandise, they can transfer it to the storehouse which they will have to establish in Mexico. This expedient alone will be sufficient to induce the Mexicans to make strenuous endeavors to be preferred in the sale at the said port, because they will not deceive the said company as they now do private persons, acting aggressively against them, in order to fix arbitrarily the prices of their goods—constrained as our merchants are to sell them, on account of the limitation of the time [of the fair], since the galleons ought to sail from the said port by the twenty-fifth of March.

43. I will conclude this chapter with the authority of the celebrated Don Geronimo Ustariz,47 who, although he disapproves the commerce [managed] by companies in España and the Americas, considers it expedient in these islands; and indeed, when his arguments against the establishment of the said companies are examined, it will be seen that they do not apply to this commerce—where, on the contrary, it will be seen that not even the least progress can be secured, unless the company of which I am speaking be formed.

44. The same author, speaking of the commerce in spices, is inclined to think that it ought to be carried on directly by the Spaniards, by the same route which other nations adopt for it, arranging the purchases in these islands in order to supply the Americas and all España by the ports of Acapulco, Panama, and Portovelo. This exhibits the utility of what I have herein set forth, for it is confirmed by the three most earnest and distinguished Spaniards of this century, to wit, the Visconde del Puerto, Don Miguel de Zabala, and Don Geronimo Ustariz. But I am surprised that

this last-named writer, who treats the subject of commerce so extensively and so acutely, with the greatest erudition and knowledge of whatever there is to be known of foreign nations and countries, should be ignorant that these islands produce in abundance cinnamon, pepper, and nutmeg, which, without the necessity of buying it from the Dutch, we can use for our benefit, in order to supply all our own dominions. This is a proof that the Spaniards of Philipinas do not apply themselves to becoming acquainted with this country, in order to make known its products; and that they would not be [thus] ignorant if the alcaldes-mayor would make reports — one to their successors, and another to the government — of the condition of each province, as I advised his Majesty in the past year of 1760.

Chapter Fifth: Of the extension which the commerce of the aforesaid company can enjoy

1–3. [Viana makes remonstrance against "the limitations and restrictions with which the commerce of the Spaniards is established." These only enable foreigners to compete with them to greater advantage, and increase the gains of foreign traders. He adduces the examples of other nations in support of his position that commerce ought to be extended and freed from restrictions, as far as possible; and complains that Spaniards only are forbidden to trade with each other, in the colonies of that monarchy. (Section 3.) "The argument for this is apparently founded on the exportation of silver, and on the opposition made by the merchants of Cadiz, who are misled by foreigners, and that of the officials at Acapulco, who find their advantage in the said limitation. Those merchants are always inveighing against the injuries that result to their trade, and the check to our [Spanish] manufactures, with which arguments they have always tried to bring about the ruin of this [Philippine] commerce; but I will see if I cannot overthrow these arguments."]

4. All the silver that is coined in the dominions of España comes to a halt in foreign kingdoms, among our greatest enemies. The treasures of the Indias pass through the aqueduct of Cadiz, without leaving even a trace on the conduits of the Spanish merchants, as can be demonstrated by [comparing] the riches that the Indias have produced, and the poverty of the Spaniards. Upon this point I refer to what Don Miguel de Zavala says in his memorial; and that which the celebrated Macanaz has written on the same subject ought to be printed on plates of gold, or, better, in the hearts of our sovereigns and their ministers of state, in order to cure the wounds of their vassals with the remedies which he proposes. For if all the silver is carried away from the dominions of España, what more will she have, whether it go by way of Acapulco or by way of Cadiz? I assert that in Cadiz

the commerce of the foreigners is greater than that of the Spaniards: the latter (with the exception of some strong business houses, which have been built up in this century) support themselves by being figureheads48 for the former, who cannot possess the commerce in their own behalf or in their own persons. This is disclosed by the "Universal dictionary of commerce," in praising the good Catholic Spaniards in this illicit mode of carrying on business — which is the same as regarding them as being, even if not traitors, at least disobedient to their king. Here is seen the interested motive for [the claim] that the silver should not be exported by way of Acapulco, but that all should go to Cadiz, into the power of the foreigners — who are the ones who, in reality and with hidden hand, have always made opposition to this commerce of Manila.

5. Those who carry away the silver from Acapulco are all Spaniards, and the greater part of it accumulates in the empire of China, which has not waged war against us, nor will she do so, with the gains that we allow her; but those who carry away the silver which reaches Cadiz are the foreigners, and it is going to remain with the powers who are harassing and ruining us with our own wealth. Let these points of difference be compared, and decide whether it is not a weak argument, that of the export [of silver from Nueva España], against which so much clamor has been made by the commerce of Cadiz — or, to speak more correctly, the convenience of the foreigners — and I believe that it will be outweighed, not only by the loss of the royal duties which are yielded to the royal treasury by the silver which goes to Cadiz, but by the injury that is caused to us by the profits which we furnish to the foreigners. Moreover, the silver carried away from Acapulco can yield the same [amount in] duties, in order to avoid the aforesaid loss, if it be considered of much importance — which it is not; for even if two millions of pesos were carried away each year, and the royal treasury deprived of the duties thereon (for which privation there is no necessity), that is not a sum which merits the great opposition, if not bitter hatred, of the commerce of Cadiz for this poor commerce [of Manila].

6. The other argument, that of the retardment which our manufactures of España would suffer [in competition] with those of China, is as easily overthrown. It is certain that our factories cannot furnish all the goods which are consumed in our dominions, and that on this account the silks, fabrics, hose, ribbons, etc., of other powers are allowed entrance therein; and what more need is there, in the case of these wares than of those of China, for declaiming against the injury which the latter, but not the former, occasion? There is no further difference except that the Spaniards trade with one class of the goods, and the foreigners with the other. Against the foreigners there is no one to raise objections, as some of them do against

our own people; and as in these clamors there is no mention of the name of Englishmen, Frenchmen, Dutch, Swedes, Danes, Irishmen, etc., but [only] of the commerce of Cadiz and of its Spanish traders, the motive for this opposition is better hidden, the injury which they exaggerate is more readily believed, the minds of people are preoccupied with impressions of this sort; and the commerce of Manila, which has neither capital nor fame nor authority, and not so much influence as that of Cadiz, is the one which always suffers, which is permitted [only] with restrictions, and which cannot repair the damages experienced by the merchants of Cadiz without knowing them.

7. Before this, I had already mentioned the great amount of silk, both raw and woven, which foreigners bring from China, and that with this they supply their own manufactures, and [likewise] obtain money from us by selling in España the fabrics from Canton as if they came from Paris, Londres, Amsterdam, etc. Is this, or is it not, detrimental to our manufactures? and, if it is, why is not an outcry made against it by the merchants of Cadiz? They will say that it is impossible to prohibit this commerce, while our own manufactures are in so backward a condition; but why will this argument not avail the Spanish merchants of Manila? They will say also that the foreigners introduce into España not fabrics from China, but those of their own manufacture; that, whether it be from one country or from another, the injury to our manufactures is the same. But what cannot be denied is, that the foreigners who obtain so great an amount of silk from China trade it in our dominions, and that we cannot do the same in order to deprive them of those enormous gains. If, then, the company of Spaniards were formed in these islands, they could convey from China a great deal of raw silk for our factories, and many special fabrics which would be of as good quality as those of Europa; they could furnish them more cheaply than the foreigners do; and, above all, the profits would remain among the Spaniards. Our commerce would steadily flourish; we would have more ships, to make our dominions safe; the marine service would be increased; and necessarily there would be diminution in the commerce of the foreigners, for which our deluded Spaniards are pleading.

8. The royal duties will be the same, if the silk and fabrics of China are carried by our ships of the company, as if they were carried by the foreigners; and even if the kindness of our sovereign makes some reduction [in the duties], in order to favor the said company and subvert those that are hostile to it, other advantages, of greater importance than the aforesaid duties, will result to the crown, in the certain knowledge that, in the present state of things, that is prohibited to the Spaniards which is allowed to foreigners — that is, the introduction of goods from China which are difficult

to recognize in España, on account of the facility with which European fabrics are imitated in Canton.

9. By allowing to the aforesaid company the importation of Chinese goods into España, while the prohibition to foreigners remains in force, the trading-fleets and galleons will be supplied; and these commodities will be purchased less from foreigners, in order that our own manufactures and commerce may gain some growth.

10. All the silk which our company will put on the market will diminish the amount sold by the foreigners; and if they have not a market for this commodity they will take on smaller cargoes of it in China, Cochinchina, Canton, Tonquin, Tripara, Bengala, and Achem, and the said company will find it easier to purchase the silk. Before the nations of Europe carried away the silk from Canton, it could be bought at very low prices; but since they began to carry on this commerce—which was in the year 1685, in which the emperor of China opened his ports to all nations—up to the present time, the prices have risen more than three hundred per cent, as some merchants of this city have informed me.

11. In the six years that I have spent in Manila, the [price of] silk has risen every time; and because so much was being sent out of the country [of China], the emperor forbade, under the most rigorous penalties, the exportation of this product—of which an enormous amount is consumed in his empire, where it was already becoming scarce in the year 759—that it might be used by his vassals, whom he regards with the most extraordinary affection.

12. Finally, when the merchants of Cadiz become shareholders in the said company there will be no more talk of the export of silver by way of Acapulco, or of the injury to our manufactures from the fabrics of China; or the only ones who will cry out against it will be the foreigners connected with the said commerce [of Cadiz], when their names are made known, for they will not [then] have Spaniards to talk, as the saying is, "through a goose's mouth." If it shall be considered expedient (as it seems to me it is) that the aforesaid company may ship freely, and without any restriction, such wares as it shall think best to the kingdom of Nueva España, the royal duties can be so adjusted that the royal treasury will not suffer a great loss, under the certainty that the goods of the said commercial company will all be duly registered, as also the silver which they bring in return; for its directors will possess no authority for anything except what is according to the rules in the like method of commerce. This legality in the declarations [of goods shipped] will result in great benefit to the aforesaid royal duties, even though these be more moderate than the duties which are exacted

from private persons whose greed for gain urges them to convey, and to bring [here], many contraband articles.

13. For greater security on this point, it could be so regulated that there would not be the slightest uncertainty, by causing the agents or directors whom it will be necessary to have in this city, to write out the invoices of what they ship, according to the entries in their cash-books, and the same with the silver and the goods that are brought back in return—information of all this being sent from here to the officials at Acapulco, and reciprocally from that port to the officials at this capital, in order that on each side any possible infraction of the law may be known, and those engaged in the commerce be restrained from committing such. This exhibition of invoices and the returns in silver can be compared with the statements which the directors of the company will furnish, in order to ascertain whether the former agree with those which will be contained in the said statements. I take for granted that in the presentation, examination, and approval of these accounts there will be the supervision of some person appointed for that purpose by our sovereign—whose royal and benevolent disposition will, it is to be believed, place some capital in the company that I have mentioned, as a foundation for this great work; and in this case it is hardly possible that the least crevice will be found by which the royal duties might suffer loss.

14. The nobility of España, from the highest rank down; the guilds of Madrid, who now form a commercial body of much importance; all the merchants of España, the kingdom of Mexico, Peru, and these islands; some foreigners; and many religious communities which have set aside the produce of their funds for pious purposes—all these will, without doubt, become shareholders in the aforesaid company, if they are convinced of the benefit of this commerce, and of the prosperity which will ensue to the Spanish nation; and when the said merchants have their gains by means of these seas assured, and a means of supplying the kingdom of Mexico with a great part of the goods which its people need, without the burden of the royal duties, it is certain that they will not desire to purchase foreign goods, except at such advantage as will prove detrimental to the foreigners.

15. It is also evident that the aforesaid company will be able to furnish its commodities at lower prices than the foreign companies do; for it does not have to incur so many expenses in maintaining troops, fortresses, etc., as do the Dutch, English, and French; nor will the costs of the navigation be so great, because the voyage is shorter. Moreover, the purchases will be [made] in China, at the same prices as those of the said foreigners; and consequently, the company transporting its merchandise to España, and being able to furnish goods at more reasonable prices than the foreigners do,

for these reasons the profits will be greater and the losses of the foreigners more certain. By carrying the goods from these islands to Nueva España, the company will hinder the illicit commerce of the said foreigners, who in sailing from India to Europa, and from Europa to their colonies in America, must incur more expense than the said Spaniards, and will not be able to furnish commodities at the same prices as the latter can.

16. The English who come to trade in China carry these goods to the ports of Inglaterra, pay there the duties on them, and afterward ship them to various regions — among these to Jamayca, from which island they carry on a very extensive illicit commerce with the Windward Islands; with Nueva España, through Honduras, and by way of the coasts of Campeche and Vera Cruz; and with Peru, through the colony of Sacramento, and various other places. The number of laden vessels which enter Jamaica every year exceeds five hundred; and by this can be estimated the value of the goods which are [thus] disposed of (for all of these are carried into our dominions), and the great amount of silver which they carry away from us, thus causing loss to the royal duties of his Majesty — which, in proportion to the said goods and the money which they produce, would be very large.

17. Sabary, whom I have cited, estimates at eight millions of pesos the illicit commerce which the English carry on, from Jamayca alone, with the Spaniards of America; and he states, to the discredit of our nation, that all the ministers and officials, from the highest to the lowest, proceed by agreement to defraud the royal duties, and to become rich at the cost of what they seize from the royal revenues.

18. Probably no less is the amount of the fraudulent commerce carried on by the Dutch from Curazao; and much greater is that which is conducted by the two nations (and even by the French) in Puerto Rico, Cartagena, Buenos Ayres, Campeche, Honduras, Portovelo, Caracas, Guayaquil, and the Canarias Islands, and the other ports of the Windward Islands and the two Americas — as also is made known by the same author whom I have already cited, besides what we all know.

19. The new and very extensive territory which the aforesaid English now possess in North America, and on the Mexican Gulf as far as the Misisipi, renders this illicit commerce much easier for them by means of that coast, especially by way of the new Santender,49 which has a good harbor for vessels of moderate size, and many rivers; it is not far distant by land from Cretaro [i.e., Queretaro] and other rich cities of Nueva España, and by sea it is not far from Vera Cruz. With these great opportunities, the illicit commerce can be pushed to the utmost; for the ambition and covetousness of the trader despises no means which may bring him profit.

20. The commodities which the English illegally introduce [into our colonies] must necessarily be cheaper than those which go in our trading-fleets by way of Vera Cruz, for the latter pay many duties, and the former none; and the very English who sell in Cadiz to the Spaniards, paying their duties, sell the same commodities in Nueva España at a lower price than in Cadiz. Therefore, if some efficacious remedy be not applied to these illicit importations, I think that our commerce will be ruined; that our trading-fleets will experience great losses; that the royal duties will be diminished; and that in Nueva España the illicit commerce will reach an even greater extent than in Perù. But it also seems to me that if the commerce from these islands to Acapulco is free to our company the aforesaid losses can be in great part averted, for the following reasons.

21. When the foreigners (and especially the English) obtain so much silk, both raw and woven, from China we must believe that they find this commerce profitable, and that the said commodity is very cheap in the said empire, compared with the prices of silks in Europa. The profit is more obvious in the woven goods, because the infinite number of people who inhabit China, and the abundance of workmen in every kind of occupation, cause their manufactures to be exceedingly cheap—as all of us who live in this part of the world know by experience, who every year send to Canton commissions for many articles, because they cost us less than to make the purchases in this city. For instance: The Chinese and the Spaniards carry silver from here to Canton, where it is worth three per cent more; and nevertheless a snuff-box, a salver, and other small articles of silver cost less there than when made here to order—which shows the great saving of [cost in the] manufacture which results from the great abundance of workmen, as I have said.

22. This advantage which the English have through the commerce of Canton—to which port usually come every year thirteen or fourteen ships—can also be enjoyed by our company; and, buying at the same prices [as the English]; it can sell its goods at lower prices in Nueva España, even after paying the royal duties. For the English are obliged to make longer and more costly voyages, as is that from Canton to Inglaterra, and from there to España and Nueva España; while the Spaniards will sail from here to Acapulco. The former pay royal duties in Inglaterra, and the latter will pay these in Acapulco, saving the expenses of the second voyage which the English make, to their colonies in America. Finally, the Spaniards are not obliged to maintain, at so great expense as do the English, fortified posts and many troops, which are supported by their profits; for these reasons, the latter will not be able to sell their goods at the same price as that of the Spanish company. Consequently, they will not make illicit importations

[into the Spanish colonies] of silks and [woolen] fabrics; and even those of their linen goads (which are most to be dreaded) can be diminished with [our importations of] the light linen goods of China [liencesillo] (which are used in Nueva España), with "elephants" and other goods from the coast, and, in due time, with the cotton cloths which will be woven in these islands. Here there is abundance of cotton, and of people for its cultivation and manufacture—especially if some masters in this art come from España, or, in case that fail, from the Coromandel or the Malabar coast; and if among the Indians be introduced the spinning-wheels which are already in use in the manufactures of España.

23. From all these arguments it will be possible to conclude whether they are as well adapted to free commerce [of these islands] with the kingdom of Peru, and to that which the two Americas can mutually and reciprocally conduct between each other, in order that all the vassals may have a share in the extension of the commerce which hitherto has been prohibited to them; that the products of all the provinces may be increased, by the market which will be provided for them; that the Southern [i.e., Pacific] coasts of the said Americas may have an abundance of vessels; that they may mutually aid and defend each other from enemies; that by this means all our dominions remote from España may be more securely preserved; that our silver may have wide circulation among the Spaniards, who, occupied in this lawful traffic, will not expose their money to the risks of the illicit commerce; that the commerce of the foreigners may be diminished, without the least loss to the royal exchequer in the duties from them; and, in fine, that with the gains [from this commerce], and with the decreased exportation of silver to the foreign kingdoms of Europa, the prosperity of our monarchy may begin, and it may come to be the most worthy of respect in all the world, with the extension of its commerce—which is the sole and only means of attaining success; for no other means has been found more effectual, by either ancient or modern geniuses.

Chapter Sixth: Of the difficulties which the aforesaid company will encounter, in order to establish and continue its commerce; and of the method for preventing these

1. The difficulties and inconveniences which the celebrated Don Miguel de Zabala mentions, and the manner in which he entirely removes them, ought to be borne in mind in this chapter (like all the rest that that great man wrote), in regard to the establishment of our commerce through companies, in order that by the said work, and by what I have set forth, even the dullest person may be convinced of the usefulness of the Spanish company in these islands. Notwithstanding that the principal difficulty, and the only one to be

feared, is the efforts of the foreign powers, I will copy exactly the remarks of the said author, for perhaps not all those who see this document will have [opportunity to see] them; and I cannot dispel these fears with arguments more weighty, or persuasion more effective.

2–18. [Zabala admits the danger that other powers, angered at the loss of their gains through the success of a Spanish company, would endeavor to destroy it; but he regrets the timidity of the Spanish merchants, who allow themselves to remain at the mercy and dictation of foreigners. The Spaniards would readily take measures to end this, if entire secrecy were possible, but they fear failure if their intentions are known by the foreigners. They should remember that not only are the Spanish colonies in the Indias strictly forbidden to trade in any way with the other powers, but that the latter themselves had consented to these arrangements, which España had a right to make for her own colonies. Those powers will not seek by force the ruin of Spanish commerce, as that would be too costly an enterprise, but will endeavor to gain this end by craft and intrigue. If a Spanish commercial company were formed, its larger capital and more extensive business would enable it to withstand losses which would ruin private persons. All of these considerations should relieve the fears which check the free and wide operation of Spanish commerce and thus keep it within the clutches of foreign traders. Zabala urges the formation of Spanish companies for commerce, on which must depend the security of gains therein and the prosperity of España.]

19. It is hardly possible that the nations of Europa will unite to hinder the company of these islands. The Dutch will not fail to appear with their pretended right of authority to prohibit to us the navigation by way of Cape Good Hope; but with the arguments which are presented in chapter 2, part ii [of this memorial], and those which our wise ministers of state can bring forward in favor of our well-known right in justice, the said Dutch will find themselves obliged to admit it, or they will fear the injury which we can inflict upon them by hindering their commerce in China, Japon, and other regions which are included in the arbitrary division and imaginary limit made by Pope Alexander Sixth.

20. On the other hand, likewise, the Dutch recognize and fear the superiority of the English, who are doing them much damage in India—as recently they experienced, in the past year of 760, in their establishments in Vengala, and even in those of the island of Ceylan, to judge by some shrewd suspicions that the English were encouraging the king of the said island

in his revolt against the Dutch. If the Spaniards establish their company, the British forces will be further diverted, in case war should break out, by those of España and Francia; the Dutch will then consider themselves more secure, and will expect some aid in case they guide those nations to appropriate some [English] establishments; for the aforesaid powers will not, for their own advantage, consent that the English attain further superiority by unjust means.

21. The French also have a like interest in the formation of the Spanish company, and they will promote it, in order to have its aid, which may be to them very important; for if they had had it in the late war they would not have lost all their establishments in India; nor would we have lost the fortified posts of Manila and Cavite, if we had had the said company.

22. The lack of a port on the coast of Africa as a landing-place for our ships is another of the difficulties which our navigation by way of Cape Good Hope may encounter; but our friendly relations with the court of Francia will open to us, without doubt, free entrance to the port of Mauritius. With a knowledge, too, of the ports on the said coast of Africa, we can establish ourselves where we think it best to, as the Dutch have done; or we can find some island, like that of Santa Elena,50 which the English occupy, or those of San Matheo and Acension, which serve the Portuguese for a way-station.

23. The last difficulty may be the greatest of all, and it consists in the probable opposition of the ministers and officials of his Majesty to the ministers and officials of the company. For I assume, in the pursuance of my plan, that there will be here ships of war, a suitable force for the safety of these towns, a governor and captain-general, a royal Audiencia, royal officials, etc.; and that the company will have likewise its own ships, the construction of them, cloth manufactures in the provinces, the working of mines, the cultivation of cinnamon, and other enterprises, which without the aid of the government are difficult, but with it very easy. The aforesaid opposition to those of the company, and the unpleasant relations which follow (or are very probable) between the directors and the government, may be a very great impediment to all the said activities. But this, it seems to me, can be corrected by making suitable regulations, and his Majesty issuing very strict orders for their punctual observance, with heavy penalties against the transgressors; also by the company having so many protectors in the court as its shareholders, especially if the shares be taken by the highest nobility, as an example to the rest. These will be so many more public prosecutors, who will raise an outcry against those who, in whatever way, oppose the

interests of the company; and who will demand punishment for him who deserves it, in order that this may serve as a warning to others—under the well-founded assumption that the growth of the aforesaid company can interest no one so much as it does our sovereign, in order that the crown and the nation may be maintained with dignity and splendor, and gain credit by our commerce, and by the riches which it will draw to us if that commerce be undertaken and continued with the ardor which is demanded by love for our country.

24. I do not dwell so much as I might on this last difficulty, because it seems to me that what I have said is alone sufficient for taking the necessary precautions. As little will I take time to enumerate the advantages which would result to his Majesty from committing to the aforesaid company the government, management, and social order of these islands, with the obligation to maintain them with sufficient forces—for this purpose, [the crown] making over to it the tributes and the royal duties, and the company furnishing some amount to the royal revenues in acknowledgment of the [royal] authority, during the time while this sort of treaty or contract should last; on this subject, I could divulge something, if I did not realize the great difficulties therein.

25. Besides this, I consider that if his Majesty place these towns and islands under the plan that I have proposed, they can bring together their considerable military forces for the furtherance of the said company, and for such assistance as it may find necessary—so that the king may increase his royal revenues and the company save much expense, which will redound in material gains to its commerce, and to obvious damage to that of the foreigners.

26. By granting to the company the privilege of proposing [the names of] persons whom it considers trustworthy, to serve in the office of alcalde-mayor for the provinces where it will have its manufactures, cultivation of crops, or operation of mines, all possible advancement will be rendered easy, and the royal exchequer will preserve the royal revenues, by means of the said persons, for whom security will be given by the said company or its directors; and even the tributes of various provinces could be arranged, by agreement, with evident advantage and benefit to the royal exchequer.

27. Finally, all matters must be regulated on a very substantial basis— questions of government, the cases in which preventive measures must be taken, the protection of the company, and the powers which must be

granted to it, as will be unavoidable in order to obviate uncertainties and injurious dissensions, in regard to which suitable advices will be given on the proper occasion.

Chapter Seventh: Of the suitability of Panama and Portovelo, in case the navigation via Cape Good Hope be impracticable

1–2. [Viana briefly restates some of the conclusions reached in foregoing chapters, and proceeds to consider the possibility of the route via the Cape of Good Hope proving impracticable, in which case he proposes as an alternative the route via Panama.]

3. God has placed an isthmus midway between the two Americas, with the port and bay of Panama on the coast of the Southern Sea, and that of Portovelo on the opposite coast; although the former is of use only for vessels of medium size, there is another, called Perico, which admits ships of the line, their lading being conveyed in small vessels to Panama, which is two leguas distant. The second, which is that of Portovelo, is one of the most beautiful and well-defended ports in America; there are disembarked the goods of the ships from España, and they are conveyed to Panama; and the gold and silver and some products of Peru, which arrive at the latter port at the time of the [Spanish] trading-fleets, are transported to that of Portovelo by land, and by the Chagre River, for the return of the ships to España.

4. The Spanish company, when established in these islands, can have its storehouses and factors at the said ports; the ships which sail from here for Panama will leave there their cargoes, and bring back the goods which the ships of Cadiz will have carried to Portovelo; and these latter will in their turn do the same, leaving their cargoes at the said port, and, for their return voyage, taking aboard whatever might be sent to them from Panama.

5. This route would, without doubt, occasion greater expenses to the Spanish company than would the navigation via Cape Good Hope, but always many advantages to its commerce would result. If war should break out, the said route will be more secure from enemies, and our coasts will be better defended by the frequent visits of our ships to the said ports on the Southern coast; in that spacious sea they are not in danger of encountering enemies, as in the straits of Sunda, Malaca, and others of the Malayan Islands, through which it is necessary to pass in order to navigate through the seas of India and of the African coast, with risk from the nations of Europa who are established in both regions.

6. If the prosperity of the said company will be as great as the circumstances here set forth promise, we ought to expect that, in order to facilitate its commerce and save transportation, some part of its gains will be employed in the improvement of the Panama route — in making the Chagre River more navigable, and perhaps in seeking the easiest mode of joining the two seas, or in finding other means for conveying the goods by water from one port to the other.51

7. The idea of facilitating the commerce of España with these islands by the said route is not a new one, nor do I claim that it should be attributed to me; for it was brought forward in the year 1621, after the dangers of the navigation via Cape Horn [Cabo de Hornos] had been recognized, and it was realized what difficulties there were in conducting the commerce through those stormy seas. Information regarding it having been asked from the president and ministers of [the Audiencia of] Panama, "they brought forward so effectual arguments why it should not be permitted" (so Don Joseph de Veytia says, in his Norte de la contratacion) "that navigation by this route ceased."

8. Before undertaking any enterprise people's minds are usually dismayed at the multitude of hindrances which present themselves to the imagination; but all these are overcome, as a rule, by assiduous application, for the success of the enterprises which always are as difficult in their first stages as they are easy and simple in the middle and end of their course. The subject of commerce has encountered in our España apparently insuperable difficulties, which have intimidated the leading ministers in its promotion; and, while it cannot be denied that our nation has devoted very little attention to that most useful study, the science of commerce, our people ought to distrust the reality of the disadvantages which have been exaggerated in other times, and investigate them in these happier days. Therein the same difficulties will not be found, or it will be possible to obviate the injury which may be feared, by effectual measures for the greater stability of the commerce, the security of our dominions, and the welfare of all the vassals.

9. In Francia there was so much distrust on the subject of commerce that, its promotion and extension being deemed impossible, every project of this kind was rejected. Cardinal Richelieu, in his political testament, regards the French as incapable of commerce, as I have said; and, before this famous minister, his predecessors discussed the matter in no other fashion. But the great Louis Fourteenth and his most zealous and able [minister], Monsieur Colvert, overcoming dangers, scorning inconveniences, and trampling on

difficulties, resolutely undertook, with magnanimous souls, to render that easy which for so many centuries had been deemed difficult, and finally they succeeded. Then why will it not be possible also to render the transaction of our commerce successful and easy by way of Panama, conquering the difficulties which will be alleged against it?

10. I am not ignorant of these hindrances; but I believe that, however strong they may be, they will not prevail over the welfare of the monarchy, and that the elevated and magnanimous royal soul of our beloved king and sovereign Don Carlos Third (whom may God preserve) and his zealous ministers will overcome the difficulties which have been hitherto considered insurmountable, and will hasten with suitable remedies to check the ruin of our dominions, which had its origin in the great amount of illicit commerce of the foreign nations. Perhaps they will form an entirely opposite idea from that of other times, regarding the conduct of our commerce by way of Panama, in order to provide from these islands the commodities which are needed for España and the Americas, to assure the royal duties, and to overthrow the foreigners—who, as I have said, will not be able to sell their merchandise at so moderate prices as the Spanish company can; and it will be the only effectual means of preventing the aforesaid illicit commerce.

11. I have set forth, sincerely and candidly, what my limited ability comprehends, and the knowledge that I have acquired of these islands; I have touched on these subjects as concisely as possible, in order not to render this document diffuse and too wearisome. I doubt not that in it will be found many defects, since the practical knowledge of commerce is remote from my profession; on these points, others who are more intelligent will be able to bring forward their arguments. I will be content if all will be convinced of my love for the nation, of my desire for its greater prosperity, of my ardent zeal, and of my loyalty to my king and sovereign; these are the only motives which have constrained me to offer the reflections which I have here stated—availing myself, for this little work, of the small amount of leisure which the arduous occupations of my office leave free for me.

May God grant that the effects and results correspond to my good intentions; and for the sake of their best success, the preservation of these islands, the extension of Spanish commerce, and the happy advancement of the monarchy, may He render prosperous for many years the life of our beloved king and sovereign Don Carlos Third (whom may God preserve) Manila, February 10, 1765.

Francisco Leandro de Viana

1 The title-page of this valuable MS. reads as follows: "Demonstration of the deplorably wretched state of the Philipinas Islands; the necessity of [either] abandoning them or maintaining them with respectable forces, with the disadvantages of the first and the advantages of the second; what the islands can produce for the royal exchequer; the navigation practiced in their commerce, and the extension and profits of the latter. With reflections, which demonstrate the benefit of forming a company, under the royal protection, in order to render the Spanish monarchy prosperous and glorious, and to deprive its enemies of the gains by which they are ruining it in both peace and war. By Don Francisco Leandro de Viana, a student in the old college of San Bartholome el Maior of the university of Salamanca; former rector of the same college; graduated by the chapter of Santa Barbara in the aforesaid university; a member of the Council of his Majesty; and his fiscal in this royal Audiencia of Manila." It is followed by a letter addressed to the governor of the islands, Francisco de la Torre, with the date of March 20, 1765; this occupies eleven closely-written pages, and serves the double purpose of an introduction to Viana's memorial and of the official delivery of the document to the governor-general, as the representative of his Majesty. This preface rehearses the needy condition of the islands since the English invasion, entreats the royal aid for these unfortunate vassals of Spain, and briefly outlines the matter and arguments of the memorial. Vindel states (Catálogo of 1896, p. 94) that the printing of this memorial was forbidden by the Council of the Indias. It is of much importance, not only as showing the condition and needs of the islands after the English invasion, but for the light it throws on the condition of Spain, her relations with the rest of Europe, and with her colonies, and the national characteristics of her people. The memorial is here presented in full, except a few passages which are briefly synopsized, as they have but minor and indirect importance. Viana writes with authority, as being royal fiscal of the islands, a man equipped with the best learning of his day, and an ardent patriot.

The university of Salamanca originated in the cathedral school, before the twelfth century; and in 1243 it was made a university under the royal protection of Ferdinand the Saint, his son Alfonso X continuing this aid, enlarging its scope, and granting it many privileges. Later kings and several popes did much to aid and strengthen Salamanca, and it became the greatest educational institution in Spain, and one of the four greatest in the world; in 1584, it had 6,778 students. In 1401 Bishop Diego de Anaya Maldonado founded the first college for poor students, which was called the college of San Bartolomé, and later "the Old College." In 1845 Salamanca and all other like institutions were secularized, and placed under the control of the government. (Ramon Ruiz Amado, in the new and monumental *Catholic Encyclopedia*, now in process of preparation.)

2 "Since our entrance into this land, the Moorish [i.e., Mahometan] following has been greatly increased—not only through the ordinary traffic which the people of Macazar carry on in it; but because the santons of Meca, proceeding by way of the strait of Moca, come to Sumatra, and from there pass, by the strait of that island, to our islanders, with a diabolical inclination; they bring Alcorans in Arabic, and by means of these instruct our natives. A great number of these books were seized in La Sabanilla, and I saw them in the hands of Sargento-mayor Ponce, in the year 1724." (Torrubia, Dissertacion, pp. 2, 3.)

3 Probably referring to the Hudson's Bay Company, although that was actually organized in 1670; and the explorations of 1746–47 here mentioned evidently allude to the expedition of William Moor and Henry Ellis in those years, "for discovering a Northwest Passage"—a discovery for which the English parliament had offered a reward of 20,000 pounds. This expedition, however, was not under the auspices of the company, whose officials, on the contrary, treated Moor and Ellis with much harshness and even inhumanity.

4 On maps of North America made in the first half of the eighteenth century may be seen the great Mer d'Ouest, or "Western Sea," evidently an exaggeration of Puget Sound, to which only the entrance had then been discovered. The explorations of Martin Aguilar were made in January, 1603, in partial conjunction with Sebastian Vizcaino, who went along the California coast with two Spanish vessels, Aguilar being in command of one of the ships. Bancroft (Northeast Coast, i, p. 140–148) thinks that Aguilar went no farther than latitude 42°. The Russians (under the lead of Vitus Bering) made various discoveries on the Alaskan coasts before 1741, and afterward

regularly hunted for furs in Alaska, sending this commodity directly, and by a shorter route, to China, where they carried on a highly profitable trade, although they undersold the English merchants there (Bancroft, ut supra, pp. 345, 346).

5 This exploration by Fuente and Bernarda is regarded by most of the authorities on this subject as being spurious. The account of it first appeared in a London periodical (the Monthly Miscellany), in 1708, and it is now supposed that it was simply a clever hoax. For more circumstantial description of it, see Bancroft's Northeast Coast, i, pp. 116–119; and Winsor's Narrative and Critical History of America, ii, pp. 462, 463.

6 Probably referring to Ricard's Traité general du commerce, of which a second edition was published at Amsterdam in 1705.

7 In Spanish text, Cabo de Hornos, but there is no information available to show whether this is simply a corruption of the Dutch explorer's name (as seems more probable), or whether the Spaniards used the name Hornos (meaning "ovens") through some accidental circumstance or association. The first discovery of Cape Horn was made by Francisco de Hoces, one of the ship-captains in Loaisa's expedition of 1525, who was driven thither by contrary winds; but the cape was first doubled from the east by the Dutch commander William Cornelisz Schouten van Hoorn in 1616—accounts of this voyage being written by both Van Hoorn and his companion Lemaire. (Winsor, Narrative and Critical History of America, viii, pp. 384, 409–412.)

8 For the text of Extracto historial, see VOLS. XXX, XLIV, and XLV of this series.

9 Marginal note by Viana. — "Don Miguel Gomes, who plays the engineer in this town, calls for four thousand men in his new plan of fortification. He regards the entire wall and its bastions as useless, and, just as if there were no defenses, he plans for a fortification [that would be] exceedingly costly, and of greater circuit or extent than the present one. One does not need to be very skilful to adapt to the site of Manila one of the many plans of fortification that are contained in Belidor and other noted authors. The skill of an engineer consists in being able to avail himself as far as possible of a wall, correcting its irregular

shape, and putting the place in a condition of defense, with an obvious saving of expense, yet not failing to observe the rules of fortification. One of these rules is, to consider the number of men who can be maintained for its garrison, and to proportion the bastions to the number of soldiers who are there to defend them; but the said Don Miguel does not order his scheme by this rule. On the contrary, he occupies much ground, and consequently increases the number of bastions; these would remain undefended, for lack of troops, a consideration which ought to induce him to diminish the extent of the fort rather than extend it.

"On the other hand, it appears that all the bastions and the curtain on the land side could be maintained as they are, without more construction than that of the esplanades, ditch, covert-ways, glacis, ravelins, etc.; for besides the wall, which is a good one, and the bastions, which are apparently well flanked, it is easy to inundate the entire locality, or reduce it to a mangrove thicket, so that it will be impenetrable to the strongest enemy — who will not be able to set up a battery, or to endure the fire from the fort while they are clearing the field from obstructions.

"The curtain along the shore of the great Pasig River is a weak one, but there is sufficient soil for strengthening it; and by inundating the ground on the opposite shore of the said river the fortress will be impregnable on that side. This inundation can be made in various ways, but the safest one, in my opinion (although most expensive, on account of the greater strength which must be given to the pillars) would be to set flood-gates in all the arches of the great bridge, and in the estuaries or rivers of Binondoc and Santa Cruz, in order that the water might overflow (as it would without difficulty) the entire locality; nor would the said inundation prevent the ingress of provisions, which always come by water and not by land. The artillery of the redoubt [*fortin*; it defended the bridge] and the fortress would defend the said flood-gates, even though the inundation might permit the enemy to approach in order to destroy them.

"The curtain on the seashore, which is exceedingly weak, and the fortress or citadel of Santiago, which is in ruins, could be repaired without so much cost as the new scheme presents;

for we have already seen that ships cannot demolish the fort. If to that advantage be added the other of cutting a good ditch between the bay shore and the wall, with its covert-way and some outpost battery, in order to harass the said ships and hinder them from landing men, the town could be made equally impregnable on that side—especially if the fort be repaired and the corresponding bastions be constructed, in order to flank well the said seashore curtain, as seems necessary. In this manner the town could be well defended, with a great saving of expense, and without the incredible cost which would be incurred by carrying out the new plan of fortification which has been presented by the aforesaid Gomes—regarding which I set forth what common sense [*la luz natural*] dictated to me, in the *expediente* which was referred to me by this superior government, proposing the measures of economy which could be employed in any work whatever, with evident advantage to the royal exchequer; since with five or six thousand pesos, which will be the cost of forty thousand cavans of rice, six thousand workmen can be maintained for a whole year."

10 Forrest cites (pp. 307, 308) Valentyn to the effect that the Mindanaos refused in 1689 to allow the Dutch to build a fort on their land, although the latter offered a large sum of money for the privilege; and that the sultan told other Dutchmen in 1694 that the same request from the English had been likewise refused, although they offered even more money. Valentyn therefore thought that Dampier had been misled in his idea that the Mindanaos would make a treaty with the English and allow them to settle.

11 A phrase which recalls the well-known order by an American railroad magnate, "charge all that the traffic will bear."

12 The term situado was also applied, among other things, to the increase (1590) of two reals on each tribute (see VOL. XIV, p. 247, and XVI, p. 160). Torrubia explains this clearly in his Dissertacion, pp. 95–98; and he makes the following statement about the fund of "the fourths:" "The said father ministers are paid from the 'fourths' of the eight reals which remain (and these are distinct from the situado), and from the former the ministers were paid before the increase of the tributes. The present method is, to collect the ten reals, as the Ordinances provide, from each entire tribute; from this two reals are taken for paying the soldiers, etc., and this is called situado. After that, the fourth part of the eight reals (that it, two reals) is taken out, and this it to pay the ministers—to whom for every

hundred tributes that are under their ministry are paid twenty or twenty-five pesos (according to various customs of provinces and tributaries, which it would be difficult to explain at this time), with which sum the support assigned to the ministers is completed. For this purpose was instituted the royal fund of 'fourths,' which is explained in the Recopilacion by ley 14, tit. 3, lib. 1; for this fund the encomenderos of tributes who, on account of being unbelievers, have no parish priest contribute (after having paid the two reals of the situado, which amount is set apart and separately administered) another two reals for every infidel tribute, which is called the 'fourth' of the eight remaining reals; thus six reals remain, which is the amount that has always been estimated for the tribute. The destination of the money from the 'fourths' was the support of hospitals and charitable funds; but such is not now its use, because, thanks to God, all the tributes in encomiendas are Christians. Accordingly, with those two reals of the 'fourths' the encomiendas pay the ministers, and hand over the two reals of the situado to the royal treasury for its fund allotted to troops, etc. This is the usual arrangement, although in some villages and encomiendas the procedure is somewhat different."

13 Verecus (for biricús): meaning "sword-belts."

14 Spanish, pandillas: one of its meanings is, "a party of persons joined together for recreation in the country, or for mischief," which is quite equivalent to the Americanism "gang."

15 Thus in the text (y vna mitad mas deloque yo regulo), but evidently thus written by some oversight; for Viana certainly meant to say here, as in other places (see allusion to the increase of the tributes, in this and subsequent paragraphs), that the Mexican impost was twice that which he was proposing to establish in Filipinas.

16 On the margin of the MS. is the following note, written in a different hand, probably by some official of the India Council, or some friend of Viana's: "It was necessary to speak thus in a country of ignorant ecclesiastics."

17 Millones: "the voluntary impost which the kingdoms had granted to the king, on the consumption of the six commodities of wine, vinegar, oil, meat, soap, and tallow candles (see VOL. XLIV, p. 299, note 91); it was renewed every six years." Sisas: "the impost on food-stuffs, reducing the measure; a tribute reputed as a nuisance — which, notwithstanding that, still exists under another appellation." (Dominguez.)

18 Marginal note by Viana.—"In the Royal Audiencia is pending the expediente of the provincial ordinances, in which I have asked for various things which are beneficial, and proper for good government."

19 Marginal note by Viana.—"In the expediente for the regulation of storehouses I explain what would be proper for checking the abuses that are detrimental to the royal treasury, and present a plan for the orderly management and accounts of all the towns and military posts of these islands, and [records of] information about them."

20 On the matter of ecclesiastical tithes in the Spanish colonies, see Recopilación de leyes de Indias, lib. i, tit. xvi; laws xi and xii declare that the Indians shall not be responsible for tithes, but that the encomenderos shall pay these on what they receive from the Indians as tribute. In the Philippines, the crown had from the first made special provision for the support of the ecclesiastical estate; and tithes were not exacted there.

21 Presumably citing the Historia of Jacques Auguste de Thou (the Elder), originally published in Latin at Paris, 1604–08, but afterward appearing in many editions and translations. This book was "the history of his own time," covering the period 1543–1607.

22 An East India company formed in Denmark sent an expedition in 1618, which formed a settlement in the state of Tanjour, India, where the Danes built Tranquebar and Fort Dannebourg; for a time they carried on a thriving trade, but the influence of the Dutch crowded them aside in India, and the company finally surrendered its charter and made over its settlements to the government. In 1670 a new company was formed; but it was even more unfortunate than the first one, and, having become bankrupt, was extinguished in 1730. Two years later, another company was organized, which obtained a charter for forty years, with many privileges, and this was extended (1772) for twenty years. See Raynal's Établissemens et commerce des Européens dans les Indes, i, pp. 548–566.

23 For full account of the discoveries, wars and conquests of the Portuguese in the East Indies, with accounts of India, China, Japan, and of the people of those countries, see Raynal's Établissemens et commerce des Européens dans les Indes (Genève, 1780), i, pp. 1–150. At the end, he states "the causes which brought on the ruin of the Portuguese in India." "This little nation, finding itself the entire mistress of the richest and most extensive commerce in the world, was soon composed of merchants, traders, and sailors, who were consumed in long navigations. She lost also the foundation of all real power—agriculture, national industry, and population; there was no proportion between her commerce and the means of continuing it. Still worse, she aimed at being a conquering power, and embraced an extent of territory which no nation in Europe could preserve without weakening itself. This little country, but moderately populous, was constantly wasting its inhabitants as soldiers, as sailors, and as colonists." "As the government soon changed its projects for commerce into schemes for conquest, the nation, which had never possessed the spirit of commerce, assumed that of brigandage. Clocks and watches, firearms, fine cloths, and some other kinds of merchandise which since have been carried to the Indias were not then at the degree of perfection which they have since attained, and the Portuguese could only carry money there. Soon they grew tired of this, and forcibly took away from the Indians what they had at first purchased from those peoples." "Of all the conquests which the Portuguese had made in the seas of Asia, there now remain to them only Macao, part of the island of Timor, Daman, Diu, and Goa. At present, Macao sends to Timor, to Siam, and to Cochinchina a few small vessels of little value. It sends five or six to Goa, laden with goods that were rejected at Canton, and most of which belong to the Chinese traders. These latter ships carry return cargoes of sandalwood, India saffron, ginger, pepper, linen goods, and all the articles for which Goa can trade on the coast of Malabar or at Surat with its sixty-gun ship, its two frigates, and its six armed shallops. As a result of this inaction,

the colony cannot furnish more than three or four cargoes a year for Europe; and the value of these does not exceed 3,175,000 livres, even since 1752, when this commerce ceased to be under the yoke of monopoly,—excepting its sugar, snuff, pepper, saltpeter, pearls, sandalwood, and eaglewood, the exclusive purchase and sale of which is carried on by the crown." "Such is the degraded state into which the Portuguese have fallen in India, [that people who furnished] the hardy navigators who discovered it, the intrepid warriors who subjugated it. The theater of their glory and opulence, it has become that of their ruin and disgrace. Formerly a viceroy, and since 1774 a governor-general, both despotic and cruel; a military force turbulent and undisciplined, composed of 6,276 soldiers, black or white; magistrates whose venality is notorious; an unjust and rapacious administration: can all these kinds of oppression, which would ruin even the most virtuous people, regenerate a nation that is idle, degraded, and corrupt?"

24 The English jurist John Selden published (London, 1635) a work that attracted great attention, entitled Mare clausum seu de dominio maris libri duo. A later edition (1636) added to this a considerable amount of matter relating to the navigation rights of the Dutch.

The Macanaz mentioned by Viana in several places was probably Melchor Rafael de Macanaz, a fiscal of Castilla early in the eighteenth century (Revue Hispanique, vi, p. 455).

25 At the foot of the MS. page is written the following comment, in the same hand as that mentioned ante, p. 249, note 130: "The author agrees to this opinion, which is contrary to his own, through fear of ignorant and angry ecclesiastics."

26 Spanish, como en un Presidio, alluding to the custom of banishing a political offender to some remote military post, from which escape was, of course, practically impossible.

27 In the text, vicias, a word which does not appear (save as a botanical term) in the Spanish dictionaries; its translation, therefore, is necessarily conjectural.

28 An alloy of copper and nickel, known as "white copper" and "German silver," and to the Chinese as Packfong and petong.

29 The Dictionnaire universel de commerce of Jacques Savary des Bruslons was published at Paris, 1723–30; it had numerous editions, and was translated into English (London, 1751–55).

30 In text, capingotes; this word is not in the dictionaries, and suggests the blunder of some amanuensis in confusing capirotes and redingotes.

31 Manungal (Samadera indica): "the wood is used in making cups which turn liquid placed in them bitter; the bitter substance has certain medicinal properties." (Official Handbook of the Philippines, p. 353.) Blanco (who named this tree Manungala, but later Niota) says that this bitter principle is successfully used in cholera morbus; and Montero y Vidal (Archipiélago filipino, p. 77), that "it was as efficacious as Peruvian bark in fevers." In the same work (pp. 389, 391) manungal is, apparently by some oversight, identified with the macabuhay (Tinospora), which latter name is also applied, according to Merrill's Dictionary of Plant Names (p. 76) to Lunasia amara.

32 In this connection should be cited the account of the Ceylon cinnamon published by Forrest in his Voyage to New Guinea, pp. 338–349; it was "communicated by the chief inspector of the Cinnamon Trade, and Manufacturer in that Island, to Albertus Seba, a noted Druggist at Amsterdam. Translated by the late Dr. Scheucher; F. R. S." Some notes on the medicinal uses of the leaves are added by Seba, and there is an engraving illustrating the appearance of the leaves, of which nine are represented, presumably those of the nine different varieties of cinnamon which are enumerated in the inspector's description. Of these but one is mentioned as having a glutinous character, and that seems to be one of the sorts inferior in quality. Some of these varieties are said to yield "camphire" [i.e., camphor].

33 The map of Mindanao made by Norton Nicols, here reproduced, is accompanied by the following inscription: "The island of Mindanao, whose inhabitants are the fatal enemies of our holy Catholic faith and who, together with the islanders of Jolo, cause the horrible ruin, martyrdoms, and thefts in the other islands belonging to his Catholic Majesty, which have cost him so huge a sum of money, and so much blood of his faithful vassals, the Indians, although as yet fruitlessly. Said island is about 150 leguas away from Manila, and about 23 from Jolo. It lies between six degrees nine minutes and nine degrees one minute, north latitude, a distance of 44 leguas from north to south. East and west it extends 128☐ leguas. Its most western point is 127 degrees 17 minutes east of Cadiz, which counting 20 leguas per degree, amounts to 2,555☐ leguas. Reckoning 15 degrees of longitude, for each hour of time, there is a time difference of 8 hours, 31 minutes, 8 seconds, so that 12 o'clock in the day here is 8 seconds 31 minutes past 8 at night there.

34 A parallel case: "Before 1744, the Philippines had not beheld on their fertile soil the growth of any of our [European] vegetables. At that time, Mahé de Villebague carried thither seeds of them, and all these useful plants had prospered, when, eight months later, the cultivator, whom the interests of his business called to go elsewhere, left his garden to another Frenchman, who was settled in these islands. The Spaniards, who could not see without jealousy that a foreigner should point out to them the path which they ought to have entered two centuries ago, rose against the inheritor of his cares, with so much violence that, in order to restore peace, the authorities felt constrained to order that these wholesome plants be torn up by the roots. Fortunately the Chinese, who are continually occupied with what can contribute to their own success, secretly preserved the plants. By degrees the people became accustomed to an innovation so beneficial; and this [sort of] cultivation is now one of the chief resources of the colony." (Raynal, Établissemens et commerce des Européens, i, pp. 607, 608.)

35 Regarding this company, see VOL. XLV, pp. 45–50.

36 In this series the only mention of German trade in the Orient has been contained in one or two slight allusions. The following note on this subject is kindly furnished us by Asa Currier Tilton, late of the historical department of the University of Wisconsin, and now one of the staff of the Wisconsin State Historical Library.

Germany and the search for the sea-route to India. — Germany was concerned in the explorations of the Portuguese and Spaniards because of her close commercial relations with those nations. The Fuggers, Welsers, and other great mercantile houses had important trade and financial relations with Spain and Portugal, and were thus able to secure the right to participate in the India trade. The first occasion when they took part in an expedition was in 1505–06, when Almeida, the first Portuguese viceroy, was sent out. The following works furnish general information on this phase of the discoveries, and also contain bibliographical material which indicates the sources for more detailed information:

General works: Heyd, Geschichte des Levantehandels in Mittelalter (Stuttgart, 1879), 2 vols.; this has also been translated into French, Histoire du commerce du Levant au moyen-âge (Leipzig, 1885–86), 2 vols. Peśchel, Geschichte des Zeitalters der Entdeckungen (Stuttgart and Augsburg, 1858). Sachse, *Pennsylvania: the German influence in its settlement and development;* part 1, "The Fatherland, 1450–1700" — published in *Proceedings and Addresses* of the Pennsylvania German Society, vol. viii (1897).

On the Fuggers and Welsers: Ehrenberg, Das Zeitalter der Fugger (Jena, 1896), 2 vols. Häbler, Die Geschichte der Fuggerschen Handlung in Spanien (Weimar, 1897); and Die überseeischen Unternehmungen der Welser und ihrer Gesellschafter (Leipzig, 1903). Hautzsch, Die überseeischen Unternehmungen der Augsburger Welser (Leipzig, 1895), a dissertation. Tagebuch des Lucas Rem aus den Jahren 1494–1541: Beitrag zur Handelsgeschichte der Stadt Augsburg; "mitgetheilt mit erläuternden Bemerkungen, und einem Anhange von noch ungedruckten Briefen und Berichten über die Entdeckungen des neuen Seewegs nach Amerika und Ostindien versehen, von B. Greiff" — published (Augsburg, 1861) in Jahresberichte 26 of the "Historische Kreisverein" in the jurisdiction of Schwaben and Neuburg; (the appendix contains documents from the collection of Dr. Conrad Peutinger); Rem was an agent of the Welsers, and represented them at Lisbon and in Spain.

On the expedition of Francisco d'Almeida: Kunstmann, Die Fahrt der ersten Deutschen nach dem Portugiesischen Indien (München, 1861). Balthasar Springers Indienfahrt, 1505–06, "wissenschaftliche Würdigung der Reiseberichte Springers zur Einführung in den Neudruck seiner Meerfahrt vom Jahre 1509, von Franz Schulze" (Strassburg, 1902); Springer went on the expedition as one of the agents of the German merchants. *The Voyage from Lisbon to India, 1505–06*, "being an account and journal by Albericus Vespuccius; translated from the contemporary Flemish, and edited" by C. H. Coote (London, 1894); this is shown by Harrisse to be nothing but a corrupt Flemish version of Springer's account; and Vespuccius had nothing to do with this voyage. Harrisse, *Americus Vespuccius* (London, 1895); besides showing the true character of Coote's book, this work contains valuable notes on the German connection with the discoveries.

37 This work (Turin, 1724–30) was written by Alvaro J. A. I. de Navia Osorio y Vigil Argüelles de la Rua, Marqués de Santa Cruz de Marcenado and Visconde del Puerto. He also wrote Comercio suelto, y en compañias, general y particular en Mexico, Perú y Filipinas, etc. (Madrid, 1732).

38 For identifications of these various woods, see VOLS. XII, p. 245 (molave), and XVIII, pp. 169–173. Tangili is the Tagálog name for various trees of the genera Dipterocarpus and Shorea, (of the same natural order). "Teak" is a corruption of the Malabar name for the tree known to botanists as Tectona grandis. According to Official Handbook (p. 356), it "exists in Mindanao,

and said to exist in Negros." Blanco gives (Flora, p. 93), the following interesting account of its habitat: "The only teak tree of which I have first-hand knowledge is the one which exists in the village of Tanay, in Laguna de Bahi [i.e., Bay]. Formerly there were two, and they were planted by a Franciscan priest; it is not known whence the seed came. The Tanay people call it ticla…. It is common in some provinces of Visayas, in Negros Island, Zambales, Mindanao, and Butuan, as has recently been ascertained. The tree whose flowers I have seen is in Tanay, and has waited twenty-three years to bloom."

39 See VOL. XVIII, p. 177. The term is applied (Official Handbook, p. 332) to the sheaths, or fibers surrounding the leaf-stems, of a species of palm, Caryota urens.

40 Representación al Rey … dirigida al mas seguro aumento del real erario (Madrid?, 1732), by Miguel de Zavala y Auñon. It is of interest to note that Viana must have been related to Zavala, since his name, in full, was Francisco Leandro de Viana Zavala Vehena Saenz de Villaverde; he was afterward made Conde de Tepa and Marqués de Prado Alegre.

41 Cacao is found throughout the archipelago; large quantities of cacao of excellent quality are produced in southern Mindanao and the district of Davao. The native product commands a better price than that imported from Singapore. Coffee is found throughout the islands; the best quality is grown in Batangas. (Official Handbook, p. 303.) Montero y Vidal says (Archipiélago Filipino, p. 61) that the islands produce cacao equal in quality to that of Caracas, and coffee that is superior in some respects to that of Mocha.

See Jagor's account of cacao in the Philippines, its history, culture, and preparation, in his Reisen, pp. 76–81.

42 Marginal note by Viana. — "At this very time, men are obtaining in this bay many of the said shells, and some pearls of good luster."

43 Marginal note by Viana. — "The mulberry trees yield wonderfully in these islands, and, by making suitable plantations of them, and bringing silkworms from China, [the production of] this valuable article of commerce can be promoted."

44 Narra is the native name of the valuable timber trees in the genus Pterocarpus, especially P. indicas; it is sometimes called "the mahogany of the Philippines." The species alluded to by Viana is probably P. Blancoi, called apálit by the Pampangos; "the decoction of the wood is nephritic" (Official Handbook).

Catbalonga (pepitas de San Ignacio) is one of the native names tor Strychnos Ignatii, one of the species from which the drug strychnine is obtained. See Jagor's interesting note on this plant (Ignatia amara, L., or Strychnos Ignatii, Berg.) in his Reisen, pp. 213, 214; he says that it is used (under the name pepita de Catbalonga) as a household remedy in many families in Filipinas, and is regarded by the superstitious as a charm against poisons of all kinds.

45 Neither Blanco nor Merrill mentions the rhubarb (Rheum) as a product of the Philippines, although the former describes a tree the soft wood of which, when chewed, has purgative properties similar to those of rhubarb; but he did not see the tree itself, which grew in the province of Laguna. Calinga is the native name of Cinnamomum pauciflorum.

46 "On account of the English invasion, it was positively prohibited that foreign vessels should land at Filipino ports. This prohibition, and that imposed in the royal decree of 1593 — which provided that no merchant of Manila should send his vessels to China, or go there to purchase his goods directly — were superlatively absurd, mischievous, and impolitic; for this constituted a [special] privilege in favor of the Chinese, who, when they appeared in the port of Manila once a year in their clumsy champans, secured for lack of competition a considerable increase in the prices for their merchandise, the valuation placed on the goods not being sufficient to diminish the monopoly which they enjoyed on those articles." This stupid procedure not only kept the Spaniards from competing with foreigners in the markets of India and China, thus surrendering all that commerce and its advantages to the latter; but these, especially the English and French, took advantage of the Chinese monopoly of trade with Manila by sending thither cargoes of their goods under the flag of some Asiatic country; some Armenian or Moor would act as owner of the vessel, the

real captain or agent being ostensibly an interpreter. (Montero y Vidal, Hist, de Filipinas, ii, pp. 120, 121.)

On one occasion Viana tried to stop this by demanding that the Audiencia punish severely the Frenchmen who were selling their cargoes in Manila, in open and reckless violation of the royal decrees; but that tribunal declined to do more than notify the Frenchmen that a repetition of the offense would be severely punished—on the ground that a lawsuit brought against them and the buyers of the goods would involve nearly all the citizens of Manila, the religious corporations, and various dignitaries. (Azcarraga y Palmero, *Libertad de comercio*, pp. 115, 116.) Azcarraga was a Filipino.

47 Referring to the book by this author entitled Theorica y practica de comercio y de marina (Madrid, 1724), an important work, which was translated into English (1751) and French (1753). Two of the chapters have the following titles: "Of the commerce which can be carried on in the Eastern Indias, by availing ourselves of the shelter and assistance of Filipinas;" and "Of the commerce with Filipinas." (Vindel's Catálogo, 1903, p. 276.)

48 Spanish, testas de fierro (in modern form, testaferros); meaning "those who lend their names to a contract, claim, or other business when it belongs to another person" (Dominguez).

49 Referring to the town of Nuevo Santander, near the eastern coast of Mexico; it was founded in 1749 by José de Escandon, a Spanish officer, who in that year conquered and colonized the province of Tamaulipas. This town is on the Santander River, about 120 miles north of Tampico, and is now the capital of the province.

50 St. Helena Island, famous as the place of Napoleon's last exile. The British government has withdrawn (October 27–29, 1906) the military forces there.

51 Bancroft states (Hist. Central America, ii, pp. 246–250) that the first project for an interoceanic canal across the Isthmus of Panama was broached probably by Charles V, who ordered that a survey be made of the ground and estimates of the cost of such route be made; this was done in 1534, and the scheme appeared so costly that it could not be undertaken. The first road across the isthmus was made about 1520. By the middle of the century Panama had become the most important city of America, and was the seat and channel of untold wealth; it was the object of attack, more than once by the enemies of Spain and by pirates, and before 1671 (when Old Panama was burned) it was four times sacked and partially destroyed. By the end of the sixteenth century the importance and population of this city had greatly declined, for various reasons: the depredations of buccaneers; the diminishing receipts of treasure from the mines of both North and South America, and the consequent decline of commerce; the unhealthful climate; and, most important of all, the unwise and short-sighted restrictions imposed on commerce by the Spanish government. Portobello also became a rival of Panama in 1597, when it was made a port of entry in place of Nombre de Dios. Destroyed by buccaneers in 1671, Panama was immediately rebuilt in a more salubrious location, and fortified so that it was regarded as impregnable. Until 1718 the provinces of the isthmus were subject to the viceroy of Peru, and then were incorporated with the kingdom of Nueva Granada. After 1748 Spain had but little intercourse with her South American colonies except via Cape Horn, the despatch of fleets to the isthmus was discontinued; its commerce became insignificant; and Panama became of but slight importance. (Ut supra, pp. 390–403, 464–481, 517–542, 570–594.)

BIBLIOGRAPHICAL DATA

The documents in the present volume are obtained from the following sources:

1. *Usurpation of Indian lands.* — From *La Democracia* (Manila), November 25, 1901; from a copy in the possession of James A. LeRoy, Durango, Mexico.

2. *Moro raids.* — From a rare pamphlet published at Manila (1755), from a copy in the possession of Edward E. Ayer, Chicago.

3. *Augustinian parishes, 1760.* — From an original MS. in possession of Edward E. Ayer.

4. *Later missions.* — From Mozo's *Noticia histórico natural* (Madrid, 1763), and a rare pamphlet by Ustáriz (1745), both from copies in the Library of Congress.

5. *Events in Filipinas, 1739–62.* — This is compiled from Zúñiga's *Historia* (Sampaloc, 1803), pp. 546–601, and Concepcion's *Hist. de Philipinas*, xi, pp. 89–237; and fully annotated from other writers.

6. *Viana's Memorial of 1765.* — From a MS. — apparently a duplicate copy of the first original, and bearing Viana's autograph signature — in the possession of Edward E. Ayer.